Authentic Christianity

Volume 1

D. MARTYN LLOYD-JONES

Authentic Christianity

꧁꧂

SERMONS ON THE ACTS
OF THE APOSTLES

꧁꧂

Volume 1
Acts 1–3

THE BANNER OF TRUTH TRUST

THE BANNER OF TRUTH TRUST
3 Murrayfield Road, Edinburgh EH12 6EL

*

© Lady Catherwood and Mrs Ann Beatt 1999
First published 1999
ISBN 0 85151 776 5

*

Typeset in 11/13 pt Palatino at
The Banner of Truth Trust, Edinburgh
Printed in Great Britain by
The Bath Press

Contents

Publisher's Foreword

This is the first of a series of volumes which will contain sermons by Dr Lloyd-Jones on texts from the Acts of the Apostles. Most of them were preached in evening services at Westminster Chapel during 1965. They are therefore evangelistic in character, but all of them have something of great importance to say to Christian people as well.

The Doctor saw how much people needed 'to know exactly what Christianity is and what the Christian church is', and claimed that the early chapters of Acts met that need because they presented 'authentic Christianity and nothing else'. Hence the title which has been given to this series. The need is no less today, and, barring the recurrence of something like the Day of Pentecost, it is certain to become more urgent still.

It was the Doctor's conviction that it was the outpouring of the Spirit on the Day of Pentecost, unique, but with aspects which were repeatable, which alone explained the history of the Christian church recorded in Acts. The church's survival was stupendous, and its growth, over against the power of Jerusalem and Rome, was nothing short of miraculous. But, in reality, it was the 'noise from heaven' (*Acts* 2:2) which 'turned the world upside down' (*Acts* 17:6).

The Publisher

1

Christianity – The Only Hope

The former treatise have I made, O Theophilus, of all that Jesus began both to do and teach until the day in which he was taken up, after that he through the Holy Ghost had given commandments unto the apostles whom he had chosen: to whom also he showed himself alive after his passion by many infallible proofs, being seen of them forty days and speaking of the things pertaining to the kingdom of God (Acts 1:1–3).

There can be no more urgent question at this present time than just this: What is Christianity? I say that because this gospel is the only hope in the world today. Everything else has been tried and found wanting. Everything else has failed. You will not find hope with the philosophers or with the statesmen, and you will not find it in the so-called religions of the world. Here is hope, and here alone.

'But,' someone may say, 'surely you can't claim that there is any hope in the gospel either, because it has been tried now for two thousand years and has obviously failed quite as much as the various other things to which you've referred?'

And the only reply to that is the one that was given so perfectly by the late G. K. Chesterton when he reminded us, 'Christianity has not been tried and found wanting; it has been found difficult and not tried.' That is the simple truth. The world, speaking generally, has never *tried* Christianity. It has talked a lot about it, but it has not really tried it. So I argue that this is still the only hope for the world. Therefore it is urgent that we should ask what Christianity is. Or, to put the question another way: What is the Christian church? What is her business and what is her message?

It can be put like this: Why am I, or why is anyone else, a preacher of the gospel? There is only one answer to that question. I am a preacher because I believe I have been called; because in my little way God has given me a burden; because I know by personal experience, by the experience of others and by experience garnered from the reading of history, that there is nothing under heaven that can enable men and women to conquer and to master life, and to have a hope that cannot be dimmed, but this gospel. Therefore, the most urgent task in the world today is to make the gospel known to men and women. And this is the function of the Christian church.

But, as we all know, the great tragedy is that there is utter confusion with regard to what the gospel is, what the church is, and what Christians are supposed to do. I call your attention to this, God knows, not because I am anxious to be controversial, but because I have a burden for the souls of men and women. I would not be a preacher were it not for that. That is what originally put me in the ministry, and makes me go on. I see the confusion. I see men and women bewildered, asking, 'What is Christianity? What is the church?' And I am not surprised that they are bewildered.

Furthermore, this confusion is not confined to men and women outside the church – indeed, I have an increasing fear that the confusion of those outside has been produced mainly by the so-called Christian church herself. A man who has held the highest position in one of the religious denominations, and is well known as one who speaks in the name of Christianity, has recently said that he thinks that certain things should be done at once, and the first is that the church must give up the foolish habit of having two services on a Sunday. 'One is enough,' he says, 'and let's have it at nine o'clock in the morning so that having got that out of the way, we can then give ourselves to what we want to do.' He also says that if he had the power, he would decree that there should be no reading of the Bible at all for twelve months – this in the name of the church and of Christianity! And then he says that any preaching that is done in this one and only service at nine o'clock in the morning should, for at least a year, be on a political text alone.

Now I simply call attention to this because it is so typical of what is being said at the present time. Is it surprising that men and women are in a state of confusion? Speaking generally, the current idea is that the Christian message is, after all, nothing but a kind of teaching with regard to how our affairs should be ordered – that is why it is held that all texts should be political. It is said that the main business of the church is to deal with injustices and do the work of reform and that in the Sermon on the Mount we have a kind of social charter.

People who say this are never interested in the Old Testament, they generally dismiss it *in toto*, and they have no use for the apostle Paul. Instead, they point to the ethical teaching of Jesus. 'There's your political programme,' they say. 'There's your political charter, and all you must do is apply it as best you can.' You must not even read the Bible, but pick up these general principles, and try to put them into practice.

Others say that Christianity is mainly an elevated, optimistic view of life, a sort of philosophy. Having found out how life can be lived on a higher plane, and having experienced a moral uplift, you try to get others to adopt these principles.

And then there are others who, perhaps nearer to the Christian position, regard Christianity as being mainly a matter of morals and of conduct. They say that what makes people Christians is that they have adopted this ethical teaching and put it into practice. So, by living a good life, they have made themselves Christians.

Common to all those teachings is the view that what really matters is the kernel of moral teaching that is to be found in this book which we call the Bible. Unfortunately, the Bible is cluttered up with a lot of unimportant history. Most of it is false with a lot about miracles which obviously are not true and which no one with any scientific understanding can possibly believe for a moment. We must get rid of all that, they say, and find this kernel that is hidden away in all the husk and straw. Having extracted this kernel, we can ignore the Bible and start with the political or moral situation. Then we must try to persuade people to put these things into practice. That is the common idea of the Christian message and the common notion with respect to the function of the Christian church.

Now I want to deal with all this and that is why I am calling your attention to the first three verses in the book of the Acts of the Apostles. Look at it like this: What is the origin of the Christian church? Surely that is the question to ask. You do not start with the twentieth century. Here is something that can be traced back nearly two thousand years. So, surely, if you want to know what the church is and what Christianity is, your bounden duty is to go back to the very beginning and discover how the church started and what she did.

I think you will agree with me that the question of authority is primary and fundamental. When people think they have the right to announce, 'This is what I think Christianity is, and this is what the church should do,' then we have the right to ask, 'Can that be fitted into what we have here in the book of Acts?' What is our authority in these matters? Are we competent to decide what the Christian church is? Can we divorce ourselves from the history of nearly two thousand years and say that we do not care what happened in the past, this is what *we* say now? Of course, you can say that if you like, but the question is: Have you any right to call that Christianity?

Surely common honesty demands that we should say that we have only one authority on the origin of the church, and it is the authority of the Bible. Here in the Acts of the Apostles a man is writing who is undoubtedly Luke, the evangelist. He says, 'The former treatise have I made, O Theophilus.' This is a reference to the Gospel of Luke which has a similar introduction. In Luke 1:1–4, Luke writes:

Forasmuch as many have taken in hand to set forth in order a declaration of those things which are most surely believed among us, even as they delivered them unto us, which from the beginning were eye-witnesses, and ministers of the word; it seemed good to me also, having had perfect understanding of all things from the very first, to write unto thee in order, most excellent Theophilus, that thou mightest know the certainty of those things wherein thou hast been instructed.

That is why these books were written. We do not have exact information concerning Theophilus, but it is generally assumed that he was a man in some prominent position, a man of culture and of learning, who had heard various reports about Christianity and wanted to know more. He found Luke, a doctor and a most competent historian, who had accompanied the apostle Paul and so was in a very good position to know exactly what the story was. They got in touch, and Luke wrote to Theophilus saying in effect, 'I will give you an account of exactly what happened. I will tell you why we believe what we believe. I will tell you the story.' And he did it in two parts: the first, the Gospel, and the second, this book of the Acts of the Apostles. And my argument is that we must go back and consider this story. We are not only honour-bound to do that, but we must, if we want to understand it.

What is the story? Well, there were just a handful of people whom the authorities in Jerusalem regarded as ordinary, simple, unlettered and ignorant men and women. There were just twelve men essentially, and a number of others with them. They had nothing to recommend them, no great names, no degrees, no money, no means of communication and of advertising. They had nothing at all – they were nobodies. And yet what we know to be a fact is that this handful of ignorant and unlettered people 'turned the world upside down', to use Luke's phrase in chapter 17. Within about two centuries, Christianity became the most powerful force in the great Roman Empire. By the beginning of the third century, it had become such a powerful force that a Roman emperor named Constantine deemed it a wise move to make the Roman Empire officially Christian.

I am not concerned to consider that fact now. All I want to ask is: How was it that this small group of people ever got into a position in which they could shake the whole of the Roman Empire so that it became officially Christian within such a short space of time? Was it because they preached politics that these people turned the ancient world upside down?

Now Christianity is a phenomenon of history. It is a fact. The Christian church is one of the most vital facts in the total history of the world. We cannot understand that history without bringing in the story of the church. But does this modern idea as to what the church is and what her message is, account for what has already happened? My answer is that it does not. So not only do honesty and common sense tell us to come back to Acts, but if we really want to have an understanding of what Christianity means, we are compelled to come back here. Only one thing can account for the phenomenon of the Christian church and this amazing history that has come down through the running centuries, in spite of the world, the flesh and the devil and the malignity of men and of hell, and that is the explanation given in this book.

Therefore I propose to hold the message of Acts before you. I shall not preach systematically through the book, but I shall pick out certain themes that are put before us here. I feel that the modern world is very much in the position of Theophilus. At any rate, anyone considering these things who is not a Christian is in the position of Theophilus. You have become interested. You want to know what Christianity is. Perhaps you are in trouble in your moral life or in your married life. Perhaps you have some running sore of the soul, something that gets you down. And you say, 'I've tried this and that, I wonder what the Christian church has to offer?'

All right, Theophilus, you want to know, and fortunately we are able to tell you. I am not here to tell you what I think about Christianity. I am not here to tell you what I think the Christian church should do. I am in the position of Charles Wesley, saying, 'O for a thousand tongues to sing my great Redeemer's praise.' My own personal opinion is that even two services on a Sunday are not enough. How can people be satisfied with but one statement? The world is dying round about us, and it needs to hear. These early Christians went everywhere, and they spoke and they preached, and that is the explanation of this tremendous phenomenon of the church.

So let us see what Acts has to say to us. Fortunately there is no difficulty about this. First, what was the message that these people preached? Luke told Theophilus quite plainly. He said:

The former treatise have I made, O Theophilus, of all that Jesus began both to do and to teach, until the day in which he was taken up, after that he through the Holy Ghost had given commandments unto the apostles whom he had chosen: to whom also he shewed himself alive after his passion by many infallible proofs, being seen of them forty days, and speaking of the things pertaining to the kingdom of God (Acts 1:1–3).

That is a summary of the whole of the Gospel of Luke and also of the other Gospels. What does it mean? Here are some of the great principles.

The starting point, the fundamental thing, is that Christianity is about Jesus. 'I've written to you already about him,' said Luke in effect, 'and I'm going to tell you more about him.' Christianity is not a teaching, it is a person. It is not merely a moral outlook that is to be applied in the realm of politics. You start with a historical person. Luke was a pure historian. He was giving an account of events and of facts.

The Lord Jesus Christ was the theme of the preaching of the early church. He is the theme of the Gospel of Luke. He is the theme of the Acts of the Apostles. This is the tragic thing that has been forgotten at the present time. 'What we want,' people say, 'is the application of his teaching.' But it is not. What you need is to know *him* and to come into a relationship with *him*. You do not start with his teaching – you start with him. This is the message: 'All that Jesus began both to do and teach.' Our Lord himself said to his disciples, 'Ye shall be witnesses unto me' (*Acts* 1:8). He was sending these men out to preach. He said: You are not simply going to preach my teaching. You are going to preach about me.

And as you read this book of Acts, you will find that our Lord's disciples always preached 'Jesus, and the resurrection' (*Acts* 17:18). They went to people and told them about this person. This was the whole of their teaching. You never find them starting with the political or social situations. They said: Listen, we have something to tell you about a person whose name is Jesus.

And what did the disciples say about him? Well, the facts are all-important. In the Gospel, Luke gave facts, and here in Acts he gives them again. But he does not stop at that; he is equally concerned about the meaning, the significance of these facts. And he expounds that. He writes not only about all that Jesus did, but also all that he taught. The two must always go together: our Lord's acts and his teaching.

And there is this most extraordinary addition which our Lord himself made: 'Ye shall be witnesses unto me both in Jerusalem, and in all Judaea, and in Samaria, and unto the uttermost part of the earth' (*Acts* 1:8). This is truly staggering. Here was a Jew, born in poverty, one who worked as a carpenter, who began to preach at the age of thirty and after some three years was crucified on a cross dying in utter weakness, and was laid in a tomb. But here he was, telling these men that they would be witnesses to him 'unto the uttermost part of the earth'. Here is a message for the whole world.

Now I emphasize that because there are people who say that the Christian faith is all right if you happen to be interested in religion, but if you do not happen to have a religious mentality and outlook, then that does not matter, you just take up what you like. But, you see, that is given the lie direct by our Lord's words. Here is a message that is to be proclaimed to the ends of the earth. Why? Because something happened in this person, Jesus, that affects every single individual that ever has been or ever shall be in this world of time.

Now if Christianity were merely a philosophy or a political idea, then no one would be bound to believe it. There are rival schools of philosophy, there are rival teachings and theories, and one person believes this and another that. But what we are facing here is not what you and I believe, but facts, and the facts are this person called Jesus, what he did and what he said, and the meaning of his person. So there is nothing more tragic than that men and women should say, 'Shut your Bibles, the facts don't matter at all. What does it matter whether Jesus was a man, or God as well as man? The teaching is the thing that we need.' No, they have got it all wrong. It is the person who matters.

So let us go on and follow what Luke says. We have seen that he begins, 'The former treatise have I made, O Theophilus, of all that Jesus began both to do and teach.' And that word 'began' is emphatic. Luke is saying to Theophilus that all that he has written in the Gospel is nothing but the beginning. This is vital. It is why Luke wrote his Gospel. Here was a man interested in Christianity who wanted to know what it was all about. 'I'll tell you,' said Luke. And he told the story that is unfolded in the twenty-four chapters of his Gospel. And here he sums it all up in two words – it is all that Jesus began both to *do* and to *teach*.

I want to hold this before you. You may say to me that you know about Jesus. Do you? Do you realize what his life means? Do you realize its significance? What did Jesus begin to do? In his Gospel Luke tells us who Jesus was. And the first thing we want to know is how he was born. Was he a man like every other man? Luke's answer is that he was not. Luke tells us how the angel Gabriel went to Mary and told her that she was supremely blessed among women; that she was going to bear the Son of the Highest, and that he would be great. He would occupy the throne of his father David and of his kingdom there would be no end. Read it all in the first chapter of Luke's Gospel. Mary was perplexed and asked how this could be since she was a virgin.

Gabriel said: 'The Holy Ghost shall come upon thee, and the power of the Highest shall overshadow thee: therefore also that holy thing which shall be born of thee shall be called the Son of God' (*Luke* 1:35).

That is what Luke tells us and this means that Jesus *came* into the world. He was not just born like everybody else. He came out of eternity into time; he came from heaven to earth. This is Christianity. Whatever may be your moral and political views, the question confronting you is this: How are you related to the fact that the babe of Bethlehem is the eternal Son of God?

But he not only came into the world, he did many other things. He worked miracles. Oh yes, that is an essential part of the gospel message.

'But,' you say, 'modern men and women don't believe in miracles. They can't. They have a scientific outlook.' Yet Luke refers Theophilus back to his first treatise, the Gospel, where he told him about our Lord's miracles. Our Lord attracted attention. The miracles were signs and people came and watched. Luke tells us that when certain Pharisees went to see him one day, 'the power of the Lord was present to heal' (*Luke* 5:17), and he created a great stir. There is no Christianity apart from these things.

But our Lord also did something else. Though he knew that his enemies in Jerusalem hated him and were determined to kill him, and though he knew that Herod the king, who would be in Jerusalem for the Passover, wanted to kill him, nevertheless, 'He stedfastly set his face to go to Jerusalem' (*Luke* 9:51). He went there and was arrested. At his trial he would not speak, and was condemned to death. He was made to carry a cross through Jerusalem until he staggered and it had to be put on the back of somebody else. Then they nailed him to the cross and he died. Two of his friends took down his body and laid it in a tomb. But he burst asunder the bands of death. He arose triumphantly out of that tomb. He appeared to a chosen number of his disciples and other people, as Luke tells us here: 'To whom also he shewed himself alive after his passion by many infallible proofs, being seen of them forty days, and speaking of the things pertaining to the kingdom of God' (*Acts* 1:3). And then, standing with them on the Mount of Olives, he ascended from their midst into heaven.

It is all here. This is history. Luke the physician, Luke the historian, wanted to help this intelligent man, Theophilus. Theophilus had said: I'd love to know what Christianity is. I'm amazed at you people. I see what has happened to you and I hear you preaching. I can see the effects. I want to know what this is.

So Luke said: Theophilus, if you want to know, listen. This is it. It is Jesus. This is what he began to do. He came. He taught. He worked miracles. He gave himself. He died. He was buried. He rose again, and he ascended into heaven.

Luke emphasizes the resurrection. There would be no Christian church were it not for the resurrection. Here in Acts is the history of the church. Here is the account of this amazing institution that turned the world upside down and has continued throughout the centuries. It is all due to the fact that Jesus who was dead is alive again and has given many infallible proofs of it. These are facts.

'Theophilus,' says Luke in effect, 'you must believe these facts. There is no explanation except Jesus. This is what he began to do.'

But Jesus also began to *teach,* and again I can do nothing but summarize this teaching for you. It is all in the Gospels. He taught concerning himself. He said, 'Before Abraham was, I am' (*John* 8:58). He called himself 'the Son of man'. He said, 'Ye have heard that it was said by them of old time . . . but I say unto you' (*Matt.* 5:21). He claimed a unique authority. He claimed, indeed, to be the Son of God. That is what he began to teach.

He went on to tell his followers why he had come into the world. This is the most staggering event that has ever happened. Why did he do it? 'The Son of man,' he said, 'came not to be ministered unto, but to minister, and to give his life a ransom for many' (*Mark* 10:45). He said that he had come into the world because it was the only way by which anybody could be saved. He said he was sent by his Father: 'God so loved the world, that he gave his only begotten Son, that whosoever believeth in him should not perish, but have everlasting life' (*John* 3:16).

But nobody understood him. Luke had reminded Theophilus of that in the Gospel. In chapter 24, two people were walking on a road from Jerusalem to Emmaus. They had been with him and had believed in him, but now, after his death, they were utterly cast down. Then suddenly, as they were walking along, Jesus, the risen Jesus, joined them, and listened to their conversation. Earlier that day, certain women who belonged to their company had been in the garden where Jesus had been put in the tomb and had reported to the disciples that the tomb was empty, and this is what we read: 'Their words seemed to them as idle tales, and they believed them not' (*Luke* 24:11).

The two people walking to Emmaus did not recognize Jesus when he joined them. They told this stranger what had happened, and said, 'But we trusted that it had been he which should have redeemed Israel' (*Luke* 24:21). They had thought his teaching was so wonderful; they had seen his miracles. They had said that this must be the Messiah. But he could not be, of course. He had been crucified. He was dead.

And then our Lord began to speak to them: 'O fools, and slow of heart to believe all that the prophets have spoken: ought not the Christ to have suffered these things, and to enter into his glory? And beginning at Moses and all the prophets, he expounded unto them in all the scriptures the things concerning himself' (*Luke* 24:25–26).

Later that evening, in Jerusalem, our Lord came among the disciples. They were terrified; they could not believe it. He had told them repeatedly that he was going to die and to rise again, but they had never taken it in. Yet here he was appearing among them, and he said, 'Why are ye troubled? And why do thoughts arise in your hearts? Behold my hands and my feet, it is I myself: handle me, and see; for a spirit hath not flesh and bones, as ye see me have.' And he ate a bit of broiled fish and honey.

Then he began to speak again. 'These are the words which I spake unto you, while I was yet with you, that all things must be fulfilled, which were written in the law of Moses, and in the prophets, and in the psalms, concerning me' (*Luke* 24:44). If you want to understand Christianity, do not shut your Bible – open it, read it! Read the books of Moses, the prophets, the Psalms; they all point to him. Study your Bible. It is ignorance that blinds men and women of this generation and keeps them outside Christ. So do not have a hurried service at nine o'clock so that you can go out and play golf and bathe in the sea – listen for your life! Here is the only message of hope for you.

Then our Lord went on telling his disciples the meaning of his coming. Luke writes: 'Then opened he their understanding, that they might understand the scriptures, and said unto them, Thus it is written, and thus it behoved Christ to suffer, and to rise from the dead the third day: and that repentance and remission of sins should be preached in his name among all the nations, beginning at Jerusalem' (verses 45–47).There is his own explanation of why he came and why he did all he did. It is the only way anybody can be saved. Every one of us is born in sin. We are born under the wrath of God. We do not know him and we are evil by nature. Our greatest need is to be reconciled to God, to have our sins forgiven, to know God as our Father, to be blessed by him and to start as a child of God. And Jesus came in order that men and women might know this. This is his message – not that you improve the world but that you and I be redeemed. You set out with your long political programme. You say: 'Now, if we can get this on to the statute book this year, then that, then the other . . .' but you may be dead before tomorrow morning and be in eternity facing God and the judgment. But how can this message be made known?

And the answer is this: Jesus. In effect, he said to the disciples, 'I'm going to send you out to preach and I want you to tell people that repentance and remission of sins is only possible in my name. Preach it among all nations, beginning at Jerusalem. I do not care what colour, class, or creed people are, the human race is one, humanity is one in sin, one under the wrath of God, one in its deserving of hell, and there is only one Saviour. Tell them about me and be witnesses to me.'

That is what Christianity is all about, said Luke to Theophilus. That is what I told you in my former treatise, but now I want to tell you a little bit more. 'The former treatise have I made, O Theophilus, of all that Jesus began both to do and teach.' This is the vital emphasis – 'all that Jesus *began*'. It means he has not finished! He is going on with it.

Luke said: Listen, Theophilus, I've got a second treatise. I've told you what he began to do; you've got it, you've read it – that's the Gospel. I want to tell you now what he's continuing to do.

Now this is important because the modern teaching that Jesus of Nazareth was just a man, though a very fine moral and political teacher, would have us believe that he was like other teachers – Plato, Socrates and all the rest. He was in the world and he died. 'Well,' people say, 'that's all right if you're interested in people, but the thing that really matters, of course, is the teaching.' And they may prove to you that Plato and Jesus never existed. 'But it doesn't matter,' they insist, we've got the teaching. All that remains is for us to apply it.'

But the answer to that is that he is still active. It is what *he* does that matters, not what we do, and the message of the Christian church is not only of what he *has done* but of what he *is doing*. He is going on. And the book of Acts tells us about the further acts of Jesus. Some people say it ought to be called the Acts of the Holy Spirit. That is quite wrong. It is *Jesus* who dominates.

How is Christ still active? Well, this book tells us that he is seated at the right hand of God in the glory everlasting. After his resurrection he himself told us something that is demonstrated so clearly in this book. He said to those men, 'All power is given unto me in heaven and in earth. Go ye therefore, and teach all nations' (*Matt.* 28:18–19). They were to preach the gospel and disciple the nations.

I know of nothing more comforting and encouraging than that wonderful, blessed statement. This world is not in the hands of the politicians only, it is in the hands of this living Jesus, this risen Christ. This is the message: God the eternal Father, the Creator, and the Owner of all things has handed over the business of this world and its redemption to his Son. And *he* has all power in heaven and in earth.

And in this wonderful book of Acts we see Jesus demonstrating some of that power. He sent the Holy Spirit down upon the early church. That was a manifestation of his power. Then he began to give power to his disciples. We shall see Peter and John walking up to the temple one afternoon at the hour of prayer, and healing a man who lay paralysed on a mat so that he went into the temple walking and leaping and praising God. That is Christianity. Not simply a political, moral programme, no, no – this living Jesus with all power, giving power.

What else did our Lord go on to do? Well, there was a man called Saul of Tarsus, a Pharisee and a bitter opponent of the first Christians. Here was a man who hated our Lord and hated his cause and did his best to put it to an end by going out and having believers thrown into prison and even put to death. Saul was so keen on this persecution that he went to the high priest at Jerusalem and asked for authority to go down to Damascus to exterminate the little Christian church there. So they gave him authority and off he went, 'breathing out threatenings and slaughter' (*Acts* 9:1), confident that he would be able to destroy the church.

What happened? Ah, this Jesus revealed himself to Saul of Tarsus. About midday Saul saw a light in the heavens 'above the brightness of the sun' (*Acts* 26:13). Paul said, 'Who art thou, Lord?' And the answer came back, 'I am Jesus whom thou persecutest' (*Acts* 9:5). Jesus was continuing to act. He floored Paul. He humbled him. He cast him down. He led him to repentance. Jesus saved him.

So the story does not end at the ascension. He continues to act with all power. Nothing is impossible for him, and here he is, calling out men and women, saving them, building up his kingdom. He instructed them after his resurrection, 'speaking of the things pertaining to the kingdom of God' (*Acts* 1:3). He said, in effect, 'This is how it will happen. I am sending you out, just a little handful, but I will be with you. I am with you all the way, even until the end of the ages of ages – go out and disciple the nations, bear witness to me.'

But, thank God, Jesus does not stop even at that. We have a word in the Bible which tells us that in heaven, 'He ever liveth to make intercession for them' (*Heb.* 7:25). He has taken human nature back with him into heaven and there he is seated at the right hand of God. He is our representative, our great High Priest. He takes our feeble, unworthy prayers and he transmutes them with all the glory of his own intercession at the very throne of God. He still remembers our weak and fallible frame. 'He was in all points tempted like as we are, yet without sin' (*Heb.* 4:15). And why? It was to 'succour them that are tempted' – you and me (*Heb.* 2:18).

So when you read your New Testament you will find the apostle Paul able to say this: Yes, I was on trial, and all my friends forsook me, 'But the Lord stood with me, and strengthened me' (*2 Tim.* 4:17). In the court the Lord stood by his servant and Paul knew that he was there. What did it matter that all Paul's helpers had forsaken him, Demas and the rest of them? The Lord stood by him. Paul was able to say, 'I can do all things through Christ which strengtheneth me' (*Phil.* 4:13). And our Lord will continue to act 'till his enemies be made his footstool' (*Heb.* 10:13). That is the message.

And when we read the book of Revelation, we see Jesus continuing to act, and we see what he will yet do. His people are persecuted and killed, the whole church seems to be disappearing, but he intervenes, and there is judgment – eventually he will come, riding that blessed white horse. He is at the present time saving us as individuals out of this present evil world, putting us into his glorious kingdom, preparing us for the Day that is coming when he will return.

And what then? In Acts 1:10–11 we read: 'Two men stood by them in white apparel; which also said, Ye men of Galilee, why stand ye gazing up into heaven? This same Jesus, which is taken up from you into heaven, shall so come in like manner as ye have seen him go into heaven.' If you think that Jesus finished when he died and was buried, listen to the message of Luke, listen to this treatise written to Theophilus – it is written to you. He will come again, even as he went. He will return, in bodily, visible fashion, riding the clouds of heaven, surrounded by the holy angels. And he will judge the world in righteousness and set up his glorious kingdom, to which there shall be no end.

That is the message of Christianity. That is what has made the church what it is. Do men and women need to be told about some kind of programme that will give them better conditions? That is not our greatest need. Our greatest need is to know God. If we were all given a fortune, would that solve our problems? Would that solve our moral problem? Would that solve the problem of death? Would that solve the problem of eternity?

Of course not. The message of Christianity is not about improving the world, but about changing people in spite of the world, preparing them for the glory that is yet to come. This Jesus is active and acting to that end, and he will go on until all the redeemed are gathered in, and then he will return and the final judgment will take place, and his kingdom will stretch from shore to shore.

That is the message that turned that ancient world upside down. It is the only message, and I want to ask you a simple question: What does this message mean to you? What is your idea of Christianity? What do you think the business of the church is? Do you say, 'I don't want your sermons, I don't want your argumentation, I just want to feel that I've said my prayers and paid my respects, as it were, to God, before I go out and do what I like'? Is that it?

Do you think that Christianity is something that you can take up and use as a minimum, just in the hope that it will somehow put you right? Or is it the most amazing and astounding thing that ever happened or ever will happen? Is it the thing by which you live, the thing which you long to know and to experience more and more?

Do you realize that this Jesus came into the world to save you from hell, from the punishment that your sins and mine so richly deserve? Do you realize now that the essence of Christianity is not that it calls you to do something, but rather that it tells you what Jesus came into the world to do for you?

2

The God Who Acts

And when the day of Pentecost was fully come, they were all with one accord in one place. And suddenly there came a sound from heaven as of a rushing mighty wind, and it filled all the house where they were sitting (Acts 2:1–2).

I have pinpointed the two verses above, but we shall be considering together the first twenty-one verses of Acts chapter 2. We are going back to this book of Acts because it is the only authoritative account that we have of the beginning, the origin, of the Christian church. Let me remind you that I am calling your attention to this because I believe that the most vital need of the world today is the need to know exactly what the Christian message is. And that in turn leads us to seek to know what the church is, the church which delivers this message.

There is a real confusion today about Christianity and about the Christian church – her nature, her task and her message. This is a great tragedy. Think of the problems harassing people today, individually and collectively. Think of the unhappiness, the heartbreak and the cynicism and bitterness in life. We are all aware of these human problems, as they are called. But if only people were truly Christian, most of those problems would immediately be solved. And it is the same with our international tensions and difficulties. Enmity and war and strife are due to the fact that men and women are in a wrong relationship with God, and they will only find out how to enter into a true relationship by knowing, believing, accepting, and submitting themselves to the message of the Christian church, the message of the gospel.

Now we have seen that the great message of the church is, as Luke puts it here at the very beginning of Acts, a message about the Lord Jesus Christ. This is Christianity: 'All that Jesus began both to do and teach' – what he is doing and what he is yet going to do. So now we continue from there because we see that our Lord addressed these men, these apostles of his, and gave them a commission. So we come, in this second chapter, to the origin of the Christian church. Here it is before us. This is what throws light on the nature of the church, what she has been commissioned to do and how she does it. And here it is emphasized that the whole thing is the action of God. This is not something that was done by this handful of people. We are told so often about them and so often they say about themselves that they were nobodies. We never tire of hearing how they were dismissed by the learned people, by the authorities, as 'unlearned and ignorant men' (*Acts* 4:13), and that is what they were.

Now it seems to me to be simply ludicrous to suggest that such men, without learning, without any influence or authority, without any money behind them, with none of the means of propaganda that we are familiar with today, that such men by their own efforts and abilities could succeed in doing what we read of in the pages of this book. How did it come about? There is only one answer. The world was turned upside down not because of what they did, but because of what God did to them, in them, and by means of them – and that is the essential message concerning the Christian church, her meaning, her function; her message, her purpose.

So here before us is the beginning, but if you take the trouble to read the long history of the Christian church, you will find that it continues in the same way. Indeed, I want to show you that the history of the church has been a great fight between two ideas: the false human idea as to what the church is, and the true one, which is God acting in the church.

So let us look at all this in the light of what we are told in these first twenty-one verses of Acts chapter 2. What is Christianity? What is the church? First of all, we must remind ourselves of what it is not, and oh, how urgently this reminder is needed today! I am more and more convinced that the masses of people are outside the Christian church because they have a totally wrong conception of what she is. Mark you – I want to be honest – I do not blame them. They just believe what they are told, and that is this false view which I shall put before you. If they only knew what the church really is, if they only knew what is being offered them in the gospel, they would not be outside. Like the people at Jerusalem, they would come crowding to listen.

First, then, Christianity is not dead religion. The greatest enemy of true Christianity has always been *religion*, and this is as true today as it has ever been. It is religion that confuses the minds of men and women. They would be right to reject Christianity if it were a religion. But it is not. Christianity is not a state religion; it is not an official religion in any sense at all. But that is the idea that many people have of it. They identify the church simply with what happens on certain great ceremonial occasions – a coronation, the burial of a monarch or of a great statesman, or some official action. In the Second World War, people in Britain thought of the church in terms of national days of prayer. They did not think about Christianity at any other time, but when things went wrong and we were losing every battle, then there would be a national day of prayer. But that is national religion, it has nothing to do with Christianity.

Then again, people think of the Christian church in terms of formal occasions – a christening, for example. A baby is born and people who have perhaps not thought about Christianity for years insist on having the child christened. Then they forget all about the church again. Or there is a marriage and a service in the church – 'So much better than the registry office, more dignity' – or someone dies and it is said there must be a church funeral. So the church is seen as an institution to provide what is needed for these so-called 'rites of passage'.

But again, that has nothing to do with Christianity. I almost feel like summarizing it like this: Christianity is not what the media seem to think it is. I say that with all respect to any great man, and, as one who is interested in the affairs of this country, I am second to none in my admiration of human greatness, but a man is not necessarily a Christian just because he is a great man. And the

Christian church does not revolve around any person, however great and distinguished. That is religion, something entirely different.

We must get rid of this notion that the church is a national institution or any other form of human institution. She is not a club or a society where people meet together and do certain things. I never like to hear people referring to a building as a church. 'I'm going down to the church,' they say. But the church does not consist of a building, it consists of people, living souls with the Lord in their midst. We must get rid of this external notion, this idea of just paying a kind of formal visit upon God, and then forgetting all about him. That is religion, the very antithesis of the Christian faith.

Any notion that Christianity is mainly the result of something that we do is always completely, fatally wrong. We must cast off any idea that the Christian church is the result of our action and that we are perpetuating some tradition. If that is our view of Christianity, it is false. That was the curse of the Jews who finally crucified the Lord Jesus Christ. They were traditional religionists, and such have always been – and are today – the greatest enemies of the true church and of the true Christian faith and message. But how much of so-called Christianity is just this!

Let me ask you a serious question: Why do you attend a place of worship? Have you thought enough about it even to ask that question? Are you going simply because it is a tradition? People, you say, have always gone to church on Sundays. But church attendance is something *you* do. You are simply perpetuating a tradition. Large numbers of people have gone to church out of a sense of duty, hoping each week that the service will not be too long. Each week they have felt nothing at all; the service has been absolutely lifeless, the singing miserable, the intoning of the Scriptures boring. There has been no power, no vigour. And because they have thought that that is Christianity, they have turned their backs upon it. And they are perfectly right. That is the logical step. God knows, I myself did that many years ago. And I would not be in a Christian pulpit now but for the fact that I saw through that false view. You cannot fit that into the book of Acts. That is traditional, formal religion, whatever form it may chance to take and in whatever denomination it may appear.

And let me be still more specific. There are some people who seem to have seen through the formality and who compensate for it by producing an exciting kind of worship and have stunts and entertainment to make services lively and bright. But that does not make the slightest difference because it is still men and women who are organizing it. True Christianity is always the activity of God. 'Suddenly there came a sound from heaven as of a rushing mighty wind' – God. So bright services, and an entertaining and varied programme is not Christianity either. It is livelier, but the life is not the life of the Spirit. Anything controlled by us, whether lifeless or lively, is not Christianity. Christianity is that which controls us, which masters us, which happens to us.

My second negative is that in Christianity the God who is worshipped is not an unknown God. The God of religion is always an unknown God. A classic description of this is given by Luke in the seventeenth chapter of Acts where he describes the visit of the great apostle Paul to Athens. Paul saw the place cluttered up with all sorts of temples to Jupiter, Mercury and the rest, but he came across an intriguing and fascinating altar which had a most peculiar inscription over it. The inscription was this: 'To the unknown God'. Having accounted for the gods of love and war and peace and so on, the philosophers felt there was still another power that they could not cater for. They did not know him, so they said that he was the unknown god, and he seemed to be the most powerful of all. And Paul said, 'Whom therefore ye ignorantly worship, him declare I unto you' (*Acts* 17:23).

The god of religion is always unknown. There are many people who have never really thought about God at all. I do not usually adopt the language of people whose views I totally dissent from, but they are perfectly right when they say that large numbers of people are worshipping a 'father figure', projecting some idea of fatherhood and making that their god. It is possible for us to say our prayers mechanically without even thinking about God and who God is. And to many people he is entirely unknown, some kind of superstition.

But then there is another group of people who are very popular, even notorious, and it is most interesting to observe them. They are great critics of the first group who, they agree, are worshipping religion and tradition. What, then, do they say people should worship? Now here we come to what one may call the god of the philosophers. 'God,' they say, 'is the ground of being.' Or they describe him as the 'Absolute' or the 'Ultimate'. He is the vague power that is somewhere behind the universe; he is 'Force'. God, they say, is love, and by that many of them really mean – that love is God, and wherever you find love you find God. So they tell you not to go to a church to find God, but to go out into the world, into the pubs, and there you will find kindness shown by one person to another. And that is God.

So God becomes something abstract, some general benevolence, some vague activity or power, and this, we are told, is what we must substitute for that old superstitious notion of God. This is religion up to date. This is down to earth; this is honest to God; this is the truly intellectual view. God is the ground of all being, so do not talk about a person. But you cannot pray to such a god; you cannot pray to goodness or to love or to power. But that, we are told by so many today, is the living truth and real Christianity, and the result is that we are left not only very much in the same position as those people in the first group, but if anything even worse because it is almost impossible to follow their intellectual arguments, and almost impossible to know what you believe; and, certainly, everything is all still left to you.

Yet we are told that this is the religion for twentieth-century men and women who, in this post-war atomic, scientific age think in terms of 'the ground of being' and talk about 'the Absolute'. They dismiss traditional Christianity by saying, 'Of course, it's all right when people are ignorant and unintelligent. Primitive peoples have always been superstitious and therefore they've always been religious.' So they dismiss Christianity by saying that it is for ignorant people and therefore has nothing to do with them. Real Christianity is for the philosophers, for the specialists, for the thinkers, those who can read scientific journals and have understanding.

The basic notion is that the Christian faith is something that one arrives at as the result of one's own reasoning processes. You do not accept any tradition or teaching, but starting with your own reason, you examine everything. That is the method followed in the realm of science, so why not here? So you apply your mind, and only believe what you can understand. As the result of your own reason and effort, you arrive at a knowledge of the truth. You enquire, you do your research, helped by others who are on the same quest, and at last you arrive at some satisfaction. You say, 'I've got it! God is the ground of all being!' With your great mind you have arrived at this saving formula.

But this is only for certain types of people. I am almost tempted to say that if I had the power of dictatorship in these matters, I would compel everybody to read some of the latest books on this whole subject because, I tell you now, they will not understand them. So the masses of people are not interested; they are not concerned. They see these clever men bringing out their books, and arguing and debating with one another, and their verdict on it all is: 'I couldn't care less. No doubt they make money out of it. No doubt it helps to keep their jobs going.'

I am telling you what the man in the street is saying, and this is one of the greatest problems facing western Christians today. Our Christianity has become a middle-class movement; the so-called working classes are not touched by it. But this is wrong. A message that only appeals to a certain type, a certain class, is not the Christian gospel. There is something wrong somewhere. Christianity, by definition and by the example of history, is not confined to a certain type, a certain class of person.

So much for the negatives – now let us turn to the positives. What is Christianity? What is the Christian church? What is her message? How did she come into being? How has she acted? How has she persisted?

The first thing that should strike anybody who reads the Bible, a chapter such as Acts 2, or any other, is that the starting point is the living God, the Creator, and not human beings. The first verse in the Bible is, 'In the beginning God created. . .' God! The whole book starts with God and is dominated by God. I am convinced that the trouble with the world today is that it does not believe in God. And so much of our evangelism goes wrong because it starts with the Lord Jesus Christ. But you must not; you must start with God the Father, God the Creator, one whose glory fills the heavens, who is over all. With reverence I say that you cannot understand the Lord Jesus Christ, and indeed, there is a sense in which there is no meaning to him and to the message about him, unless you start with God the Father.

Christianity puts this before us in this way: 'God in three Persons, blessed Trinity', God the Father, God the Son, God the Holy Spirit. God – a God who is personal, a God who can say, 'I am' (*Exod.* 3:14); and 'I will . . .' (*Exod.* 3:17). He is a God who, because he is a living God, reveals himself. Contrary to modern teaching, God is not an abstraction. He is not the mere 'ground of all being'. He is not 'the Absolute'. He is a God who thinks, a God who speaks, a God who makes proclamations. Or, looking at it the other way round, he is a God to whom we can pray, a God whose help we can seek. This is the whole message throughout the Bible.

I could give you many illustrations. As we have seen, that was the very message which the apostle Paul preached to the people in Athens. We are told that 'his spirit was stirred in him, when he saw the city wholly given to idolatry' (*Acts* 17:16). Oh, Paul said, I can't stand this, I must tell these people they're worshipping nothing. They're worshipping idols which they made themselves, mere projections of their own minds. There are no such gods. These people know nothing about the living, the true God. This is what he said to them:

Ye men of Athens, I perceive that in all things ye are too superstitious. For as I passed by, and beheld your devotions, I found an altar with this inscription, TO THE UNKNOWN GOD. Whom therefore ye ignorantly worship, him declare I unto you. God that made the world and all things therein, seeing that he is Lord of heaven and earth, dwelleth not in temples made with hands; neither is worshipped with men's hands, as though he needed any thing, seeing he giveth to all life, and breath, and all things; and hath made of one blood all nations of men for to dwell on all the face of the earth, and hath determined the times before appointed, and the bounds of their habitation (Acts 17:22–26).

And down in Thessalonica, Paul proclaimed the same message. In his letter to the Thessalonians, he later wrote, 'Ye turned to God from idols to serve the living and true God' (*1 Thess.* 1:9). Christianity is no dead religion; we serve a living God.

But God is not only a living God, he is a God who acts, and this is the point I want to make. Here it is again: 'When the day of Pentecost was fully come, they were all with one accord in one place.' They had come together and were praying together; they were waiting. And in the end, people can do nothing but wait.

'And suddenly there came a sound from heaven as of a rushing mighty wind, and it filled all the house where they were sitting.' Now that is the truth about God. This is the special point about the Christian message, the thing that differentiates it from every other message. Every other religion worships a dead god. Take the so-called great religions of the East. Their adherents have no living God to turn to, no God who acts. They talk about Nirvana, about being absorbed into the absolute, and people think it is intelligent to believe in something like that. All is dead and a matter of passivity.

Christianity is the exact opposite. The people in Jerusalem, Jews from Crete, Arabia and all the other places, were astonished, and exclaimed, 'We do hear them speak in our tongues' – what? – 'the wonderful works of God' (*Acts* 2:11). This is the whole message of the Bible and of the Christian church. These men, filled with the Holy Spirit, were not protesting against the tyranny of the Roman Empire; they were not deciding what resolutions they should send up to the Emperor or to their representatives, their senators and others; they were not expressing their opinion on current affairs. No, no: 'The wonderful works of God'. The Christian message is a proclamation to men and women fumbling and stumbling, even at noonday, trying in the darkness to solve their problems and understand the mystery of life. It is a proclamation that this is God's world, that God has made it. It has not just evolved. 'In the beginning God' – and he created.

But God not only made the world, he owns it and controls it. Read Psalm 104 and that will tell you how he gives breath and life to everything and how, when he withdraws the breath of life, all creatures collapse and die. God is over all, not men and women, not even the greatest of them, but God, who has made everything and who gives every gift. Even the greatest people have nothing to boast of, they have nothing but what they have received. They have not generated it or produced it. 'Every good gift and every perfect gift is from above, and cometh down from the Father of lights' (*James* 1:17).

Furthermore, God is actively interested in this world. He is not some god in the distance, in the vagueness of impersonal religion. No, no! He looks down upon the world which he has made and is concerned about it. And the great message of the Bible, as it was the immediate message of the early Christian church, is to tell men and women something about 'the wonderful works' which God has done upon this earth.

Let me emphasize some of these works for you. God has not abandoned this world. It is in a terrible mess; it has been in a mess since Adam and Eve rebelled against God in the Garden of Eden. All our troubles have come out of that. But the message is that it is not men and women who will redeem the world and lift it up again. They have been trying to do that for many centuries, and that is the story of civilization and of political activity. I am not here to criticize them. Let them do their best: They are meant to preserve order as far as they can in the chaos, but they will never redeem this world.

But the God that Christianity preaches came down into the garden in the cool of the evening. This is a God who is concerned. He came down and spoke to the man and woman, exposing their evil and punishing them, but he gave them a promise, and if I did not have this promise I would not be a preacher. The promise reveals that God is concerned about this world and its affairs and is doing something about it.

The Bible is the book of God, the history of the activity of God. After the account of the fall, we go on to read that men and women turned their backs upon God and sank so deeply into sin that they were living not only a materialistic, immoral life, but an amoral life, and God visited the world with the punishment of the flood. And that is the sort of world we are living in now.

And then later on, in their cleverness, men and women said, 'Let us build a city and a tower, whose top may reach unto heaven' (*Gen.* 11:4). That is the time in the Old Testament that seems to me to correspond most clearly to the twentieth century: Build a temple, build a tower that will reach into heaven. We'll do it with our scientific knowledge. We're going to get right into heaven.

But God acted. He came down and confused it all. The same God acted in Sodom and Gomorrah, and in many a similar society, and in Babylon, too. All these great places have gone down; they all turned to rubble.

But, thank God, that is only one side. There is another – he is the God of Abraham. How did the great Old Testament story of the Jews ever come to pass? The answer is that God looked on a man called Abraham, living in paganism in Ur of the Chaldees. He spoke to him and called him out, and Abraham went out 'not knowing whither he went' (*Heb.* 11:8), simply obeying the call of God. It is all of God. This is the essence of Christianity, this is the true message: Not you and I dragging ourselves to a church service in which we do everything and feel nothing, while God is some abstraction, away in some infinity.

There was a man called Jacob, a pretty poor character. He had a twin brother called Esau who, as a natural man, was much nicer and a better fellow. But Jacob, disguised as Esau, received the blessing that his dying father had intended for Esau. So Jacob had to run for his life. On the first night of his escape, he lay on the ground and put a stone under his head as a pillow, and there he had a most amazing dream. God spoke to him. This is it! God interfering in a man's life, God addressing him, a ladder sent down and traffic between heaven and earth – God and man. Jacob awoke, astonished and amazed, and said, 'This is none other but the house of God' (*Gen.* 28:17). 'I didn't realize it,' he said in effect. 'I thought I was in a wilderness and I put my head upon a stone, but I'm in the house of God, and at the very gateway and doorway of heaven. I've met with God.' And he had. This is Christianity.

Or take another illustration, this time from the third chapter of the book of Exodus. Here was a man who had been a shepherd for forty years. His name was Moses, and he was a great man. Because of something he had done in Egypt, Moses, too, had had to escape, and he was apparently destined to spend the rest of his life as a simple shepherd. But one afternoon he took his sheep to the back side of a mountain, not expecting anything at all, and, 'The angel of the Lord appeared unto him in a flame of fire out of the midst of a bush: and he looked, and, behold, the bush burned with fire, and the bush was not consumed' (*Exod.* 3:2). We would never have heard the story of the exodus of the children of Israel from Egypt to Canaan but for this. It was not an idea that suddenly occurred to Moses. He did not plan and scheme and order it – far from it!

God appeared to him and poor Moses fumbled, hesitated and did not understand. When Moses first saw the bush, he said, 'I will now turn aside, and see this great sight, why the bush is not burnt.' He was going to investigate. He was a modern man, you see, a scientist. What is this? What is this phenomenon? I'm going to understand it.

But God called out of the middle of the bush and said, 'Moses, Moses . . . Draw not nigh hither: put off thy shoes from off thy feet, for the place whereon thou standest is holy ground . . . I am the God of thy father, the God of Abraham, the God of Isaac, and the God of Jacob' (*Exod.* 3:4–6). Then we are told that Moses hid his face for he was afraid to look upon God – and rightly so. And the Lord said – and oh, if this were not true, there would be no message, no hope – 'I have surely seen the affliction of my people which are in Egypt.' He is not some ground of reality, not some impersonal force or idea or mere love or goodness or kindness. He is *personal* – 'I have seen . . . and have heard their cry by reason of their taskmasters; for I know their sorrows . . .' (He is 'touched with the feeling of our infirmities' [*Heb.* 4:15]) '. . . And I am come down to deliver them' (*Exod.* 3:3–8), And he did.

Then the great story follows. Let me urge you to read your Old Testament. Go on to the fourteenth chapter of that book of Exodus and there you will find that Moses and the people, having gone out of Egypt, now found themselves with sea in front and the hosts of Pharaoh behind. They felt they were on the point of being annihilated. Then Moses turned to God, not knowing what to do. And God said, 'The Lord shall fight for you . . . Wherefore criest thou unto me? Speak unto the children of Israel, that they go forward' (*Exod.* 14:14–15). And they went – the God who acts! Then God went on to speak to Moses on Mount Sinai, revealing his character, giving the Ten Commandments and the moral law.

Oh, I am like the author of the epistle to the Hebrews. Time would fail me to tell you all these great stories: David, the prophets, Elijah on Mount Carmel in the great trial. There they were, the eight hundred and fifty false prophets with one true prophet – Elijah, the man of God. He challenged them and said, 'The God that answereth by fire, let him be God' (*1 Kings* 18:24). The false prophets said that they had a god, Baal.

Very well, said Elijah. We'll test our gods. We'll see which of them is God. Kill a bullock, cut it in pieces, put the pieces on a pile of wood on an altar, and then ask your god Baal to send down fire to consume the offering. So they began, the eight hundred and fifty false prophets, and Elijah was watching them. He knew the result before they began. He spoke to them now and again and said: Why doesn't your god answer you? Perhaps he's gone on a journey, or perhaps he's asleep and can't hear you. Shout a little louder!

That is the way to deal with false prophets. Let them produce their god, let them show the results of their 'living' god – where is he? That is why chapels and churches are empty. People are not worshipping the true and living God, but mere projections of their own minds and philosophies.

And on Mount Carmel nothing happened. The prophets cut themselves with knives and lancets and went into a frenzy. But they failed completely. Then Elijah stepped quietly forward and offered a simple prayer to God. He began, 'Lord God of Abraham, Isaac, and of Israel, let it be known this day that thou art God in Israel' (verse 36). And God answered by fire. He is the living God. He is the active God. He is the true God.

In one way, the story of the New Testament begins in Luke 3: 'Now in the fifteenth year of the reign of Tiberius Caesar, Pontius Pilate being governor of Judaea, and Herod being tetrarch of Galilee' – what happened? – 'the word of God came unto John the son of Zacharias in the wilderness.' There had been no word for about four hundred years, not since the prophet Malachi, but now here was John the Baptist. He was in the wilderness and the word of God came to him. That is the whole story: It is always God acting and sending his word. But the climax is this: 'When the fulness of the time was come, God sent forth his Son, made of a woman, made under the law' (*Gal.* 4:4). 'God so loved the world, that he gave his only begotten Son' (*John* 3:16). Jesus of Nazareth is the Son of God, sent into the world, appearing among men – God sending, God acting.

And here, in Acts 2, God is starting the Christian church: 'And when the day of Pentecost was fully come, they were all with one accord in one place.' And there they would have remained until they died were it not for this: 'And suddenly there came a sound from heaven as of a rushing mighty wind, and it filled all the house where they were sitting.' God was continuing, acting in them and through them. And it is quite certain that we should not be considering this now were it not for the fact that God has continued to act. Men and women in their blindness and sin have done their very best to ruin the Christian church. If she were our creation, she would have finished long ago, like many another institution. People have misunderstood; they have gone wrong; they have preached error, and the church would have died. So why is there still a church? There is only one answer: God comes in revival. God sends his Spirit again. Look at the Protestant Reformation. God, as he sent his word to John the Baptist, sent it to Martin Luther, and when God sends his word even to one man, and gives him great power, he can turn over a great church with fifteen centuries of tradition behind it. One man – it was enough – Martin Luther, called of God, given the message and filled with God's Spirit overthrew a Church which had become quite pagan in its teaching.

God, the living, active God, sent the rushing, mighty wind. Why does he do it? It is for salvation. 'It shall come to pass, that whosoever shall call on the name of the Lord shall be saved' (*Acts* 2:21).Everyone needs to be saved, however great, however illustrious. We are all sinners. We are all born in sin, 'shapen in iniquity' (*Psa.* 51:5). 'There is none righteous, no, not one' (*Rom.* 3:10). The wrath of God is on us all. 'All flesh is as grass, and all the glory of man as the flower of grass. The grass withereth, and the flower thereof falleth away' (*1 Pet.* 1:24). The greatest lose their faculties. Final illness and decay come to each of us.

> *The boast of heraldry, the pomp of power,*
> *And all that beauty, all that wealth e'er gave,*
> *Await alike the inevitable hour,*
> *The paths of glory lead but to the grave.*
>
> Thomas Gray

Oh, there is no hope in humanity, the only hope is that God is, and that he is the God who comes down, the God who offers salvation. He sent his only Son into the world, even to the cross to die, his body to be broken, his blood to be shed, so that 'whosoever believeth in him should not perish, but have everlasting life' (*John* 3:16).

This is Christianity: It is the message that you need to be saved and that God has provided the means whereby you can be saved. It is all his action. It is a supernatural action, a miraculous action. I am not telling you to be good, I know you cannot be. I am not telling you to read books of philosophy in order to arrive at a knowledge of God and learn how to live – I know it is all useless. My message is that God 'hath visited and redeemed his people' (*Luke* 1:68). It is no use anyone telling us to pull ourselves together – that is the one thing we cannot do. We are mastered by lust and passions and evil desire. We are victims; we need to be delivered. And thank God he does deliver us. That is our message. It is surprising. Like the visitors to Jerusalem, people today ask, 'What meaneth this?' (*Acts* 2:12). Of course. We cannot understand. It is powerful. It was a mighty rushing wind. And it is a transforming power. It changes people. It changed these disciples so that from being weak, frightened, alarmed, helpless and useless they became mighty men of God.

But above everything else, Christianity is entirely beyond understanding. 'What meaneth this?' they asked. Of course they did. If you can understand your religion it is a proof it is not Christianity. If you are in control of your religion, it is not Christianity. If you can take it up in a bag on Sunday morning when you go to church and then put it down again, that is not Christianity. Christianity is a miracle. It is a marvel. It astonishes people.

When Blaise Pascal, the French thinker, had a great experience of God, he said, 'The God of Abraham, the God of Isaac, the God of Jacob'. Then, negatively, 'Not the God of the philosophers and seers and thinkers'. That is the contrast. The God of the Bible is the God who reveals himself in all the glory and the wonder of his miraculous, eternal power. Thank God for such a message, such a gospel. It made the church. This is what she preached, and on the day of Pentecost three thousand men and women were added to the church.

But, finally, because all this is true, Christianity is a message for all people: 'Whosoever shall call on the name of the Lord shall be saved' (*Acts* 2:21). You will need to be very clever to understand these modern books about God, but thank God, you do not need to be clever to be a Christian. 'The common people heard him gladly,' wrote Mark (*Mark* 12:37). 'Not many wise men after the flesh, not many mighty, not many noble, are called,' says the apostle Paul (*1 Cor.* 1:26). No, 'God hath chosen the foolish things of the world to confound the wise; and God hath chosen the weak things of the world to confound the things which are mighty . . .

and things which are not, to bring to nought things that are' (verses 27–28). There is a hope for all who realize their need, and cry out to him.

Is that your idea of Christianity? Do you know this living God, this true God, this active God, this God who intervenes and comes? Have you ever met him in any shape or form, as Moses met him in the burning bush, as Jacob met him at Peniel, as Elijah met him on Mount Carmel?

Have you ever felt the touch of God upon your soul? Are you aware that you have been dealt with, that God has entered into your life and has done something that you could not do? Do you know that you are what you are by the grace of God? Do you say, 'I can't explain, all I know is that God has done something to me in Christ'? If you can say that, you are a Christian, but if all you have is what you do and what you think, I am afraid you are not a Christian. God's coming to you need not be the rushing, mighty wind, but it is always the power of God. It is always the hand of God. It always brings the knowledge that God has had pity upon you and has come down in the person of his Son to enter even into your life, to save you and set you free. Oh that men and women might know the living God and his power unto salvation in Jesus Christ our Lord!

3

The Great Fact of Prophecy

But Peter, standing up with the eleven, lifted up his voice, and said unto them, Ye men of Judaea, and all ye that dwell at Jerusalem, be this known unto you, and hearken to my words: for these are not drunken, as ye suppose, seeing it is but the third hour of the day, but this is that which was spoken by the prophet Joel; And it shall come to pass in the last days, saith God, I will pour out of my Spirit upon all flesh: and your sons and your daughters shall prophesy, and your young men shall see visions, and your old men shall dream dreams: and on my servants and on my handmaidens I will pour out in those days of my Spirit; and they shall prophesy: and I will shew wonders in heaven above, and signs in the earth beneath; blood, and fire, and vapour of smoke: the sun shall be turned into darkness, and the moon into blood, before that great and notable day of the Lord come: and it shall come to pass, that whosoever shall call on the name of the Lord shall be saved.

Ye men of Israel, hear these words; Jesus of Nazareth, a man approved of God among you by miracles and wonders and signs, which God did by him in the midst of you, as ye yourselves also know: him, being delivered by the determinate counsel and foreknowledge of God, ye have taken, and by wicked hands have crucified and slain: whom God hath raised up, having loosed the pains of death: because it was not possible that he should be holden of it. For David speaketh concerning him, I foresaw the Lord always before my face, for he is on my right hand, that I should not be moved: therefore did my heart rejoice, and my tongue was glad; moreover also my flesh shall rest in hope: because thou wilt not leave my soul in hell, neither wilt thou suffer thine Holy One to see corruption. Thou hast made known to me the ways of life; thou shalt make me full of joy with thy countenance.

*Men and brethren, let me freely speak unto you of the patriarch David
that he is both dead and buried, and his sepulchre is with us unto this
day. Therefore being a prophet, and knowing that God had sworn with an
oath to him, that of the fruit of his loins, according to the flesh, he would
raise up Christ to sit on his throne; he seeing this before spake of the
resurrection of Christ, that his soul was not left in hell, neither his flesh
did see corruption. This Jesus hath God raised up, whereof we all are
witnesses. Therefore being by the right hand of God exalted, and having
received of the Father the promise of the Holy Ghost, he hath shed forth
this, which ye now see and hear. For David is not ascended into the
heavens: but he saith himself, The Lord said unto my Lord, Sit thou on
my right hand, until I make thy foes thy footstool. Therefore let all the
house of Israel know assuredly, that God hath made that same Jesus,
whom ye have crucified, both Lord and Christ* (Acts 2:14–36).

The day of Pentecost was a most notable and vital day for the
Christian church, and it was also one of the great turning
points in the history of the world. Without understanding it, it is
quite impossible to have any correct notion as to the character and
nature of the Christian church and the Christian message. In Acts
2 we have the first sermon that was ever preached under the
auspices of the church, and therefore it is of unusual importance.

I am calling attention to Peter's sermon because we are confronted by the tragic fact that the world, speaking generally, is not
interested in this message. Now that is particularly staggering
since we now find ourselves in a world which we understand less
and less. The other day, I was reading an article in a learned
journal which pointed out that towards the last quarter of the
nineteenth century scientists had become exceedingly confident
and optimistic. Even a great and sane man like Lord Kelvin did
not hesitate to say that it was merely a matter of time before all the
secrets of nature were discovered. Discoveries and inventions had
led men and women to believe that scientific research and endeavour held the key to unlocking the secrets of life. But the article
went on to point out, quite rightly, that in a very short time indeed
all such notions were exploded.

By what? Well, by further discoveries of science! The discovery
of x-rays shattered nineteenth-century optimism and dispelled
the idea that all the mysteries of the universe would soon

be fathomed. The discovery of radium increased the sense of mystery, and then later research in the twentieth century, on the nature of the atom and so on, completely destroyed this idea. The universe has become mysterious.

But apart from that, what is life itself? What is the purpose of it all? What are we doing here? And then, of course, there is death, this inevitable event towards which everybody is moving. What is it? What lies behind it? We are only here for a short while – threescore years and ten, says the Bible – some are taken beyond that, yes, to ninety and even more, but death is bound to come.

So is it not amazing that, confronted by such ignorance about the universe, about ourselves, about life, death, and eternity, the majority of men and women will still not consider the only book, the only teaching, that gives us even a modicum of explanation and understanding? It is astounding that people in the world can still go on in their fatal optimism in spite of facts which are shaking their world, even in the face of their own discoveries, and even when confronted by the sort of event which is undoubtedly uppermost in the minds of all the people of this country at present.[1] But this is the truth that is before us, and I assert once more that the only help and guidance we have is to be found here, in the pages of the Bible.

When we come to the Bible, we come to something which is entirely different from what passes for Christianity in the minds of so many people, both with regard to the nature of the church and the character of her message. But because people do not know that, they are not interested in it, and turn away from it. They are left to their own misery, disturbed by events, shaken for a moment when they stand over an open grave, but rushing away to take a drink or plunge into pleasure or watch the television in an attempt to forget all about it. Now apart from anything else, that is not intelligent. It is foolish to dismiss these fears by brushing them away and turning your back upon them. Here is a message that asks us all to think, and to face solid facts of history, and that is why I come back to it once more.

Now one reason which people very often give to explain why they are not interested in Christianity is that it can be understood and dismissed finally and completely – so they say – in terms of

[1] Sir Winston Churchill, the great British wartime leader, died on 24 January 1965.

psychology. This argument takes many different forms. Some say, 'You Christians claim to have religious experiences, and people like you have claimed this throughout the centuries. It used to be thought, of course, that all this was real, but now we know otherwise.' (Incidentally, with reference to Lord Kelvin's confident assertion, which I quoted earlier, he was answered not only by the discovery of x-rays, but perhaps quite as much by the theories of Freud and his school of psychology.) The argument is this: 'Of course, we are not all the same. We have different temperaments and we react in different ways to the same set of facts. Furthermore, people's own minds can produce things. People used to think that there was a great God in the heavens. Of course, we have now discovered, as the result of psychological research, that there is nothing there at all, but people have conjured up the idea of some powerful father figure, some great being outside us. When they say there is a God, they are merely projecting their own feelings, their own sensations. And that is the essence of religion.

We are asked to look at the science of the development of religions – the philosophy of religion, as it is called. And we are told that the further back we go in the story of the human race, and the more primitive people are, and the more superstitious they are, then the more frightened they are of life. Primitive natives are always frightened of everything, and they tend to personalize everything. They hear a thunder clap and say, 'Oh, there's some great being up there, who has just roared,' and they see a flash of lightning and add, 'He struck some tinder or something.' And so they turn every natural event they do not understand into the work of a god. That is primitive man.

Then we are told that as societies develop and people become more sophisticated, religious belief becomes less crude. If we go up the scale, we find fewer and fewer gods and eventually we arrive at the Jews who reached the topmost pinnacle, maintaining that there is only one God and that the others are not gods at all. But of course, the theory continues, even the Jews were wrong. They had advanced tremendously – it is a great advance to have only one god instead of dozens – but we know now that there is not even one god. And even the most intelligent people, not only the Jews but Christian people also, are still just doing the same old thing, objectifying their fears and phobias, and putting them all together into a being, a person, whom they call God. To sum up, this is the sole explanation of religion, and of Christianity, which is a higher and modified form of the religion of the Jews.

So that is the argument, and I am very concerned about this because I often find that Christian people do not know how to answer it; indeed, they have even lent their support to that argument. Back in 1935 I had the privilege of taking part in a summer school for ministers. One evening we had a discussion which I was leading, and I was most interested to notice that certain men, who were arguing from the same position as I was, were almost giving me more trouble than the people with whom we were arguing. They got up one after another and they said something like this (and how often one has heard it!): 'Now it doesn't matter what you say, I don't care what scientific evidence you produce, you can argue as you like, you can ridicule my Bible with your learning and take most of it from me, and maintain that science can prove this and that, but you will never take my experience from me.'

These men thought that in that way they were answering the scientists, but they were simply delivering themselves lock, stock and barrel into the arms of the psychologists! 'Quite so,' says the psychologist. 'That's exactly the trouble with you religious people. You shut your eyes to the facts. You say, "my experience", but of course, we can explain your experience quite simply. Think of the man who says he has had an experience of God and has felt awe in his presence. Now if you were to psychoanalyse that man, you would probably find that as a child he was once terrified by his own father. He had done something wrong, so his father had reprimanded him very severely and perhaps smacked him. This began to rankle and to build up until it became his idea of God.' That is the kind of response you may get when you base the whole of your position upon your experience. Yet so many Christians do that.

Do not misunderstand me. I believe in the objective validity of religious experiences. All I am trying to show is that you cannot base the Christian message on experiences because people explain them away like that. Sometimes they go further and say, 'Of course, you say that the only explanation of these experiences is your Christian message, but of course we know something about the cults. We've heard similar things about Christian Scientists, for example, who claim that whereas they used to be worried and troubled, now, since they've taken up this teaching, they are no longer ill or worried.' So if you put the Christian case in terms of some wonderful experience you have had, or in terms of an appeal like, 'Come to Jesus and you will find a friend,' or, 'Come to Jesus and you will get physical healing,' or, 'Come to Jesus and you will receive guidance,' or, 'Come to Jesus and you will discover peace and joy,' if you put it like that, you are just opening the door to a psychological explanation of your faith.

Or again, some people may say that though they are very glad that others have had these experiences of healing and deliverance from various troubles, they themselves have never been worried by such things. 'I'm very glad that you are better than you used to be,' they may say, 'I'm thankful for any kind of agency that can deliver people from their troubles. I think you may be wrong in your explanation, but as long as it makes you feel better, well and good, carry on. I'm obviously a different kind of person and I don't need what you're talking about. Life is going very happily and smoothly. I've a good job, I'm earning good money, I've a wife and children, we've a wonderful home, there's nothing that I desire. So when you come with your great stories and ask me to take this, that and the other, the answer is, thank you, but I don't need it!' And many people are in precisely that position.

The answer to all these comments is Peter's sermon on the day of Pentecost. Why did Peter preach? It was to give an explanation. The people in Jerusalem were suddenly confronted by a group of men and women, some of whom they may have already known, and who were obviously very simple people – fishermen and others – who were suddenly entirely changed. Something astounding had happened to them, and the people of Jerusalem 'were all amazed and marvelled, saying one to another, Behold, are not all these which speak Galilaeans? And how hear we every man in our own tongue?' (*Acts* 2:7–8). And some said that the disciples were full of new wine. The crowd was confronted by a phenomenon, an experience, by a change in the lives of men and women, so the whole question was: What has done this? And in his sermon Peter gave the answer to that question.

The Great Fact of Prophecy

Notice first of all that Peter did not just talk about his experience, or say, 'This is wonderful and you people can have this same thing.' No, he said, 'This is that which was spoken . . .' and he quoted a prophet, and then another prophet, and he expounded the Scriptures. In addition, he expounded the Scriptures in terms of certain facts. The whole of this sermon is a recital of facts and an explanation of them, put in this most interesting manner.

Peter said, 'This Jesus hath God raised up, whereof we all are witnesses' (verse 32). Indeed, he addressed them, 'Ye men of Israel, hear these words; Jesus of Nazareth, a man approved of God among you by miracles and wonders and signs, which God did by him in the midst of you, as ye yourselves also know. Him, being delivered by the determinate counsel and foreknowledge of God, ye have taken, and by wicked hands have crucified and slain: whom God hath raised up, having loosed the pains of death: because it was not possible that he should be holden of it' (verses 22–24). Peter pointed his listeners to objective facts and then worked out his great argument. And the essence is this: You are asking what this is, and I can only explain it to you in terms of a person called Jesus of Nazareth. He is the sole explanation.

'If you want to understand what has happened to us,' said Peter in effect, 'if you want to understand this amazing phenomenon, you have to look at that person, Jesus of Nazareth.' So Peter told them about our Lord's birth and his life, about his teaching and especially about his death upon the cross, his burial in the tomb and then his resurrection and ascension. Then, finally, he explained this thing which had just happened on the day of Pentecost.

Now the apostle's argument is that the events on the day of Pentecost would not have happened were it not for those facts. Were it not that our Lord had risen from the dead and appeared to his disciples, nothing would have happened. Peter was claiming that this Jesus of Nazareth is the only begotten Son of God and that that is proved by his resurrection from the dead. So Peter gave a long quotation from David. He said that David had foreseen this event and prophesied it. He could not have been talking about himself because, said Peter, 'he is both dead and buried, and his sepulchre is with us unto this day' (verse 29), whereas Christ, having died, had been raised, and had ascended to heaven from where, 'being by the right hand of God exalted, and having received of the Father the promise of the Holy Ghost, he hath shed forth this, which ye now see and hear' (verse 33). Christ, said Peter, had sent down this power, even as he had promised he would. And that, Peter argued, was the sole explanation of what had happened to them. Now you will notice that Peter did not answer in terms of a theory; he did not make a psychological analysis; he did not try to explain it. He said: I have only one explanation and it is Jesus whom you have seen and heard and whose miracles you have witnessed.

So I say to you that it does not matter what your temperament is, it does not matter what your psychological make-up may or may not be. Like Peter, it is my task to remind you of certain historical facts. May I put it like this to fix it in your mind? This age may well be known as the age of Winston Churchill – a fact of history. There has been an age of Cromwell; there was an age of Julius Caesar. These are facts – these people were historical personages. And Jesus of Nazareth is an historical personage.

I am not trying to explain some experience or a theory. I start with certain events that have taken place and belong solidly to history. That was Peter's argument. That was how he started his sermon. But he put it in a most interesting way. He put it in terms of this next element that I want to emphasize – prophecy. 'This,' he said, 'is that which was spoken by the prophet Joel' (verse 16) and then he proceeded to quote that prophet who had lived many centuries earlier.

That Jesus' life and death is the fulfilment of prophecy is one of the main arguments in this sermon and I want to show you its importance. It is very interesting to notice how these preachers repeated themselves. Much later on, when Peter came to write a letter and was talking about this great salvation, he said:

Of which salvation the prophets have enquired and searched diligently, who prophesied of the grace that should come unto you: searching what, or what manner of time the Spirit of Christ which was in them did signify, when it testified beforehand the sufferings of Christ, and the glory that should follow. Unto whom it was revealed, that not unto themselves, but unto us they did minister the things, which are now reported unto you by them that have preached the gospel unto you with the Holy

Ghost sent down from heaven; which things the angels desire to look into (1 Pet. 1:10–12).

And in Peter's second letter, when he reminds his readers that he is an old man, he says:

I will not be negligent to put you always in remembrance of these things, though ye know them, and be established in the present truth. Yea, I think it meet, as long as I am in this tabernacle, to stir you up by putting you in remembrance; knowing that shortly I must put off this my tabernacle, even as our Lord Jesus Christ hath shewed me (2 Pet. 1: 12–14)

Peter's body was but a tent and he says: I am going to put it off; I am going on to the realm of the spiritual. So what was Peter reminding his readers of? Well, he says:

For we have not followed cunningly devised fables, when we made known unto you the power and coming of our Lord Jesus Christ, but were eyewitnesses of his majesty. For he received from God the Father honour and glory, when there came such a voice to him from the excellent glory, This is my beloved Son, in whom I am well pleased. And this voice which came from heaven we heard, when we were with him in the holy mount. We have also a more sure word of prophecy; whereunto ye do well that ye take heed, as unto a light that shineth in a dark place, until the day dawn, and the day star arise in your hearts (2 Pet. 1:16–19).

You see, the old man is saying: I am going to die and shall not be with you much longer. So I want you to hold on to those things that you have heard, because you are living in a difficult world and you are confronted by the world, the flesh, and the devil. You yourselves have to die, and I am thinking of your having an abundant entry into the everlasting kingdom of God when you come to die. The only way to have this is to hold on to the truth you have heard.

But somebody may say, 'Why should we believe it? On what grounds do we believe it?'

Well, says Peter, I am by way of being a witness. I remember the day when this Jesus of Nazareth turned to James and John and to me and said, 'Come along, I want you to go with me to the top of the mountain.' So we went up, leaving the other disciples at the foot, and you know, I shall never forget it. There the three of us were with him on top of this mountain, and suddenly the place was overshadowed by a bright, shining cloud, and as we looked at him, he was entirely transfigured. He began to shine with an amazing luminosity, even his clothing was shining and a radiance of heaven came into it. Two men appeared, speaking to him – Moses and Elijah – and we heard a voice speaking from heaven saying, 'This is my beloved Son: hear him.'

Now, continues Peter, I am an old man, on the verge of the grave, but I testify to you that I was there. I heard it. I am a witness to it and so were my brethren, James and John. We heard that voice on the holy mount, we heard God speaking about this Jesus. We have not followed cunningly devised fables. We have not been telling you fairy tales. We have had to suffer for this, and I know that I am going to suffer. He told me, he prophesied that I was going to die in a most extraordinary way.

Jesus had predicted that when Peter came to die, he would be crucified (see John 21:18) and according to tradition he was crucified upside down. So here is an old man knowing that that is coming, and he says: I tell you in the presence of God, I heard the voice. But notice that in his letter Peter does not stop at that. The facts are there, and they are important, but he also says, 'We have also a more sure word of prophecy.' If you do not believe my testimony, says Peter, if you do not believe my witness, then I have another bit of evidence – prophecy, verified prophecy.

So at the end of his life Peter was, in a sense, preaching the same sermon as his very first sermon on the day of Pentecost when he reminded these people of Jerusalem: '. . . as ye yourselves also know . . . This Jesus hath God raised up, whereof we all are witnesses,' but also said: 'This is that which was spoken by the prophet Joel.'

In his sermon in Acts 2, Peter quoted two prophecies in particular: the prophecy of the prophet Joel, and that of David, who, because he was a man of God who was at times illumined by the Spirit, also prophesied and wrote his prophecies in the form of psalms. And the apostle's argument is that prophecy is a fact. These prophecies were written centuries before the birth of Jesus Christ. So it does not make the slightest difference whether you are volatile or quiet, whether you are an optimist or a pessimist. It is a solid fact of history that many centuries before the birth of

Christ, various men wrote down, in documents that were preserved, prophecies about a person who was going to come. They gave the most extraordinary details concerning him – details about his birth in Bethlehem, about his poverty and about the character of his life. They told of his ride into Jerusalem on the foal of an ass, of the betrayal for thirty pieces of silver, and they said that he would be 'led as a lamb to the slaughter' (*Isa.* 53:7) and killed. They said he would die, yes, but that he would rise again and would ascend and send down the Holy Spirit. All that was prophesied.

This is the basis of the Christian faith. I do not simply preach experiences to you. Thank God, I have had experiences, but I do not tell you what has happened to me. I do not talk about myself. With the apostle Paul I say, 'We preach not ourselves, but Christ Jesus the Lord' (*2 Cor.* 4:5). That is why I never believe in just putting up people to give their testimonies and say, 'Come to Jesus and you will get the same thing.' No, no, my task is to hold these facts before you, the facts recorded in the Gospels, and, behind them, the fact of prophecy.

But how do you explain prophecy? How did it come about that so many centuries before the events these men were able to tell us about them in such detail? The answer is given by Peter in that last letter of his when he says, 'Knowing this first, that no prophecy of the scripture is of any private interpretation' (*2 Pet.* 1:20). This means that no man ever wrote a prophecy which he simply conjured up out of his own mind or imagination. The prophet was not just a man who sat down and thought philosophically about life, trying with his insight to understand it, and then had a brilliant idea. He could not. A human being cannot by himself foretell facts. He can give theories, he can make a forecast, though it is generally wrong rather than right, but that is all. These men, however, were right, and right in detail. If they had told a one-off fact, you could say it was a coincidence, but there are dozens of details. It is extraordinary. How do you explain it? Peter said, '. . . for the prophecy came not in old time by the will of man: but holy men of God spake as they were moved by the Holy Ghost' (*2 Pet.* 1:21). That is the only explanation: It is God who was behind everything, revealing it, making it known, and that is what the prophets say – read their words for yourselves. They do not say,

'I've suddenly had a bright idea.' No, it is: 'The word of the Lord came unto me'; 'the burden of the Lord'; 'the Lord spake unto me'. They were given the words to say.

Jesus' life, death and resurrection were a fulfilment of prophecy. This was the basis of Peter's message, and I suggest to you that that is unanswerable. So let me summarize what it all means. First and foremost, it reminds us of the living God. He is not an abstraction. He is not a philosophic 'x' about which you argue and debate. No, no, he is a living God who gives revelation, gives knowledge, imparts information.

Peter also made this striking point: In those revelations which God gave to the prophets, he was revealing that he has a great plan and purpose with respect to this world. That is the message of Christianity, and that is really why I am a preacher. It is because there is no other hope. Princes and lords may flourish, but then they fade. The great statesman dies; the great leader goes. There is an enemy that conquers all – death. Today is an historic occasion, it is a great day that will go down in history – 24 January 1965, the death of Sir Winston Churchill. So let us look at history. What does it tell us? It tells us that great men arise, that they give an impetus to the human race and solve certain problems. But they die and they leave us in a world of tragedy and pain.

Churchill said that he did not believe he had been called to preside over the liquidation of the British Empire, but he witnessed it, did he not? And that is the whole message of history. Men and women come, they strive, they cut great figures on the stage of history, then out they go, even the greatest of them, and the problems remain. I am not detracting from them in saying that. All honour to great men and women, but it has nothing to do with Christianity. The message of Christianity is that *God* has a plan and purpose.

In his sermon, Peter, referring to the death of our Lord, said, 'Him, being delivered by the determinate counsel and fore-knowledge of God, ye have taken, and by wicked hands have crucified and slain.' Notice the words, 'the determinate counsel and foreknowledge of God'. That is what the Christian message is about. It tells us that the death of Christ on the cross was not an accident, that ultimately it was not even something achieved by men, but was part of the plan and purpose of God. So whatever your temperament, whether you are an optimist or a pessimist, whether you are mercurial or phlegmatic, and with all your scientific and psychological knowledge, listen to this: The great eternal God who revealed the plan hundreds of years ago, is carrying it out, and as part of his plan, he sent his Son into this world, even to the death of the cross.

And the object of this plan? It is to save. The end of the quotation from Joel is this: 'And it shall come to pass, that whosoever shall call on the name of the Lord shall be saved' (verse 21). Saved from what? Saved from eternal misery, which is the punishment we all so richly deserve from God, against whom we have rebelled and whom we have offended. And we are saved for a positive knowledge of God, for a new, a fuller life, an expanding life, a life that leads to glory everlasting. That is God's plan, and that is what he revealed through the prophets all those centuries before the events. Isaiah said: It is all right. Listen: 'Comfort ye, comfort ye my people, saith your God' (*Isa.* 40:1). All eyes would see God's salvation.

And God would bring about this salvation by sending his Son into the world. The prophets had foretold that a baby would be born of a virgin in Bethlehem. He was coming, the Deliverer, the Messiah. They were to wait for him. That was the message of the prophets.

God would send a Deliverer, but how would he bring about deliverance? Would it be by giving us an example, by saying, 'Follow me. Imitate that'? Thank God, that is not the message. Who can imitate God? It is easy for the philosophers to talk and write about it, but have you ever tried to do it? No, no, God's Deliverer did not come merely to teach us; he did not come and tell us, 'Do this, and you will save yourselves.' He knew we could not. It was because the whole world lies guilty before God that he came. 'All have sinned, and come short of the glory of God' (*Rom.* 3:23). He came because man could not save himself.

No, this is the answer: 'Him, being delivered by the determinate counsel and foreknowledge of God.' God sent his Son into this world to bear the guilt of our sins. God punished our sins in his Son. It was God who contrived the cross. The cruel hands of men actually knocked in the nails, but it was by the predetermined counsel and foreknowledge of God. It is God's way of saving, in his Son and by his death, and to prove it, he raised his Son. Our Lord was big enough and strong enough to bear all our sin: 'Whom God hath raised up, having loosed the pains of death: because it was not possible that he should be holden of it.' Why? Because he was God the Son in the flesh and he could not die. He is divine; he is eternal. He rose, bursting asunder the bands of death.

And so Peter taught the people and that is the Christian message: that we all of us need to be delivered from the guilt and the bondage and the power and captivity of sin, and that it is Christ alone who can deliver us. This is God's plan, determined and purposed before the foundation and creation of the world.

But finally, not only has God a plan, it is a plan which is certain; nothing can stop it. The Pharisees and Sadducees and scribes and all the others were against him. They all delivered him up to death. He was a danger, a nuisance, and they regarded him as a political agitator. Away with him,' they shouted. The unintelligent mob crucified him, and they thought it was the end, but they did not know that even as they were hammering in the nails, they were carrying out God's will. The God I preach to you can use his enemies and he has often done so. They do not know what is happening, but he does. He used his enemies to carry out his own plan. Human malignity could not frustrate it. Our Lord's enemies thought that when they crucified him and saw his body taken to a tomb, that would be the end of him, but it was not. Hell had let itself loose, man and devil had done their utmost, but God smashed it all. God raised him from the dead. He is over all, he triumphed over all, even over all his enemies, even the devil and hell and everything that was against him. All are to be defeated: He has announced it by the resurrection.

So the apostle says here, 'Therefore let all the house of Israel know assuredly, that God hath made that same Jesus, whom ye have crucified, both Lord and Christ' (verse 36). It is a solemn thought that we are face to face with God. You may say, 'I'm all right. I'm happy. I have all I want. It's a wonderful life.' Yes, but how do you explain these facts concerning Jesus of Nazareth? Why did it happen? Why did it *have* to happen? Why did God send him? Why was this God's plan? You are a living soul, and this has happened in your world, and it has happened with respect to you, as it has with respect to everybody else, because, in spite of our differences, in one respect we are all the same: We are all sinners in the sight of God. 'There is none righteous, no, not one' (*Rom.* 3:10).

The issue cannot be evaded by talking about psychology and temperament and by quoting experiences. Every one of us is confronted by the fact of this Jesus of Nazareth. Yes, it is Sunday, 24 January 1965. Why? Not because Sir Winston Churchill died but because Jesus of Nazareth was born and lived and taught and died and rose again and sent down the Spirit. It is 1965 AD – Anno Domini – the year of our Lord. That is what we must all face. It does not matter who you are. It does not matter whether you are able or whether you are lacking in talent, whether you are learned or ignorant. It does not matter what you have been, nor what your constitution is. Nothing matters except that you are a human being and that God sent his only begotten Son into a world of human beings.

So the question confronting you is not what you need, but who this person is. Why did the prophets write about him, and, especially, why did God ever send him to die? Has this got anything to do with me? That is your question. That is the way to face history. That is the way to face the history even of a great man. You do not just say, 'How wonderful he was!' You say, 'What has all this got to do with me?' You relate yourself to history, and that is right and good; we should all be trying to do it. But here is the supreme fact of history: Why Jesus Christ? Why Bethlehem? Why Golgotha? Why the tomb? Why the resurrection? Why the descent of the Holy Spirit? Why the church? Why all these things?

Have you ever asked those questions? It is because men and women never face the fact of Christ and the fact of prophecy that they continue in the darkness and the misery of sin, not knowing where they are going, not understanding life, not ready to die, afraid of the eternal future. So today, make use of history. Ask yourself this fundamental question: Who is this Jesus? And if you do that seriously, you will come to see that he is everything to do with you for he came 'to seek and to save that which was lost' (*Luke* 19:10). He came 'to give his life a ransom for many' (*Mark* 10:45). My dear friends, look at the facts, and especially this great fact of prophecy, of which the facts are a verification.

4

Becoming a Christian

Now when they heard this, they were pricked in their heart, and said unto Peter and to the rest of the apostles, Men and brethren, what shall we do? Then Peter said unto them, Repent, and be baptized every one of you in the name of Jesus Christ for the remission of sins, and ye shall receive the gift of the Holy Ghost. For the promise is unto you, and to your children, and to all that are afar off, even as many as the Lord our God shall call. And with many other words did he testify and exhort, saying, Save yourselves from this untoward generation (Acts 2:37–40).

The Bible is a very honest book. At the end of the various Gospels we are given a picture of the disciples, our Lord's innermost circle, and it is a most dismal picture. There they were: Their leader had been taken, condemned and crucified. His body had been put in a tomb, and they were utterly cast down. Now the Bible tells us that about them and shows them fumbling. Peter at last said: Let's go and fish. Let's get some relief, at any rate. So he tried fishing and he could not even do that.

So how do you think people like that could start the Christian church? The idea is ludicrous. No, the church is not a human society; it is not something brought about by human beings. The church is not a branch of the state. Of course not! There is only one explanation for the existence of the church and her persistence, and that is given in this book.

We have looked at the biblical picture of the church and her message in general. Now we take a further step and consider this vital question: How does one become a part of this spiritual society called the Christian church? How does one become a member of this community of living people that we find in the book of Acts? How does one become a Christian? I want to impress upon you not only the urgency of this question, but also its solemnity. Ultimately, when we consider our final destiny in this world, does anything matter but this?

Again, as we come to look at the question of what it is to become a Christian, we shall find a complete contrast between the teaching here in Acts and the popular understanding today. How does one become a Christian? The answer that we find here is that it is not something vague and indefinite but concrete and clear. There is a time when one is not a Christian, and then one is. We are told here that three thousand people were added to the church as the result of that one sermon by the apostle Peter. Now something happened to those people, they moved from one position to another: They were 'added' to the church. First they did not belong, and then they did. There is nothing uncertain about that.

Christians, according to the New Testament, are men and women who know exactly where they are and what they believe. As the apostle Peter put it when he wrote a letter to Christians later on in his life: 'Be ready always to give an answer to every man that asketh you a reason of the hope that is in you' (*1 Pet.* 3:15). That is the basic point from which we start.

But if you say to many people who call themselves Christians: 'What does it mean to become a Christian?', they do not know. They have a vague notion that somehow or other you sometimes think about God and about religious matters, and then try to do a bit of good and live a good life, and, well, that is it, you are a Christian. Or perhaps you were taken to church when you were young and you have just gone on. They think that Christianity is a spirit of friendship and benevolence and a desire to do good. As we have seen, some modern writers say that whenever you find love or kindness, you find God. But, I repeat, that is far removed from what we find in the book of Acts. Here is something entirely different. Here are three thousand people who passed from there to here, from this to that – what happened to them?

The first thing is that the three thousand people underwent a complete change. Their whole position was revolutionized. Their thinking, their actions, their outlook were all changed. It is as complete as that – and that is Christianity. There is nothing more definite than being a Christian, according to the New Testament, and people who do not know what it is to be a Christian, or cannot tell you why they are Christians, by definition, are not Christians at all. There is something unique, special, specific about being a Christian. You can find many men and women who are not Christians, who do a lot of good, who think noble thoughts, and are ready to make great sacrifices. But they will tell you they are not Christians, and they are not. The so-called humanist will say, 'Everything you people stand for and do, I can do, without any of your doctrine and your shibboleths, without all your accretions and all those myths that you add on to your teaching.'

I was reading an article recently by one of the leading humanists at the present time in which the author was commenting on the programmes she listens to on the radio and watches on the television. She said, 'I notice that they [the Christians] are very shy about mentioning God and the Lord Jesus Christ. They are all so anxious to show that after all what they have got is so much like that which is best in the world' – and she is perfectly right. It is not surprising that the vast majority of people are outside the church. But that is not Christianity. As we have seen, Luke starts off the book of Acts by saying, 'The former treatise have I made, O Theophilus, of all that Jesus began both to do and teach, until the day in which he was taken up.' It is all about him. And if you do not speak about him, but simply talk about good ideas and good thoughts and how to do this and that, what you are talking about is not Christianity.

So we find here that these people underwent a complete change. How did it happen? It was not the preaching of Peter. If you read Peter's sermon, you see that he quotes his Scriptures, he develops certain arguments. Quite right. Logically sound. He makes his case and you cannot contradict it. But Peter's sermon, read in cold print, does not account for the fact that something vital happened to three thousand people! No, what accounts for that is the action of the Holy Spirit. 'They were pricked in their heart' (*Acts* 2:37). The men and women standing there and listening to an exposition of certain Old Testament Scriptures were in trouble. They were disturbed and they cried out. This was the work of the Holy Spirit, and there would never have been a Christian church but for this. This is what makes her; this is what causes her to persist. This is the explanation of the revivals and reformations of all the centuries.

Now this is something that we cannot understand. It is something that happens to us, something that takes place in us, and we ourselves are amazed at it. It is not something *we* do. Let me make this perfectly clear. You cannot 'take up' Christianity. You can take up Christian Science; you can take up many cults; you can take up many movements; you can even join a church, but you cannot take up Christianity. By definition, Christianity is something that takes you up. It is not primarily something you do, but something that is done to you. You cannot explain it. You cannot dissect it or analyse it. It is the power of the Holy Spirit.

And this incomprehensible work of God is seen in its classic form in this second chapter of Acts. The conversion of the three thousand people was entirely because of the descent of the Holy Spirit and the power of the Spirit using the words of a frail, ignorant man, driving them into the minds and hearts and consciences of those listening.

The New Testament is full of examples and teaching on the same subject. Take the great statement in 1 Corinthians 2:1, 'And I, brethren' – Paul reminds those Corinthians to whom he had first gone to preach the gospel – 'And I, brethren, when I came to you, came not with excellency of speech or of wisdom, declaring unto you the testimony of God.' Now do not misunderstand this. The apostle could have spoken 'with excellency of speech or of wisdom'. He was a learned man, a great thinker; he knew their poets and so on. But he rejected that approach. Why? Because, 'I determined not to know anything among you, save Jesus Christ, and him crucified' (verse 2).

Then Paul goes on to say, 'I was with you in weakness, and in fear, and in much trembling. And my speech and my preaching was not with enticing words of man's wisdom, but in demonstration of the Spirit and of power: that your faith should not stand in the wisdom of men, but in the power of God.' Becoming a Christian is, I repeat, primarily and essentially something that happens to us. We are conscious that we are being dealt with and that a power greater than ourselves is taking us in hand.

So there is no explanation of the Christian church but that – none at all. We have seen how the apostles themselves underwent this great change, especially after the baptism of the Spirit. They were transformed, made entirely new. And this is the story of the centuries, the story of all the revivals and of all the great saints. 'You', says Paul to the Ephesians, 'hath he quickened, who were dead in trespasses and sins . . . and were by nature the children of wrath, even as others. But God, who is rich in mercy, for his great love wherewith he loved us, even when we were dead in sins, hath quickened us together with Christ, (by grace ye are saved)' (*Eph.* 2:1–5).

This is the first thing that strikes us. Something happened to these people, to the three thousand. A work went on within them. The Holy Spirit of God was using the Scriptures and applying it to them. He is a powerful influence, an influence that baffles our understanding, defying analysis and explanation, but we just know it has happened.

But what exactly is it that the Spirit does to us? Now at this point some people may go off at a tangent and say, 'Of course, that's typical of you Christian preachers, you are just advocating intellectual suicide. You stop thinking and abandon yourselves to the unseen, and strange things happen. I've always thought that of you, that's why I've dismissed you. You are admitting now that you do not know. Of course, it is this other power. People can get great and strange experiences. I know all about that. I'm interested in extra-sensory perception and psychology. So I'm not surprised that those of you who abandon yourselves like this have strange experiences as a result.'

Wait a minute! All I am saying is that the ultimate explanation of the Christian is the power of God, the work of the Holy Spirit, that it is something that he does to a man or woman. But *what* does he do? Here is the interesting point. The first thing the Holy Spirit does to people when he comes upon them in this powerful manner is make them think! How do I find that? Well, the apostle, applying his sermon, said, 'Therefore let all the house of Israel know assuredly, that God hath made that same Jesus, whom ye have crucified, both Lord and Christ.' And then we read, 'Now when they heard this, they were pricked in their heart, and said unto Peter and to the rest of the apostles, Men and brethren, what shall we do?' And they said that because they had been made to think.

This is most remarkable. Look at these three thousand people. They were a part of the crowd that, but a few weeks before, when Jesus of Nazareth was on trial, had cried out, 'Away with him! Crucify him! Give us Barabbas.' The Pharisees and Sadducees and the doctors of the law, these clever men, these politicians, these ecclesiastics, had seen themselves getting into trouble because of the ministry and the teaching of Jesus of Nazareth. So they had said: Let's get rid of this man who would save the nation! Let them punish him and then we'll be all right.

So these religious leaders had incited and manipulated the crowd, which earlier had almost worshipped our Lord, surrounding him as he rode into Jerusalem on the foal of an ass and singing, 'Hosanna to the Son of David.' The thoughtless, heedless crowd, dupes of the 'thing to say', carried away by the clichés, not thinking at all, changed their opinions, blinded by 'the god of this world', and cried out, 'Crucify him!'

That is how these people had been, but a great change came over them, and the first thing in the change is that they began to think, and to think about this Jesus. Those who had shouted against him were now beginning to think about him. Oh, the Bible is full of this! What Christianity does, what the gospel does, is save us, it delivers' us, as Paul puts it to the Galatians, 'from this present evil world' (*Gal.* 1:4). And what is the main characteristic of this present evil world? It is that it does not think, that it cannot think, that it is carried away by mob emotion. It exaggerates; it goes to extremes. It does not know what it is saying. It has no understanding. It is the victim of the powers that are ready to manipulate it.

Now I am preaching out of the second chapter of Acts, but I could illustrate this perfectly with a parallel example in the last chapter. When Paul was being taken as a prisoner to Rome, there was a shipwreck and eventually the ship's crew and prisoners landed on the island of Malta. Here, we are told:

The barbarous people shewed us no little kindness: for they kindled a fire, and received us every one, because of the present rain, and because of the cold. And when Paul had gathered a bundle of sticks, and laid them on the fire, there came a viper out of the heat, and fastened on his hand. And when the barbarians saw the venomous beast hang on his hand, they said among themselves, No doubt this man is a murderer, whom, though he hath escaped the sea, yet vengeance suffereth not to live. And he shook off the beast into the fire, and felt no harm. Howbeit, they looked when he should have swollen, or fallen down dead suddenly: but after they had looked a great while, and saw no harm come to him, they changed their minds, and said that he was a god (Acts 28:2–6).

You see the relevance of my quotation? That is the mind of this world. That is the mob. At one moment they said he was a murderer who was getting what should come to him, the next they exclaimed, 'This man is a god!' The crowd does not think. At one time it says of a certain man, 'He's a warmonger, impossible to work with. He's a bad-tempered individualist. He just wants to be a dictator. Keep him out. Keep him out of the government. Have nothing to do with him. He's dangerous.' But perhaps today they tend to say that he was a god![1] And they are wrong on both occasions. They are always wrong. They were wrong before the war, they are wrong now – the unthinking, heedless, ignorant mob. And the masses in this country today are dismissing Christianity as the Jerusalem crowd dismissed the Lord. So I repeat that the first thing that happens to people when the Holy Spirit begins to deal with them is that they begin to think and to look at things as they have never done before.

I emphasize this for this good reason: I know the silly argument that people are not Christians because they are thinkers. The Rationalist Press Association publishes books. What are they called? 'The Thinker's Library'! They are the only people who think! And Christians, what are they? Well, they are people who are ignorant and brainless and thoughtless. They have swallowed this 'dope' – 'the dope of the masses', 'the opium of the people', call it what you like. Christianity, we are told, is just a drug to stop people thinking and to keep them down. It has been the greatest enemy of the working classes, and if you want freedom you must shake off this incubus, this drug, and think for yourselves. But the facts are the exact opposite of that.

[1] The reference is to Sir Winston Churchill. This sermon was preached on 31 January 1965, the Sunday after his funeral.

Now I want to be fair. False religion is nothing but a dope. You are merely aware of some great solemnity which is very wonderful, massive and beautiful. But what is it? Well, you do not know but somehow in its immensity it gives a kind of comfort. So you do not trouble to understand it. That is false religion; that is pagan religion. Pagan religion is always unintelligent. It is a religion of fear, a religion of pomp and ceremony, a religion that lacks a doctrine and a vital truth. People are merely awed by something luminous that they do not understand. I am not here to defend that for a second. That is undoubtedly the opium of the masses, and it is not Christianity.

So the first effect of Christianity is to make people stop and think. They are not simply overawed by some great occasion. They say, 'No, I must face this. I must think.' That is the work of the Spirit. The people in Acts thought again. They repented – the Greek word for repentance is *metanoia* – they changed their mind completely. The Spirit always leads people to think and, as I have been showing you, the greatest trouble is that men and women go through life without thinking. Or they think for a moment but find it painful, so they stop and turn to a bottle of whisky, or the television, or something else – anything to forget.

Is it not obvious that the world, speaking spiritually and intellectually, is in a doped condition? In all sorts of ways men and women evade the facts. They can do this with great energy, they can be very intellectual, but ultimately they always end up with nothing.

What does the Spirit make us think about? Well, not first and foremost about ourselves. I must emphasize that Christianity does not start with us. It does not say: Do you want to get rid of that sin that is getting you down? Do you want happiness? Do you want peace? Do you want guidance? That is not Christianity. That, again, is the approach of the cults. No, these people in Jerusalem were made to think about – Jesus Christ! They were given the objective, historical facts about this person. Peter had just said to them, 'Therefore let all the house of Israel know assuredly, that God hath made that same Jesus, whom ye have crucified, both Lord and Christ.'

The next verse continues, 'Now when they heard this' – they were not thinking about themselves, but were beginning to think about him. That is always the message of the Christian church. The true Christian message brings us face to face with the historical facts. I repeat this once again because false religions make people think about everything except Jesus Christ. But when you come to a truly Christian church, it is Jesus Christ who takes the highest position – nobody else, however great, however wonderful. Jesus Christ dominates, and the Spirit dominates us. The first thing we have to face is the person of Jesus Christ – his life, his death, his resurrection, these great historical events. 'When they heard this' – when they were reminded of what they had done – 'they were pricked in their heart, and said unto Peter and to the rest of the apostles, Men and brethren, what shall we do?'

The next point is that the power of the Spirit upon the message makes us consider this person, but does not stop at that. The Spirit now makes us go on to realize the relevance of Jesus Christ, and everything concerning him, to ourselves personally.

You can sit in a chair and read a book about Jesus Christ, you can read about him in your Bible, and you can read books of theology. Very interesting. To an intelligent person there is no study more entrancing. It has been the occupation of some of the greatest minds of the centuries. But you can do all that and still not be a Christian. It is the Holy Spirit who makes each of us see the relevance of Jesus to ourselves, so that we are no longer spectators, no longer critics, no longer people taking a wonderful objective view. No, no, I am under criticism myself. The relevance of this has come to me. I see that I am involved in all this and I had not realized it.

That was the trouble with these people in Acts. There they had been, but a few weeks back, shouting with all their might: 'Away with him! Crucify him! Give us Barabbas. Who is this Jesus? What's all this fuss about? What's all this nonsense? Are we going to get into trouble with the Roman authorities because of this crackbrained man who sets himself up as some great deliverer and messiah? Nonsense! He has nothing to do with us.' And so they went back and they drank and had a wonderful evening together and the jokes had never been so good.

But now, suddenly, they realized, listening to Peter, that this Jesus whom they had thus dismissed and so easily got rid of, as they had thought, was one with whom they were vitally concerned. They understood what everyone who becomes a Christian must understand, because you cannot be a Christian without realizing this, they understood that this Jesus was 'made . . . both Lord and Christ'. They saw that they had therefore been fighting against God and rejecting his Christ. Their voices had done it. They had urged the authorities to crucify him. The crucifixion had been carried out by popular verdict.

And this is still the message of Christianity. This is still the Christian gospel, and it is addressed to everybody in the whole world today. You may say to me, 'But I can understand it in the case of those people. They had literally shouted, 'Away with him!' In a sense, they were responsible for his murder. But I have never done that!' I agree, but remember this: If up to now you have been unconcerned about Jesus Christ and who he is, then you have rejected him. By doing nothing about him, you reject him. You cannot be neutral in this matter. So I say to the respectable people, the humanists and others, some of whom may live very good lives, and think they are all right, that if they are not related to this person, and if they are not for him, they are against him. And when people are convicted by the Holy Spirit, they begin to realize it.

People have said so far, 'Well, I'm living a good life, aren't I? I've never committed adultery. I've never got drunk. I've never done any of these things. I really am trying to help people. I'm paying my full dues morally – what more do you want?' But the Holy Spirit shows them that Jesus Christ came into the world to save sinners and that the whole world is in a state of sin, and that includes them.

There is no greater sin than not to see any need of Jesus Christ. The greatest sinners in the world today are those who do not think about Christ at all. They are much worse than the vilest, foulest blackguards who think they need salvation and who come to the minister and say, 'Is there hope for me?' The most hopeless people in the Gospels are the Pharisees, not the publicans and sinners, and that is because they see no need of him. And is not that the tragedy today?

Not to accept Jesus is to reject him, and to reject him is to reject God. It is God, said Peter, who has made Jesus both Lord and Christ. The people of Jerusalem saw that by agreeing with the authorities, they had been fighting against God. Jesus Christ is the Son of God, and they had crucified him. Jesus Christ is the greatest manifestation of God's love, and they had said, 'Crucify him!' Jesus Christ is the very pivot and centre of God's eternal plan and purpose of world redemption, and they had rejected him. They were suddenly awakened to this. They had shouted thoughtlessly, but now it was brought home to them and they were made to think. And that, of course, leads to conviction, and conviction leads to fear.

Do you not hear the fear in the voices of those people of Jerusalem? 'They were pricked in their heart, and said . . . Men and brethren , what shall we do?' This is no intellectual interest in Jesus, no bandying about of opinions: 'Well, indeed, I do think after all that he is a very good man who said some fine things and he is a great leader and we want more of that spirit'! No, no! They were aware that they were in trouble. They were 'pricked in their heart'. They were convicted and afraid. Why? Because they had asked themselves certain questions. And this is how people become Christians.

Have you ever put these questions to yourselves? Have you ever asked: Why is it that I have been so unconcerned about Jesus Christ? How long have I lived in this world? How much have I thought about him? Has he been central in my thinking? Is my life dominated by the historical fact that nearly two thousand years ago God sent his only Son into this world? Have you stopped to ask: Who was this Jesus? Why are the years numbered according to him – Before Christ, After Christ?

And you suddenly realize that you have never asked those questions. You have never been concerned. 'Jesus Christ? Of course, I know all about him!' But you have never read the Gospels. You have never read the Bible through. You think you know, but you do not. Now when we are awakened, and stop, and ask those questions, it is because of the work of the Spirit. This is conviction. We sit down and say: Why have I been so unconcerned? What was the matter with me? Here is a great historical fact. I'm interested in history. I know about great men. I know about great kings and princes and leaders and prime ministers.

Now I am not saying there is anything wrong in knowing about the great people of history. All I am trying to say to you is that if you are interested in history and in historical personages, why have you not been interested in Jesus Christ? Why has he meant so little to you? Why have the great men of the world meant more to you than Jesus Christ? Why have they influenced your life more than he has? Here is this great historic personage who came into this world and died and rose again, who sent down the Spirit, and established the church, why are you so unconcerned? Why are you aware of the facts, but no more? Why has it never really gripped you? You say, 'I read of men like the apostle Paul, and these other apostles to whom Christ was everything. They were thrilled by the gospel. They were ready to die for it. Why isn't it everything to me?'

And if you come down the running centuries you will read of others. There is Augustine, that brilliant philosopher, a great flowering genius. He was once living an evil life and did not accept the truth of Christianity, but then he heard the call of God. Thereafter he lived for the gospel. He preached it, taught it and expounded it in his own amazing manner. You will read about the martyrs and confessors, the giants of the Protestant Reformation. You will read of those great Christians in the Puritan era, the Covenanters in Scotland – men and women who gladly preferred to die rather than deny Jesus Christ and who died triumphant, glorious, knowing they were going to be with him.

Why do you not say to yourself, 'Why am I not like that? I know about it, but it makes no difference to me. I've never been thrilled by him. I've never been moved by him. If you could blot him out of history, it would not make any difference to me. I'm not ready to die for him and his teaching! Why not?' Have you ever asked those questions? That is what you are made to do by the Spirit.

Then another question is this: Why have I never seen my need of him? He says, 'The Son of man is come to seek and to save that which was lost' (*Luke* 19:10). We are meeting on a great and solemn occasion when people are thinking about life and death, so I will ask you a simple question: Have you ever seen your need of Jesus Christ? Have you ever realized that he came into the world because of you and because of everybody else who is exactly the same as you? Why is it that you have never even considered the consequences of rejecting him? Now the Spirit makes you ask those questions and they are painful. You are thinking now. Before you simply said, 'There's nothing in Christianity. It's played out. Away with him! He's nobody. Get him out of the way. Christianity is outmoded. He doesn't count.' But now you say, 'Had I been wiser, I would have been saying: Here it is. He is a fact. What does he mean? What is his relevance to me?'

The moment you ask yourself those questions, you will find the answers. You will say to yourself, 'I've never thought about him, and I've never seen my need of him, for one reason only, and that is my ignorance – and first, my ignorance of God!' How often do we think of God? Where has the world come from? What keeps it going? What accounts for all its marvel and perfection? Is it all the result of chance?

And, secondly, you will see that you have been ignorant of your own true nature. People today never ask, What is man? They go on saying that people are wonderful and twentieth-century man the most wonderful of all. They just go on repeating the clichés they are told every day in the newspapers and on the television. We are always being praised and are praising one another. But do we stop to ask what people have made of the world? Do we even stop to ask what is a human being? What is the meaning of life? What are we doing in this world?

Thirdly, you will see that you have been ignorant of the meaning of death. 'Death,' you used to say, 'is the end of life. It's the end of a great career. Death is just the end.' Death makes people feel solemn, but they do not think about it. But now the Holy Spirit makes you think about death. What does it lead to? And the Bible answers: 'It is appointed unto men once to die, but after this the judgment' (*Heb.* 9:27). The soul goes on, and stands in the presence of the eternal God who made us and holds us responsible. We stand before the one from whom we have received all we have – oh, the greatness of man! What is this greatness? It is not what men and women do, but that they are made in the image of God and were meant to be God's companions. It is that God holds them responsible for what they do with the gift of life and the gift of the soul.

You see that you have been ignorant about all this, and that is why you have not been interested in Jesus Christ. That is the end, a magnificence and pomp and splendour.[2] But no, no! Beyond!

[2] Again, the reference is to Sir Winston Churchill's funeral.

Judgment! God! Eternal destiny! And there is only one of two destinies open to us all. It is either to be with God or to be outside him. It is either to enjoy the pleasures of God to all eternity among the righteous and 'the spirits of just men made perfect' (*Heb.* 12:23) and all the holy angels, or it is to be in a state of torment, misery and pain.

And added to ignorance you see that you have been spiritually dead. That is the state of the world. Even when these facts are put before us, we shake them off, do we not? We are not alive to spiritual things. We say, 'You preachers go on saying all that, but I couldn't care less, it's got nothing to do with me.' The apostle Paul describes our spiritual deadness in these famous words: 'The natural man receiveth not the things of the Spirit of God: for they are foolishness unto him: neither can he know them, because they are spiritually discerned' (*1 Cor.* 2:14). And in the same chapter Paul says that when the Lord Jesus Christ came into this world, the princes of this world did not know him, 'For had they known it, they would not have crucified the Lord of glory' (*1 Cor.* 2:8). Why did they not know him? Not because of lack of intelligence, but because of spiritual deadness. They saw nothing but the carpenter of Galilee.

The Holy Spirit makes you come to the terrible realization, 'I must be spiritually dead! I must be lifeless. I must have a heart of stone! There's something wrong with me. I'm in trouble. What can I do?' Those people in Jerusalem now realized that their rejection of Jesus was based upon ignorance and deadness, and that as a result they were terribly guilty before God. They realized that they belonged to this 'untoward generation' from which Peter told them to save themselves (verse 40). They saw that they were blind fools with no excuse. There were damned, and could do nothing about it.

Now they saw that there was only one thing left for them to do – they could cry out unto the Lord. And they started by addressing a question to his representatives, Peter and the others: 'Men and brethren, what shall we do?'

And the Holy Spirit makes each of us realize that we are guilty. We see the relevance of the gospel to us. We realize that we must die and that we cannot escape. Listen to the poet Dryden. His philosophy is wrong, but it has a lesson to teach us:

Since ev'ry man who lives is born to die,
And none can boast sincere felicity,
With equal mind, what happens let us bear,
Nor joy nor grieve too much for things beyond our care.
Like pilgrims to th' appointed place we tend;
The world's an inn, and death the journey's end.

John Dryden

We are all pilgrims. Where are we going after death? There is a Bladon for each of us.[3] There is a Bladon for you, and you are moving towards it, my friend. You cannot escape it. You will have to leave behind you the world and the cleverness of the world, and your soul will go out on that last journey – alone! Where to?

Have you ever asked that question? It is madness not to, but that is what the heedless, thoughtless crowd never does. Death is not the journey's end. Death is certain, unavoidable, inexorable, but where do I go? You do not know? So are you not afraid? Do you not think it is about time you began to be concerned? Cry out, 'Men and brethren, what shall we do?'

There is only one final point and it is quite simple. All you must do is obey the message that is given to you. In answer to their question, Peter said to the people in Jerusalem, 'Repent' – think again, change your minds – 'and be baptized every one of you in the name of Jesus Christ for the remission of sins, and ye shall receive the gift of the Holy Ghost.'

If you have seen what I have been putting before you, tell God about it, acknowledge and confess it to him. Confess that you have been a fool, that all your boasted cleverness is rubbish. Acknowledge all your arrogance. Admit that you have sinned against him. That is repentance: You simply make an open confession, without any reservations at all, and cast yourself entirely upon God's mercy and love.

Tell God that you have lived to the world and its passing glory. Tell him that you have put other people before him. Fall before him and confess that you deserve nothing but punishment, that you have nothing to plead, you have no excuse. That is repentance. That is 'calling upon the Lord'. Joel had prophesied,

---

[3] The place where Sir Winston Churchill was buried.

Becoming a Christian

'Whosoever shall call on the name of the Lord shall be delivered' (*Joel* 2:32). And the moment you call upon God in repentance, he will look upon you and will smile upon you, and will say: It is all right! I sent my only Son into the world for you. Believe on him. Believe that he died for you and for your sins and thank him.

Then give yourself and your life to him. Submit yourself to him, whatever the cost, and be baptized. It was not a small thing for those new Jerusalem believers to be baptized. It cost them dearly in persecution, and the renunciation of family, and ostracism, and a thousand and one other things. It probably meant death for many of them as, indeed, it did to many Christians in the arena in Rome. But it does not matter. Once you see this truth, you say with the writer of the hymn,

> *Love so amazing, so divine,*
> *Demands my soul, my life, my all.*
>   Isaac Watts

Beloved people, have you thought about these things? That is how one becomes a Christian.

5

Mind, Heart and Will

Now when they heard this, they were pricked in their heart, and said unto Peter and to the rest of the apostles, Men and brethren, what shall we do? Then Peter said unto them, Repent, and be baptized every one of you in the name of Jesus Christ for the remission of sins, and ye shall receive the gift of the Holy Ghost. For the promise is unto you, and to your children, and to all that are afar off, even as many as the Lord our God shall call. And with many other words did he testify and exhort, saying, Save yourselves from this untoward generation. Then they that gladly received his word were baptized: and the same day there were added unto them about three thousand souls. And they continued stedfastly in the apostles' doctrine and fellowship, and in breaking of bread, and in prayers. And fear came upon every soul: and many wonders and signs were done by the apostles. And all that believed were together, and had all things common; and sold their possessions and goods, and parted them to all men, as every man had need. And they, continuing daily with one accord in the temple, and breaking bread from house to house, did eat their meat with gladness and singleness of heart, praising God, and having favour with all the people. And the Lord added to the church daily such as should be saved (Acts 2:37–47).

I am anxious to consider this entire paragraph in general before we come to a consideration of its particular statements. We are studying the book of Acts, you remember, because it is the authoritative statement as to what the Christian church is, what Christianity is, and what it really means to be a Christian; and also because we know that this is the greatest need in the world today. Here is the only message for men and women which holds out any hope at all.

Now that is not exaggeration; it is sheer fact. When we read the newspapers, we see that the world is in desperate trouble, and we all know that from personal experience. Life is a fight and a problem for all of us. But the Christian message is good news. It is the very thing that men and women need, and the supreme tragedy is that they do not know this. Often this is because their ideas of the Christian church and message are about as far removed from the real thing as anything could possibly be. There is a terrible confusion between human ideas – the teaching of philosophy – and the revelation of God. Nothing is more urgently important than that we should allow these records to speak to us so that we might find out what the church was like at the beginning and how she came into being.

We have considered together the way in which one becomes a Christian. It is not by being born in a so-called Christian country, nor by being the child of Christian parents. Living a good life does not bring it about. No, no. Each of us becomes a Christian when the Spirit of God comes in power and brings the truth home, especially the truth about this person, Jesus of Nazareth. Then we see what he means to us, and we turn to him in utter, absolute submission. We confess our sin and failure and inability, and with a simple, childlike belief we accept the message concerning him.

What follows from that? In other words: What is a Christian? Here, again, we are given an authoritative account of this matter, and let me once more emphasize the vital importance of this record here in Acts. Here is the first account of the Christian church: 'The Lord added to the church daily such as should be saved.' We are told that on the day of Pentecost, 'There were added unto them about three thousand souls.' Before that, there had been a little body of about a hundred and twenty people – that is how many were gathered together in the upper room. They were the nucleus of the church and the Spirit came down upon them. Then these others were added to them, and there was the Christian church. So what sort of people were they? Well, as we have said, here is the authoritative description of what a Christian is like, and of what it means to be a Christian.

Now I know that you can buy books and read about men and women who are described as 'the greatest Christians of the twentieth century', but they are not authoritative. We judge those people, and everybody else, including ourselves, by what we read about the men and women in the early days of the church. Here is the first gathered company of Christian people. And I ask: How do I measure up to this? Are there evidences in me of what I see so clearly here? And these verses in Acts are undoubtedly given to us that we may test and examine ourselves and make quite sure that we are Christians.

So what does it mean to be a Christian? Let me answer first of all in the negative. I am forced to deal with this because so much is being poured out that is against the truth. It is not what I want to do. I wish I could simply give a positive exposition. But I live in the same world as you, and I try to keep my eyes open. It is my duty to do so, because I cannot help people unless I know their difficulties and problems. So I read the newspapers, I listen to the radio, and I look at the television when these issues are being dealt with, and I know the impression that is given as to what it is that makes a man or woman a Christian.

Let me put it quite simply like this: What would your answer be if I gave you a sheet of paper and a pencil and told you to put down in as few words as possible your idea of what it means to be a Christian? Now as we look at this record in Acts, I think we will have to admit that the answer is very different indeed from the views that are popularly held today.

These are some of the suggestions that are put forward. The general idea is that Christianity is primarily something you take up. You decide to be a Christian. You 'go in' for it. You have tried various other things, the cults and so on, and now you try the church. There are, of course, all sorts of sub-divisions of this viewpoint. We do not have time to go into them all, but let me give you some general headings to show what I mean.

There are some people who quite clearly think that Christianity operates solely in the realm of the intellect. These are serious and able men and women who are concerned about life and its problems. They know that here is a traditional teaching and believe it their bounden duty to consider it. So they read about the Christian faith and may become very interested in it, even accepting a good deal of it. But it is all in the mind. It is all theoretical. They may greatly enjoy their study of Christianity, it may become their hobby, but it is nothing beyond that. In addition, many people devote their lives to theological study. These scholars and academics spend their time in intellectual argument, taking up religious issues, and writing their books one against another or in agreement with one another. That is their whole life.

As a result of all this, the man in the street often thinks that Christianity is just a kind of intellectual hobby. Just as some people take up art and drama, others, these odd people, take up Christianity, this intellectual matter, and there it is. 'I notice,' people say, 'that such types don't seem to agree with one another. They even have violent disagreements. Well, of course, if they like that sort of thing,' says the man in the street, 'let them carry on. But as for me, I'm not interested – not interested at all.'

At the opposite extreme, there are those for whom Christianity is purely a matter for the feelings. They have had a wonderful experience of peace, or love, or happiness, and say they need nothing else. The intellectuals, of course, condemn such people. 'It's pure emotionalism,' they say. 'They cannot argue seriously with you. They haven't read the books and cannot discuss them with you. They live on the wonderful feeling they say they've had and deliberately try to work it up again and again.' And, of course, there is a good deal of evidence that lends considerable weight to these objections.

Then there is a third group which puts the entire emphasis upon the will. According to this view, what makes a Christian is not what people think; and if they like to play with the emotions, let them do so. No, whether or not you are a Christian hinges upon what you do. It is the way in which you live that is the deciding factor. Are you living for the good of humanity? Are you ready to make sacrifices? Are you ready to put desire for a great career on one side in order to do something heroic and wonderful and sacrificial?

That is what makes people Christians. It is a question of making a deliberate decision to improve the lot of humanity and uplift the human race. This may take you into politics or into social work – the sphere is unimportant. As long as you are giving yourself in service, what does it matter what you believe? The intellect is comparatively unimportant. Indeed, you can be certain of very few things in a world like this. The important thing is your will and your desire and what you are actually doing.

A fourth view of Christianity, a view commonly held by many people who have been brought up as Christians – I myself held it for many a year, is the view that being a Christian is a task which you have to take up, and which you take up more or less reluctantly and miserably in a spirit of fear. Christianity is mainly something that spoils life. You know other people who were not brought up as Christians, and you see that they do things freely without any hesitation at all, and you wish that you could be doing the same things, but you are afraid. You have been brought up in a chapel or a church, brought up as a Christian, as it were, and though you want to do these things, you cannot. This Christianity stands between you and them.

Christianity seems to be something negative, something prohibitive and restrictive, something which you are afraid not to practise. Above everything else, it is characterized by a sense of duty. Religious practice is a solemn duty which you must go through, and the sooner it is finished, the better, and the shorter the service, the better. There is no happiness anywhere near this version of Christianity; there is no joy, quite the reverse. It is a teaching that makes you, in the words of Milton, 'scorn delights and live laborious days'. You have to go to that church meeting on a Sunday, and the trouble is that so far it has been twice on Sunday – so let us try to get a reform movement to bring it down to once on a Sunday! And make the service earlier so that at any rate you have the rest of the day free.

Now that is the attitude that many people hold. Christianity is a solemn, unhappy, uncertain and vague task which you pursue because you are afraid not to, or because you promised your parents. You do not quite know what you are doing. You are only hoping that somehow or other you are observing the right thing and it will bring you to the right place in the end. Now we must face these things. It is said that only ten per cent of the people of Britain even claim to be Christian, and I wonder how many of that number hold the view that I have just been describing? I am afraid it is alarming to contemplate the number of those who believe that Christianity is a solemn task which makes us more or less miserable and stands between us and what appears to be a life of freedom and abandon and enjoyment. Of course, such a view of Christianity is encouraged by parents compelling their children to go to Sunday school, sending them there to get rid of them. Indeed, the result is that when a child reaches adolescence, he or she says, 'No more of that. I'm going to shake myself free. I want my liberty.' Christianity is a chain, it is a law. John Bunyan got it right when in *Pilgrim's Progress* he talked of a man carrying a load on his back. And people stop at that point. They feel the burden, the misery, the unhappiness. Others, observing such people, turn their backs upon Christianity, and are not interested in it.

So we are considering these eleven verses from Acts and we see what an utter travesty this last view is of Christianity. This is what Luke wrote: 'They, continuing daily with one accord in the temple, and breaking bread from house to house, did eat their meat with gladness and singleness of heart, praising God, and having favour with all the people' (verses 46–47) Could anything be a greater contrast? But this is Christianity. How little of it there is now! That is why the world is in her present trouble. We must get back to true Christianity. I am not interested in traditions. I am only concerned to get back to this. This is the real truth, the real thing.

And it was not only true of Christianity in these early times. If you read about the great epochs in the history of the church, the times of reformation and revival, you will always find a repetition of this. These are the marks and characteristics of a gathering of Christians – of the Christian church as she is meant to be. Oh, how different from what she has become! But this is what matters, and I am not here to advocate anything else.

So, having looked at what Christianity is not, I want to show you the contrast. What makes real Christianity so different? We have already seen that becoming a Christian is primarily something that happens to us; we cannot make ourselves Christians. 'The promise is unto you, and to your children, and to all that are afar off, even as many as the Lord our God shall call' (verse 39). In his letter Peter wrote, '. . . who hath called you out of darkness into his marvellous light' (*1 Pet.* 2:9). This call of God comes to us through the word of God applied by the Holy Spirit. Our Lord Jesus said, 'Come unto me, all ye that labour and are heavy laden, and I will give you rest' (*Matt.* 11:28). Or you may hear this call as a kind of command: 'Save yourselves from this untoward generation.' Then notice this interesting term: 'The Lord added to the church daily such as *should be saved*.' This is in the Authorized

(King James) Version, but everybody is agreed that unfortunately that is a bad translation. It should read, 'The Lord added to the church daily such as *were being saved.*' They were 'being saved', and they were 'added' to the church.

As we have seen, this is a realm which is so different from the mistaken ideas I have been describing to you. Those versions of Christianity are all controlled by human beings who have decided to be religious and to live the religious life. But that religion is dead and mechanical; it is dull and filled with fear. True Christianity is charged with life and power and abandon because it is the action of God. It is the work of the Holy Spirit of God sent into the church in order to bring about God's purposes in the world. Wordsworth was not thinking of this, but he wrote such a wonderful expression that I always like it. He was thinking of nature, but this is what happens to people when they become Christians. They come to a point when they are able to say:

> *And I have felt*
> *A presence that disturbs me with the joy*
> *Of elevated thoughts.*

And no one is a Christian who has not been aware of this disturbing 'Presence', of something happening. The great God who made us at the beginning, is re-forming us, doing something in us and upon us, making something of us. And what he does, of course, is to produce a complete change.

We have already looked at the change God brings about in us when we become Christians. But I want to show you that God does not merely produce a change in us with respect to our views of the Lord Jesus Christ. We have seen that the people in Acts realized the tragic mistake they had made about Jesus, but oh, God does much more than that! When men and women become Christians, their whole condition is changed and they are moved from one position to another. The Bible is full of this. The apostle Paul reminds the Colossians that God 'hath delivered us from the power of darkness, and hath translated us into the kingdom of his dear Son' (*Col.* 1:13). And the way in which that is put here in Acts is by the use of the word 'saved', which is a most important word. 'Save yourselves from this untoward generation . . . The Lord added to the church daily such as were being saved.'

Now I know that many people react violently against this word 'saved'. They hate it, and I think I know why. We do not hear as much of it as we used to, but I remember very well that, particularly when I was a young man, I resented it, and disliked it, and my contemporaries were almost unanimous with me in rejecting it. There was no one we so hated as the man who came up to you and said, 'Are you saved?' He said it so glibly, and often he did not know fully what he was saying. People have reacted against this word because of its glib use and I do not defend that. But 'saved' is a tremendous word. Here it is before us, and it is vital that we should know what it means. The difference between a Christian and a non-Christian is that the Christian is among the saved, while the non-Christian is among those who are not saved.

It is like this: Imagine a house on fire and a number of people inside. A ladder is put up to a window and a certain number are rescued – they are saved; the rest are burnt in the fire. What a difference! Or picture a shipwreck; or a judgment in court where a charge has been brought. At the end of the trial the accused man is in one of two positions. He is either at liberty, or else he is under condemnation, sent to prison and to punishment. An illustration which appears in the New Testament is that of a slave. The slave is entirely under the control and the domination of his owner. But he can be bought out and set at liberty. He can be emancipated; he can become a free man. These are some of the thoughts and pictures that are behind the New Testament use of this particular term.

'But,' says somebody, 'that is what I object to about this term 'saved'. You Christians are claiming that you're perfect.'

No, no, we are claiming nothing of the sort. Even in this one paragraph that we have before us, that is quite clear from the tense of the verb 'saved'.

One can say of Christians that 'they have been saved', that 'they are being saved', and that 'they are going to be saved'. The apostle Peter, writing many years after he preached this sermon, brings out these aspects very clearly. He puts it like this:

That the trial of your faith, being much more precious than of gold that perisheth, though it be tried with fire, might be found unto praise and honour and glory at the appearing of Jesus Christ: whom having not seen, ye love; in whom, though now ye see him not, yet believing, ye

*rejoice with joy unspeakable and full of glory: receiving the end of your
faith, even the salvation of your souls* (1 Pet. 1:7–9).

Here Peter talks of receiving salvation, and yet he has been referring to his readers as people who have already undergone
salvation. Look at it like this. The first thing we must realize about
ourselves is that we are in a terribly dangerous position. Now this
is a state, or a condition. We are all face to face with God. Let me
take up one of those illustrations again. Look at that man standing
there in a dock in a court. There are many things to be said about
him, but the first and most important thing is that he is in a dock,
on trial before a judge. Now that man may be feeling well or ill,
but that has nothing to do with his position. He may have slept
soundly the night before, or he may not have slept a wink, it does
not make any difference at all. His position is that he is on trial, a
charge has been brought against him and he faces terrible possibilities. And that is how we must look at this question of salvation
in the first instance. You can divide men and women, if you like,
into good and bad. That is done, is it not? But it is quite irrelevant
because we are concerned about the position; and the teaching of
the Bible is that all people – whether we call them good or bad or
anything else – are in the dock with the judgment of God upon them.

We are none of us righteous by birth. We are all under condemnation. That is our status. We are all in a world on fire. We are all
in danger of eternal destruction. We are all lost. We are all in the
dock by birth and by actions. We have all sinned against God. The
law of God is the prosecuting counsel and a just and a holy God is
sitting there on the bench. We are every one of us guilty, and the
sentence on a guilty sinner is 'everlasting destruction from the
presence of the Lord' (2 Thess. 1:9).

Now the teaching is that the moment we believe on the Lord
Jesus Christ, our whole position is changed. Our standing and
status under God is entirely different. That is the first way in
which we look at salvation, and it is in that sense that we can say
of Christians that they are already saved. To use the language of
the apostle Paul, 'There is therefore now no condemnation to them
which are in Christ Jesus' (Rom. 8:1). According to this teaching,
'God so loved the world, that he gave his only begotten Son, that
whosoever believeth in him should not perish, but have everlasting life . . . He that believeth on him is not condemned: but he that

believeth not is condemned already, because he hath not believed in the name of the only begotten Son of God' (*John* 3:16, 18). We are all under the condemnation of the law until we believe, but the moment we believe, we are no longer under condemnation. We are no longer in the dock. We are set at liberty. We are introduced into the kingdom of God and the glorious liberty of the children of God. So a Christian is bound to say, 'I have been saved.'

But that does not mean that I am perfect. No, no. Having been changed in my whole standing, a process now begins in me. I need to be saved. Saved from what? Saved from my evil nature, saved from my evil tendencies, saved from the relics and the remnants of sin that remain in my mortal body. So now *I am being saved*. In the Bible, that process is called sanctification, while the first is called justification. Christians are not perfect, but they are gradually, slowly, being made perfect. There may be many ups and downs, but they are slowly being prepared for the glory to which they are going.

So Christians have been saved, they are being saved, and the day will come when they shall have been saved completely. The Bible calls that glorification. It means freedom not only from the condemnation of the law and the guilt of sin, but entire deliverance from the power and pollution of sin. A time will come when believers will be sinless; they will be perfect. This will not happen in this world, but it will be our condition in the glory that is to come.

So there are tenses to this word 'saved': 'I have been saved', 'I am being saved', 'I shall be saved', and you will find these three tenses constantly used in the New Testament writings. The whole position of these people in Acts was that they had been saved – they had been moved from one kingdom into another. That is the first thing.

But the second thing we notice about these people – and oh, how important this is! – is that this Christianity of theirs was central in their lives. It was the controlling factor of their lives. It was everything to them. This is true of every Christian and it is here that we see the contrast with those popular views of Christianity that I have tried to dismiss. The popular view is that Christianity is something that we add to our lives. The main tenor of our lives is very much the same as that of everybody else in the world, but we have one difference: On Sunday mornings we go to a place of worship for a brief service.

Now am I being unfair? Am I exaggerating? God knows, I am not. Look at the lives of these so-called Christians. Look at their interests; look at the things that excite them. They are exactly the same as everybody else in the world. But they do this odd thing at a given time once a week, perhaps not even that, sometimes only once a year. Their faith is not in the centre of their lives; it is an addition. It is like a man taking up a bag. He has a number of bags, but there is one he only takes up on Sunday morning when he goes to a place of worship. Having been there, he puts it down as quickly as he can, and back he goes to live as he was living before and as everybody else is living. Or his Christianity is like a cloak that he puts on for these odd occasions and then takes off again. Oh, this is not Christianity.

The false idea always has Christianity on the periphery. It is not the heart, it is not the vital, controlling thing, but it has its place there on the edge of life, generally as far away as possible from the centre. But it has to be there because people are afraid something may happen to them if it is not. They live as near as they can to the world but still like to feel that they do not ultimately belong to it.

Now the thing that hits us about these people in Acts is that their whole life, their whole outlook, was changed. They were now controlled by something absolutely new. Look at these people. They were the mob, the people who had cried out, 'Away with him! Crucify him!' That is where they had belonged, but now they belonged to these disciples, to the followers of this Jesus, this Galilean. They had become entirely different. This was not an outward, but an inward change, a radical and profound change. They were now ready to take any risk in order to be with the very people they had previously reviled.

They knew it was dangerous to belong to this group of believers. Had not their leader been crucified on a tree but a few weeks back? Yet they were now ready to join these people and to continue with them. They continued steadfastly with them – they would not leave them. They were risking everything. They knew that their relatives would be annoyed, that probably they would be ostracized by all who were dear to them; it did not matter. They submitted to public baptism, they aligned themselves with these despised people. Whatever happened, they must be with them.

That is Christianity! Not this miserable, doubtful, uncertain, unhappy something that you take on as a task and try to hide as best you can in case someone makes a joke about you in the office and says, 'Ah, in church last night, were you?'

The next point, also, must be emphasized in order to give the lie to a further entirely erroneous conception of what it means to be a Christian. Nothing is so obvious about these people in Acts as the fact that the whole person was involved. And there is nothing that should be emphasized more strongly than this. We have seen how some say that a person's Christianity is determined by the mind only, while others say it is the heart only, and still others that Christianity is a matter of the will only. But the glory of the true Christian faith is that it takes up the whole person – it is so big; it is so great; it is so glorious. The whole self is emancipated and captivated and taken hold of; the entire personality is engaged.

How do I see that? Well, look at the words that are used here. I read, 'Then they that gladly received his word were baptized.' They believed it. They received it with their minds. Then I read later on in verse 44, 'And all that believed were together, and had all things common.' First, they believed.

What did they believe? Do you think it is possible that if you had asked them what they believed, they could not have said anything but, 'Well, I was always brought up to do this, you know, and I think it's quite good, and I think it may help the morals of the country if we hold on to these great traditions. We mustn't let them go, you know. Things are very bad, so let's hold on.' Ask such people what they are holding on to, and they do not know. No, here in Acts we find the exact opposite. We are told, 'They continued stedfastly in the apostles' doctrine.'

Christianity does not by-pass the mind. Christians can tell you why they are Christians, and if you cannot give me a reason, if you cannot say, 'I believe this and that,' then you are not a Christian. We read here, 'They that gladly received his word' – the mind is engaged and involved and on we go to receive more and more. It is thrilling, and the mind expands.

There is nothing that I know of in the universe that is comparable with this gospel. I have often put it like this: Is there somebody with a superfluity of intellect? Are you such an intellectual that you want some exercise for your great mind? Well, I can tell you what to do – start studying the epistle of Paul to the Ephesians, and when you have finished that – if you do ever finish it – I can give you other writings of Paul's that are matchless for profundity of thought, for amazing conceptions, for vistas of truth spreading out and out and out, even into eternity itself and the glory everlasting. Here is the truth that throughout the running centuries has expanded the greatest intellects that the world has ever known.

I am reminded of the story of that old professor who lived in Scotland in the nineteenth century when this modern intellectualism and scientific thinking began to flood in. He used to preface his lectures with these words: 'Gentlemen, I suggest to you that a gospel and a teaching that were good enough and great enough for the mind of a Paul and of an Augustine, and of an Aquinas, and a Luther, and a Calvin, and a Knox, and a Pascal, and a Wesley, and a Gladstone, are at least worthy of your respectful consideration.'

I hear people saying, 'I cannot understand this,' and they reject Christianity because their minds stumble at some particular teaching. But do you imagine for a moment that you are the first ever to have seen that problem? All your problems have been known to these great intellects throughout the centuries. Most difficulties, indeed, I would say all, are dealt with somewhere or another in the Bible. There is nothing original in your problem.

But just look at it like this – before you reject Christianity, say, 'How did these men with their great intellects, receive it?' That is the answer. It is no use saying that modern knowledge has added a new understanding. It has not! It has made no difference. Modern knowledge has told us nothing new about God or about people. It has told us nothing new about death, and nothing new about eternity. Here in the Bible we read of men and women who believed the truth. They received the word that was preached. The whole intellect was engaged and began to function as never before. But Christianity does not only come to the mind. Christians are not mere dry-as-dust intellectuals or academics. The heart is involved: 'They that gladly received his word . . .' Listen to verses 46 and 47: 'They . . . did eat their meat with gladness and singleness of heart, praising God, and having favour with all the people.' This is true happiness. There is no real happiness apart from it. The idea that Christianity makes people miserable and wretched is the greatest lie that the devil has ever perpetrated. That is how he deludes people. 'Ah,' they say, 'you've become religious. You'll be miserable. You'll have to stop enjoying yourself and do all these dull and boring things – it will ruin your life. You'll be unhappy as long as you live. Come with us,' they say, 'come with the world and have life and happiness.'

Has there ever been a greater fallacy? Happiness in the world? Well, where is it? As I see people passing through the divorce courts, I do not detect much happiness. Even drink is not enough, so that more and more people are turning to drugs. There is only one thing in this world that can make people really happy, and that is the truth that these people in Jerusalem believed. They did not only accept it with their minds – they were moved; they were happy; they were released and joyful. The Holy Spirit, in whom the Christian believes, is characterized by love, joy and happiness – the very things the world stands so much in need of. The world knows so little. But these people knew. In the face of persecution and possible death they were thrilling with joy, and that has been the mark of true Christians in all eras and periods ever since. Can thinking people be truly happy in a world with bombs and sin and shame? No, they cannot. There is only one way to find happiness, and that is to be separated from this world into this other life in which you see through the world and beyond it and know the glory that is coming.

You can then say with the apostle Peter, 'Wherein ye greatly rejoice, though now for a season, if need be, ye are in heaviness through manifold temptations . . .' (*1 Pet.* 1:6). Or you say with Paul, 'We that are in this tabernacle do groan, being burdened' (*2 Cor.* 5:4). Yes, 'For in this we groan, earnestly desiring to be clothed upon with our house which is from heaven' (verse 2). Gladness! Joy! You realize you have escaped hell. You are no longer going to perdition: You are a child of God. Your heart is moved. You are living a great and a glorious and a big life and you are rejoicing in it. Peter said in his letter, 'Whom having not seen, ye love; in whom, though now ye see him not, yet believing, ye rejoice with joy unspeakable and full of glory' (*1 Pet.* 1:8). That is it; the heart is engaged. So also is the will: These early Christians were baptized. And I like these words: 'They continued stedfastly in the apostles' doctrine and fellowship . . . and they, continuing daily with one accord . . .' Their conversion was not a flash-in-the-pan experience; it was not just going forward at the end of a meeting and making a decision or signing a card. I do not ask for that sort of thing because I know that believing is the work of the Spirit, and the whole person is involved. The mind understands and knows what it is doing; the heart is moved and has its reasons that cannot be expressed through thought; and the will becomes operative. That is Christianity. It means that we have been separated from this present evil world, and separated into and unto the kingdom of God and his Christ.

Are you a Christian? I am not asking you whether you are doing a lot of good. I am not asking you whether you are a church member. I am not asking whether your parents were Christians, or whether you were born in a so-called Christian country. I am not asking you whether you were christened as a baby or even baptized as an adult. I am simply asking this: Are you like the people described in this paragraph at the end of the second chapter of Acts? They were ready even to die for their faith, and many of them did die, as Christians have had to die throughout the centuries. But they know that they are saved once and for ever from the condemnation of the law. Whatever happens to them, their position with God is right. God has forgiven them, their sins have been remitted, they are justified by God through their faith. God declares them to be free, and they know that. Their minds have seen the truth, they have received it, and received it gladly.

And they give practical demonstration of their faith by leaving the world to which they belonged, and joining, being 'added to', the church, which consists of these people who have an entirely new view of the meaning of life, a new view of themselves, a new view of the meaning of history and of why things are as they are, a new view of death, a new view of eternity, a new view of God, and a new view of Jesus of Nazareth as the Son of God and the Saviour of their souls. Oh, it is entirely new. They are controlled by this, it is at the centre. Everything they do now comes to the bar of this. They are indeed 'born again' and are children of God.

6

Separation

Now when they heard this, they were pricked in their heart, and said unto Peter and to the rest of the apostles, Men and brethren, what shall we do? Then Peter said unto them, Repent, and be baptized every one of you in the name of Jesus Christ for the remission of sins, and ye shall receive the gift of the Holy Ghost. For the promise is unto you, and to your children, and to all that are afar off, even as many as the Lord our God shall call. And with many other words did he testify and exhort, saying, Save yourselves from this untoward generation. Then they that gladly received his word were baptized: and the same day there were added unto them about three thousand souls. And they continued stedfastly in the apostles' doctrine and fellowship, and in breaking of bread, and in prayers (Acts 2:37–42).

Why are we dealing with this question of what it means to be a Christian? Is this some sort of anachronism in this modern world? Is it because we are carrying on some old tradition and perhaps have not thought enough even to stop – is that the position? No, the reason is very different indeed. It is because there is nothing today that holds out hope for men and women save this message. It is indeed, as it describes itself, 'a light that shineth in a dark place' (*2 Pet.* 1:19). The world is a cavern and here is the only light. There are speculations, I know, and men strike their little matches. They do not last very long and are denounced by the next generation. Ideas come and go and are always changing. Indeed, the most extraordinary and in many ways the most tragic aspect of all is that though the world boasts about its advances, its ideas do not progress but go round and round in circles, just like fashions, which are popular at one moment and then are discarded and ridiculed. But you wait a bit; they will come back.

Today, people no longer recognize the category of the moral. Modern men and women say, 'We have a new morality.' But that is simply a repetition of what the devil has suggested before. He puts an idea back into some cupboard, and brings out another one, and everybody forgets the old idea. He lets a century or two pass, then he brings the first one out again. 'Brand new!', people say. 'A new morality.' It is as old as Adam in sin! Nothing new at all, nothing original in any sense whatsoever. All perversions and all foulness are described here in the Bible as well as in the pages of secular history.

For many centuries, the Bible has told us, 'There is no new thing under the sun' (*Eccles.* 1:9), and there certainly is not. And all the arguments against Christianity, against this faith and way of life, have been put forward many times. So we have nothing to do but to turn back and consider this account, which is the only authority that we really have as to what it means to be a Christian.

Now we have seen that men and women become Christians because of the action of God and that as a result they undergo a profound change in mind, in heart and in will. We see that in practice here in Acts and we find the same thing stated in our Lord's own teaching and in the teaching of the apostles. Our Lord made a famous statement to Nicodemus, that ruler of the Jews, whose idea was that you added on something to what you already had. He was a teacher who thought that this Jesus had something that he had not got. He thought: I am a master of Israel, but this man works miracles and seems to have a deeper insight than I have. I must have an interview with him and find out what else I need.

And the answer Nicodemus received shook him to his foundations, as it was meant to do: 'Verily, verily, I say unto thee, Except a man be born again, he cannot see the kingdom of God' (*John* 3:3) - he cannot even see it! 'Born again' – that is it – a profound, radical change that makes a man or woman an entirely new creature. As the apostle Paul puts it, 'If any man be in Christ, he is a new creature' – not merely a trimmed up or an improved creation, but a new creation, a new creature – 'Old things are passed away; behold, all things are become new' (*2 Cor.* 5:17).

Now that, and nothing else, is Christianity. All else is religion, and I am not here to preach that. You can make yourself religious but you cannot make yourself a Christian. This is the action of God the Creator re-creating the soul. It is the Holy Spirit taking men and women, convicting them, smashing them and reassembling them on a new pattern, on the pattern of the image of the Son of God himself. Christians – to use the title of a famous book that had such influence upon George Whitefield and John and Charles Wesley two hundred years ago – Christians are those who have the life of God in their souls. That is Christianity: *The Life of God in the Soul of Man*. That stands out very clearly in this account of these first Christians who were added to the Christian church.

I want to establish yet further that this is true Christianity. Let me prove it by showing you that this change in someone's whole outlook shows itself in action. If it does not do that, then it is of no value: 'Faith, if it hath not works, is dead, being alone' (*James* 2:17). But true faith, this change leading to faith, always shows itself.

How does true faith reveal itself? Well, the first big thing we notice here in Acts is that it leads to a great separation. It separates men and women from the world, and separates them to the church. This is something that is found everywhere in the New Testament. Not one of the New Testament letters was written to people in the world; they were all written to churches, that is, to people who had been gathered out of the world and put into these new communities. Here they were; they had been 'added to the church' and 'continued stedfastly in the apostles' doctrine and fellowship, and in breaking of bread, and in prayers'. A tremendous change was taking place within them and showed itself outwardly in that they had left one position for another.

This is one of the most vital things that needs to be emphasized at this present time. The church will be useless until this separation is made clear in her life. There is no state church in the New Testament – nothing approaching it! In the New Testament we see a division. A man or woman is taken from the world and put into the realm of the church. An admixture of church and state, world and Christianity, is fatal to true Christianity. It misleads, it is wrong, and it hinders the whole work of the church. In every time of reformation and true spiritual revival this separation, this distinction, becomes plain.

Now let us be clear about the meaning of the term 'world'. As used in the Scriptures, 'world' always means the mind and the outlook of humanity without God. It does not mean the physical universe – there is nothing wrong with that – nor does it mean animal creation. No, the 'world' means human beings trying to organize themselves and their lives without God. And my contention is that when people become Christians, they are taken from the world, though they still live in it, and are joined to this other body of people whom they resemble in most essential respects: the Christian church.

Look at this as it comes out plainly in the teaching of our blessed Lord and Saviour himself. Read, for example, Matthew 10, and see how our Lord was always surprising his contemporaries, as he has surprised people ever since. The common idea about Jesus Christ, is it not, is that he is someone who came into the world to give peace, that he was the apostle of peace. So it is claimed that Christianity is a teaching that denounces war and bombs. But he himself said, 'Think not that I am come to send peace on earth: I came not to send peace, but a sword' (*Matt.* 10:34).

Now let us be fair. When our Lord said that, he did not mean that he had come into the world to make nations fight one another. Of course not! But he was nevertheless dissenting very strongly from the notion that he was just 'a pale Galilean' or 'a gentle artist'. He was not some aesthete or a moral philosopher who had come simply to bring people together, to break down barriers, and urge peace. He rejected that.

The idea that the Christian message is just a message to be nice and kind and friendly to one another is a travesty of the gospel. It is too profound for that, too radical, too strong, too fundamental. There is no sloppy sentimentality about the Christian message. It is a message with a sword, and we see this in operation right at the beginning, on the day of Pentecost. I am anxious to prove this point because the idea still persists that the church is like some sort of maiden aunt who comes in on certain special occasions with a sentimental touch. In the name of the church and of Christianity, I protest! Here is strength and power; here, I repeat, is a sword.

Separation

One day, on the road to Damascus, our Lord commissioned a man called Saul of Tarsus, and this is what he told him:

Rise, and stand upon thy feet: for I have appeared unto thee for this purpose, to make thee a minister and a witness both of these things which thou hast seen, and of those things in the which I will appear unto thee; delivering thee from the people, and from the Gentiles, unto whom I now send thee.

What for?

To open their eyes, and to turn them from darkness to light, and from the power of Satan unto God, that they may receive forgiveness of sins, and inheritance among them which are sanctified by faith that is in me. (Acts 26:16–18)

That is the commission that was given. Paul would separate the Gentiles – call them out of darkness and put them in the realm of light – this great separation from the world into the realm of the kingdom of God.

We find this repeated everywhere. 'Come out from among them,' says the apostle later on, 'and be ye separate' (*2 Cor.* 6:17). He has just written, 'What communion hath light with darkness? And what concord hath Christ with Belial?' (verses 14–15). You cannot mix light and darkness; you cannot mix Christ and Belial. And the difference between the Christian and the world is the difference between light and darkness. These things are eternal opposites. They are as different as God and the devil, heaven and hell. Here is the great contrast.

Or again, take the specific statement which Paul makes at the very beginning of his epistle to the Galatians: 'Grace be to you and peace from God the Father, and from our Lord Jesus Christ, who gave himself for our sins, that he might deliver us from this present evil world' – that is it; that is why Christ died on the cross: that he might separate us, deliver us, from this present evil world – 'according to the will of God and our Father' (*Gal.* 1:3–4).

Again, the apostle Paul writes to the Ephesians, 'This I say therefore, and testify in the Lord, that ye henceforth walk not as other Gentiles walk, in the vanity of their mind, having the understanding darkened . . . ye have not so learned Christ' (*Eph.* 4:17–18, 20). They must not go on living as they used to live, like the rest of the Gentiles to whom they belonged. They had been changed, they had 'learned Christ'. Things were different.

Paul puts it still more specifically in the next chapter:

Let no man deceive you with vain words: for because of these things cometh the wrath of God upon the children of disobedience. Be not ye therefore partakers with them. For ye were sometimes darkness, but now are ye light in the Lord: walk as children of light . . . Proving what is acceptable unto the Lord. And have no fellowship with the unfruitful works of darkness, but rather reprove them (Eph. 5:6–11).

And Paul exhorts the Christians in Philippi to be 'blameless and harmless, the sons of God, without rebuke, in the midst of a crooked and perverse nation, among whom ye shine as lights in the world' (*Phil.* 2:15). What could be stronger? He says: The difference between a Christian and a non-Christian is that the Christian is like a star in the blackness of the heavens on a dark night. Christians shine as luminaries in the heavens, in the midst of all that darkness. That is Paul's definition of a Christian.

Then, writing to the Colossians, Paul says: 'Giving thanks unto the Father, which hath made us meet to be partakers of the inheritance of the saints in light: who hath delivered us from the power of darkness, and hath translated us into the kingdom of his dear Son' (*Col.* 1:12–13). There has been a great transference, a movement of population, if you like, from one realm into another.

Then take one other statement. Listen to the apostle writing to the Thessalonians:

But ye, brethren, are not in darkness, that that day should overtake you as a thief. Ye are all the children of light, and the children of the day: we are not of the night, nor of darkness [we were, but we are not any longer]. *Therefore let us not sleep, as do others; but let us watch and be sober. For they that sleep sleep in the night; and they that be drunken are drunken in the night. But let us, who are of the day, be sober, putting on the breastplate of faith and love; and for an helmet, the hope of salvation* (1 Thess. 5:4–8).

And the apostle Peter preached exactly the same message. This is not only Pauline theology, as foolish and ignorant people would have us believe, this is the teaching of all the teachers in the New Testament. Peter writes in his letter:

Ye are a chosen generation, a royal priesthood, an holy nation, a peculiar people; that ye should shew forth the praises of him who hath called you out of darkness into his marvellous light: which in time past

were not a people, but are now the people of God: which had not obtained
mercy, but now have obtained mercy. Dearly beloved, I beseech you as
strangers and pilgrims, abstain from fleshly lusts, which war against the
soul; having your conversation honest among the Gentiles: that, whereas
they speak against you as evil-doers, they may by your good works,
which they shall behold, glorify God in the day of visitation (1 Pet.
2:9–12).

And we must not leave out the apostle John – this is the universal apostolic message. John puts it like this:

*Love not the world, neither the things that are in the world. If any man
love the world, the love of the Father is not in him. For all that is in the
world, the lust of the flesh, and the lust of the eyes, and the pride of life,
is not of the Father, but is of the world. And the world passeth away, and
the lust thereof* (1 John 2:15–17).

Is that not enough? Well, says John towards the end of his first letter, 'This is the victory that overcometh the world, even our faith' (*1 John* 5:4). And finally he says, 'We know that whosoever is born of God sinneth not; but he that is begotten of God keepeth himself, and that wicked one toucheth him not. And we know that we are of God, and the whole world lieth in wickedness [in the wicked one]' (*1 John* 5:18-19).

So there is the statement which is so plain and clear in the whole of this New Testament teaching. Once men and women are dealt with by the Holy Spirit, through this word preached, they are entirely changed, and the change reveals itself in their separation from the godless world.

But we must go a step further, and I do this in order that we may establish once and for ever that becoming a Christian is the most profound change that can ever take place in a human being. Think again about what our Lord said to his disciples: 'Think not that I am come to send peace on earth: I came not to send peace, but a sword.' Then – 'For I am come to set a man at variance against his father, and the daughter against her mother, and the daughter in law against her mother in law. And a man's foes shall be they of his own household. He that loveth father or mother more than me is not worthy of me . . . And he that taketh not his cross' – whatever it may cost and whatever separation it may involve – 'and followeth not after me, is not worthy of me' (*Matt.* 10:34–38).

This is our Lord speaking. Yet people think of him as one who just says sweet, sentimental nothings! No, no. Here is a gospel that produces heroes. Here is a gospel that produces martyrs. Here is the strongest thing in the world. But you see how it works? 'The brother shall deliver up the brother to death, and the father the child: and the children shall rise up against their parents, and cause them to be put to death. And ye shall be hated of all men for my name's sake: but he that endureth to the end shall be saved' (*Matt.* 10:21–22).

All those passages establish that when people become Christians, something so profound takes place within them that not only are they separated from the world in general, they are separated even from their nearest and dearest if they are still not Christians. Do not misunderstand this. It does not mean that a man has to leave his wife, or the wife the husband, or the father the child, but what it does mean is that whereas the members of a family had been living the same sort of life more or less in harmony, the moment one member becomes a Christian, there is an inevitable separation, and everybody knows it. The man or woman to whom it has happened knows it, and the others know it and resent it. Something has come between them – between a husband and wife, between a father and son, a mother and daughter, something has disrupted the nearest and the dearest relationships. Becoming a Christian cuts and divides even the most tender earthly associations – 'I came not to send peace, but a sword.' Our Lord's words show how thorough, how profound this change is. Now there is nothing one can say beyond that. That is what our Lord himself says, and his words have been fulfilled throughout the centuries.

But why should there be such a change? That is the great question. And the answer is right before us in the pages of the Scripture. The teaching is that we all by nature belong to the world. The human race is one. There is such a thing as the solidarity of the human race. It is one in sin; it is one in evil; it is one in its alienation from God. This is true of everybody born into the world. This is deeper than all the world's divisions. Look at all the talk today about segregation and colour and so on – why can people not see that 'one touch of nature makes the whole world kin'? All the people in the world are sinners, whatever the colour of their skin. All human beings are 'shapen in iniquity' (*Psa.* 51:5). Sin reveals itself in every continent, in every clime, in every culture. In every division of the human race we find the same things being done and the same problems arising. That is the teaching of the Bible.

Now by nature men and women are not aware of this. That is why there are these separations and divisions. We think we are superior or we feel that we are inferior and there are clashes. But whether the world knows it or not, it is just a simple fact. And when people become Christians, the Holy Spirit, using this word, opens their minds and awakens them to a realization of this tremendous truth. That is what Peter said in his exhortation at the end of his sermon. We are told, 'With many other words' – many other similar words – 'did he testify and exhort, saying, Save yourselves from this untoward generation.'

How, then, do you 'save yourself'? Well, once men and women are dealt with by the Spirit of God and begin to understand this message, their minds and understanding are awakened to the tremendous truth of the solidarity of the entire human race in sin. At first they do not know what Peter is talking about when he says, 'Save [separate] yourselves from this untoward generation.'

'I'm in the world, how can I save myself from it?', they say. 'Is Peter asking me to become a monk or an anchorite or a hermit? Is he asking me to segregate myself from society?'

No, he is simply asking you to separate yourself from all that is true about the world in the biblical sense. It works like this: when the Holy Spirit begins to work in people, as I showed you earlier, they begin to think for the first time and they find that there is such a thing as 'the mind of the world' which is opposed to God. They did not know that before. They thought that they were original thinkers! They thought that they had their own ideas and that their point of view was absolutely their own. But they wake up to the fact that it is nothing of the sort and they are just victims of the mind-set of the world. E. C. Bentley put it like this in a little poem he sent to his friend G. K. Chesterton:

> *The world was very old indeed*
> *When you and I were young.*

And how true that is.

We are all inheritors of prejudices and ways of thinking. We are all imitators, gramophone records, almost robots, repeating, repeating, repeating. Why do we do certain things? Because everybody else does them! We want to be up-to-date, abreast of the times. We want to do 'the thing to do'. We are victims of propaganda, the propaganda of the newspapers and of the television, the radio, the hoardings and plays. And this 'world mind' which makes us what we are, is opposed to God.

Now there is some interesting teaching about this in the New Testament and as men and women are dealt with by the Spirit of God, they begin to see it more and more clearly. Listen to the apostle Paul putting it so plainly to the Ephesians: 'You hath he quickened, who were dead in trespasses and sins' (*Eph.* 2:1).

'But they were alive,' you say.

Of course they were, but they were 'dead in trespasses and sins'. People can be alive physically and dead spiritually. And as we have seen, that is the trouble with all human beings, we are all spiritually dead. We are not aware of the spiritual realm. We do not think in a spiritual manner. Then Paul goes on to say:

Wherein in time past ye walked according to the course of this world, according to the prince of the power of the air, the spirit that now worketh in the children of disobedience: among whom we all had our conversation in times past in the lusts of our flesh, fulfilling the desires of the flesh and of the mind; and were by nature the children of wrath, even as others (Eph. 2:2–3).

There is no such thing as freedom of the mind. We all inherit a prejudice against God. We all have this worldly outlook. A young man reaches a certain age and he says, 'I've been made to go to Sunday school and to chapel; no more! I'm going to think for myself!' Then he begins to say things which he thinks are brilliantly new, absolutely original. His father did exactly the same thing, and his father before him, and it has been done ever since Adam and Eve fell, away back at the dawn of history.

But then the question is: What is it that controls the mind of the world? What controls this outlook which people have upon life and upon God and upon death and upon themselves and eternity? Well, according to the apostle and according to the whole of the Bible, all this is controlled by the devil. Yes, I still preach the existence of the devil! And I do so because it is in the Scriptures. But even if it were not, I would still do it because there is no other explanation for the state of the world. What is it that thwarts all the efforts of humanity to put itself right? Why does every civilization fail? Why is it that the world is still struggling, as it has throughout recorded history, to deliver itself, and cannot?

There is only one answer – the devil, the 'god of this world' (*2 Cor.* 4:4), 'the prince of the power of the air, the spirit that now worketh in the children of disobedience' (*Eph.* 2:2). And the world is as it is because it does not know that. It is because of the devil that all our efforts are vain and futile and nothing can deliver us. A tremendous, unseen, spiritual power is paralysing and blinding the minds of men and women. The apostle Paul says, 'If our gospel be hid, it is hid to them that are lost: in whom the god of this world hath blinded the minds of them which believe not, lest the light of the glorious gospel of Christ . . . should shine unto them' (*2 Cor.* 4:3–4).

But now, under the influence of the Spirit and this teaching, people begin to understand.

They suddenly see the awful prejudice, the spiritual tyranny. They see that there is no such thing as a 'free thinker'. Then people ask, 'So how has all this happened? When did it start?' And there is only one adequate answer. It is all due to the fact that man in his folly rebelled against God. Before the fall, the world was in harmony with God. Man enjoyed fellowship with God and God blessed him. The change came about like this: the devil asked, 'Did God say?' Why did God say that? God said it to keep you down and to rob you of your privileges as a man. Assert yourself and you will become as God.

That is the outlook of the world. And its author is the devil. Worldliness started in the original rebellion and fall and sin of Adam. And as they realize these things, men and women begin to see that they are victims, and especially when they try to fight against it, they find they somehow cannot. They make their resolutions, only to break them. They are always in a state of defeat. Then the Holy Spirit shows them that the explanation is that the world is controlled by the devil and they cannot get free.

'Save yourselves,' says the apostle, 'from this untoward generation.' The word 'untoward' is the biblical description of a person in sin. It means crooked, intractable, not manageable. It means that men and women have a twist in them, they are perverted. John the Baptist made the same point, quoting Isaiah: 'The crooked shall be made straight' (*Luke* 3:5), and, according to the Bible, this is what people see as they are beginning to become Christians, as they come under conviction. It is not only the world, it is they themselves. They and the world are all twisted and perverted. There is nothing straight, nothing pure, nothing clean.

If you want a description of the crookedness of men and women as they are by nature, and the world as it is apart from God, then you will find it all in the opening chapter of Paul's letter to the Romans, in the terrifying words that are to be found there:

Because that, when they knew God, they glorified him not as God, neither were thankful; but became vain in their imaginations, and their foolish heart was darkened. Professing themselves to be wise, they became fools, and changed the glory of the incorruptible God into an image made like to corruptible man, and to birds, and fourfooted beasts, and creeping things [worshipping mascots, worshipping idols, and so on]. *Wherefore God also gave them up to uncleanness through the lusts of their own hearts, to dishonour their own bodies between themselves: who changed the truth of God into a lie, and worshipped and served the creature more than the Creator, who is blessed for ever. Amen. For this cause God gave them up unto vile affections: for even their women did change the natural use into that which is against nature: and likewise also the men, leaving the natural use of the woman, burned in their lust one toward another; men with men working that which is unseemly, and receiving in themselves that recompence of their error which was meet* (Rom. 1:21–27).

Here is a summary of it:

Being filled with all unrighteousness, fornication, wickedness, covetousness, maliciousness; full of envy, murder, debate, deceit, malignity; whisperers, backbiters, haters of God, despiteful, proud, boasters, inventors of evil things, disobedient to parents, without understanding, covenant breakers, without natural affection, implacable, unmerciful: who knowing the judgment of God, that they which commit such things are worthy of death, not only do the same, but have pleasure in them that do them (Rom. 1:29–32).

That is a description of any big city without God! That is the life of the rich as well as the poor. Here is humanity without God, slaves of sin and evil, foul, debased, disgusting, vile. 'Untoward generation'! Twisted! Perverted!

So when men and women are under the conviction of the Holy Spirit, they begin to see these things and to understand them. They find a vileness in themselves, an ugliness and a foulness – evil imaginations, evil thoughts and actions. They say, 'What's the matter with me? I'm a mass of corruption, what can I do?' That is what happened to the people at Jerusalem and made them cry out, 'Men and brethren, what shall we do?'

And then the gospel message goes on to tell us that we were never meant to be like that and that the world was never meant to be as it is today. This is not the world as God made it. This is the result of man's rebellion and foulness and evil. I am not what I was meant to be, as I was originally made in the image of God. But I see another view of humanity; I see another possibility. The gospel alone gives it me, and I am convinced of it.

And then the gospel reveals to me the fate that awaits the world as it is without God, and antagonistic to him, and it is a terrifying fate. That is why Peter cried out on the day of Pentecost, 'Save yourselves from this untoward generation.' What did he mean? John the apostle puts it in these words, 'Love not the world, neither the things that are in the world,' because, he says, '. . . the world passeth away, and the lust thereof: but he that doeth the will of God abideth for ever' (*1 John* 2:15, 17).

The message that came home to these people at Pentecost was that. They were a part of the world that had sinned against God, and the wrath of God was upon it – God had pronounced judgment on the world. According to the prophecy of the Son of God himself, far from getting better and better, the world would get worse and worse. He said, 'Ye shall hear of wars and rumours of wars' (*Matt.* 24:6). Today many people don rose-tinted spectacles and promise us an era of universal peace but their words are a delusion and snare of Satan. The world will fight and war. Evil and sin, lust and foulness will increase in spite of modern civilization, until the Son of God returns in mighty judgment.

God has revealed the coming judgment throughout the history of the human race. He revealed it in the flood; he revealed it in the destruction of the Tower of Babel; he revealed it in the destruction of Sodom and Gomorrah; he revealed it in the destruction of Jerusalem in AD 70, and I believe he is revealing it in the wars of this twentieth century. We are making a mockery of our civilization, of our great advancement. The state of the world is a manifestation of the wrath of God. He has handed us over to evil. He is allowing us to stew in our own juice. He is withdrawing his restraining power in order to warn us to save ourselves from this untoward generation, in order to warn us to 'flee from the wrath to come' (*Matt.* 3:7).

The people in Acts 2 heard the warning. Peter preached, 'Save yourselves,' and they said, 'What shall we do?' And the answer that Peter gave was that God had sent his only Son into this world. What for? To start a new humanity, to start a new human race. Adam failed and fell and we reap the consequences. But God has sent his Son, the second, the last Adam, and he is 'the firstborn among many brethren' (*Rom.* 8:29).

We can be forgiven. We can be rescued. We can live in this world and yet not be of it. We can have a new life, a new nature, a new start. We can become the sons of God and look forward to the glory everlasting. That is the message, and all we are called upon to do is to believe it, to believe in the Lord Jesus Christ and at all costs to follow him, leaving the world, taking up the cross and following him wherever he may lead.

This may mean misunderstanding in the family; but what does it matter? My soul is at stake. I was once in sin with them, but God has chosen to reveal to me that my soul matters. They will die, I will die, what of my soul? What is the value of the good opinion of your family, or of a country, or what is the value of a state funeral and a magnificent procession, or the tributes of the universe, if your soul is lost and you are a stranger from God and you go to everlasting misery and perdition and suffering and loss?

'What shall it profit a man, if he shall gain the whole world, and lose his own soul?' (*Mark* 8:36). This message tells us that we must be separated, that the sword must come and divide us. And it tells us that we must ask him to use the sword to set us free. He came into the world in order to do that. He said, 'If the Son therefore shall make you free, ye shall be free indeed' (*John* 8:36). Here is a message, a truth, coming in the power of the Spirit, that separates us from the kingdom of darkness and translates us into the kingdom of God's dear Son. People show that they have become Christians when they leave the world and all it represents and join the body of God's people and continue among them. This is not a mere intellectual change. Having seen this truth, they hate the world.

> *I hate the sins that made Thee mourn,*
> *That drove Thee from my breast.*
> William Cowper

They want to be delivered. They want to be like Christ. Not only is the mind affected, but the heart and will as well. Becoming a Christian, as I said at the beginning, is the profoundest and the most radical thing that can ever happen to a man or woman.

So I end by again asking the same old question: Has the sword of the Son of God been exercised in your case? Has it divided and separated you from the world? Do you differ from the mind and the outlook and the desires of the world? Have you seen its baseness, its foulness, its pretence, and utter emptiness? Have you seen that if you die like that you are under the judgment of God? Have you given proof that you have seen it by separating from the world and by giving yourself to the Son of God and joining in the life and fellowship of his people? Do you know anything of the 'gladness' that came into the life of these first believers and the 'joy unspeakable and full of glory'?

Oh, may God by his Spirit bring home and apply this truth to all who hitherto have been ignorant of these things!

7

Continuing Steadfastly

Then they that gladly received his word were baptized: and the same day there were added unto them about three thousand souls. And they continued stedfastly in the apostles' doctrine and fellowship, and in breaking of bread, and in prayers. And fear came upon every soul: and many wonders and signs were done by the apostles. And all that believed were together, and had all things common; and sold their possessions and goods, and parted them to all men, as every man had need. And they, continuing daily with one accord in the temple, and breaking bread from house to house, did eat their meat with gladness and singleness of heart, praising God, and having favour with all the people. And the Lord added to the church daily such as should be saved (Acts 2:41–47).

As we have been considering these verses in Acts, we have seen that by nature we are all under the wrath of God and the world is as it is because of that, too. A blind man once said a very true thing to our Lord's enemies: 'God heareth not sinners' (*John* 9:31). It is no use expecting God to bless men and women who deliberately flout him and rebel against him and insult his holy name. And undoubtedly the world is as it is because 'the wrath of God is revealed from heaven against all ungodliness and unrighteousness of men, who hold the truth in unrighteousness' (*Rom.* 1:18). God withdraws his restraining power. At times, he hands the world over to a reprobate mind. He allows men and women to reap the consequences of their own foolish thinking.

They say that there is no God, and that they can live without a god, that they can manage their own affairs. Well, they are being allowed to see what happens when they do. That is one of the ways in which God manifests his wrath upon the rebellion and the arrogance of men and women.

But we also believe and preach that the only hope for any individual, the only hope in the world today, is the gospel of our Lord and Saviour Jesus Christ, and that the Christian church is the institution formed, founded by the Lord himself, in order to preach and to propagate his message. So we have been looking at the account of the early church, and have seen how men and women become Christians and how they are completely changed so that they are new creatures with the life of God in their souls.

And we have seen that this new life immediately expresses itself. Indeed, life always expresses itself – it is bound to do so. The moment a child is born he expresses the fact that he is alive; he moves, he desires food, and so on. A dummy would not do that, but a live child does. By definition, life has a vitality about it. And that, as we have seen, is equally true of this new life that is in our Lord Jesus Christ. So everything that Christians are and do is an expression of this new life that is in them. I do not mean their every single action, but the main bent and characteristic of their lives. Or, to put it the other way round, Christians are people who can only be explained in terms of the fact that they have new life in them, that they have the life of God in them. Did not our Lord say, 'I am come that they might have life, and that they might have it more abundantly' (*John* 10:10)? Without him, we do not have life; we exist, no more. He alone gives life.

We are in the process of considering the ways in which that new life reveals itself. So far we have considered only one aspect of that new life and that is negative – the first thing men and women do when they become Christians is separate themselves from the world – and we gave reasons for that. But how does this new life manifest itself in a positive manner? Again, I want to show you that it does so in a way that is almost the exact opposite of what people imagine it to be. Why is it that with an open Bible in front of them, and with a record such as this in Acts, men and women think instinctively about the Christian and about Christianity and the church in a manner that is the exact contradiction of what we find here? Now there is only one answer to that: It is because of sin. As we have seen, the Bible says that sin *blinds* us. It confuses the understanding, so that, though you put truth before people, they cannot see it. There is no other explanation.

So now let us look at the positive expressions of faith, seen here in Acts. Again, as I begin, I trust that it is plain and clear that this becomes a very real test for every one of us. Do we conform to this picture? Is this true of us? Is this the sort of thing we are doing? These things are absolutes. There is no getting away from them. We are either Christians or else we are not, and we know which we are in the light of this truth. Now it is put to us here in a number of phrases:

Verse 42: 'They continued stedfastly in the apostles' doctrine and fellowship, and in breaking of bread, and in prayers.'

Verse 44: 'And all that believed were together, and had all things common.'

Verse 45: 'And sold their possessions and goods, and parted them to all men, as every man had need.'

Verse 46: 'And they, continuing daily with one accord in the temple, and breaking bread from house to house, did eat their meat with gladness and singleness of heart.'

Now I want to emphasize particularly verses 42 and 46. These men and women had become Christians. How did they show it? Negatively, they separated themselves from what they had been. Positively, they joined the church and continued in the church. Let me divide this up. The first thing we are told is that they came together constantly – 'they continued stedfastly'; 'and they, continuing daily'. All who believed these things, all who were Christians, were constantly to be found together. So here is my first proposition. One of the first tests that you must apply to yourself, or to anybody else, in order to discover whether or not you are a Christian is to put the question: Do you want to come together with other Christians? If you do not feel this desire, then there is only one explanation: You are not a Christian. Now one would have thought that it would be unnecessary to say a thing like that, but, sadly, this warning is needed.

When I am preaching a series of sermons like this, it always interests me to see how often the newspapers provide me with just the illustration that I need. There may be some people – and I am sure there are – even certain churchgoers, who begin to say to themselves, 'Why is he doing all this? Isn't all this so obvious? Isn't he setting up some imaginary Aunt Sallies in order to knock them down?' In case there is somebody who thinks like that, let me read to you what I found in a recent newspaper. Here is a bold heading and a photograph of a clergyman, with a statement attributed to a man called Mr Brooks. Although Mr Brooks and his wife do not attend a church, they had been anxious that their child should be christened. However, the clergyman had refused. He said he would only go ahead with the christening if Mr and Mrs Brooks and the godparents would agree to attend a class of instruction on the purpose of baptism. He told them that he wanted them to be quite clear in their minds about what they were doing.

Mr Brooks commented like this to the *Evening Standard* reporter: 'Although I am a Christian, I am strictly the non-churchgoing type, believing' – *believing*! But he has not finished – 'believing that most churchgoers are hypocrites and go merely for convention's sake.'

The reporter adds, 'It seems to me that, as a recent innovation, this desire, this request that they should attend this instruction class, represents a desperate last-ditch attempt to bring people into the churches in exchange for priestly favours.' And the article concludes: 'The vicar says that his offer was adamantly refused and Mr Brooks told him he thought a person who did not attend church was as good a Christian as a regular communicant.'

So that is why I hold these things before you. Here is a man who says that you can be a Christian even when you are 'strictly the non-churchgoing type', and that, indeed, he himself is a better Christian than those who do go to church. Those who go to church are just hypocrites, who attend out of mere tradition and for convention's sake. He says, 'I'm a fine Christian, but I don't go to church. I'm not that type.'

Now according to the book of Acts, such a man – I do not know him but I can tell you this about him – such a man is not a Christian. I say that, not because of the insulting remarks he makes about those who do attend a place of worship – let us be as fair as we can to Mr Brooks and grant that many who go to church *are* hypocrites. I am not here to defend such people. I know that there are people who are mere traditionalists and that there are men and women in churches who have no idea why they go, nor what it means to be a Christian. Yes, we will grant Mr Brooks all that, though we do not agree that that is true of all churchgoers. No, I say that he is not a Christian because he maintains something which is the exact opposite of what we are told in the New Testament. He is behaving in a manner that is a direct denial and contradiction of what those first Christians did, and what all other true Christians have always done.

The first indication of new, divine life is a drawing together of people who have this life in common. You see what a contradiction that is of the modern idea that preachers today are simply concerned with their own livelihood and are trying somehow, anyhow, to get a congregation? The man in the interview goes on to maintain that if preachers continue to refuse to christen the children of non-churchgoers, soon they will not have any congregations at all! According to him, Christianity is just a social formality. But when the apostle Peter preached his sermon, he was not concerned to gather a congregation; his concern was to save souls. That is the business of the Christian church: It is to proclaim the truth to men and women.

My difficulty, as I shall show you, is that so often the church herself violates the principle of her own being and behaves in a manner that justifies the kind of statement made by Mr Brooks. But that is not seen in the New Testament and I am not interested in the organized church as such, only in the church of the living God, the New Testament church. I recognize no other. I am not here to defend institutions. I am here to show what the true church is and what the true gospel is. And men and women who never attend a place of worship are by definition not Christians because they are revealing that they do not have God's life in them.

Secondly, I would also say that those who merely go to church occasionally are, to put it at its highest, only very doubtful Christians. There are many people who attend church infrequently. When they have nothing better to do, they go to a place of worship. Can you fit that in to what you read here? But this is the only standard; we have no other way to measure people. It is not what you or I or Mr Brooks think that makes men and women Christians. It would be interesting to know what Mr

Brooks's idea of a Christian is. He probably thinks a Christian is a good, moral person who is, therefore, much better than those hypocrites who go to church. You see, the poor man knows nothing about Christianity. He thinks he does, but his spirit and, even more, his actions, prove he does not.

But as I said, this applies not only to a man like Mr Brooks, but also to people who only go to church occasionally. They keep up the membership, as it were, pay the subscription once a year, and think they are church members. They think they are Christians. They think they belong to the true church. Can you fit that in with what we read in Acts?

Let me give you a third possibility: What about those who only go to church as a status symbol? Going to church can be nothing but a part of the social round. One often hears of this sort of thing. People go to a morning service and then they have their sherry party together before they go back to lunch. A social custom! But is it not patently clear here, on the very surface of Acts 2, that when people become Christians, when they are born again, when they have this new life in them, this association with other Christians is the biggest thing, the very centre of their lives? 'And they, continuing daily with one accord in the temple, and breaking bread from house to house . . .' If that is not there, can you say there is evidence of Christianity?

The second proposition is that these men and women not only came together regularly, they came together willingly. They did not come reluctantly or in a spirit of fear; they did not come merely to perform a task or a duty. I remember very well that in the days when I attended a place of worship even though I was most certainly not a Christian, quite often I used to hear sermons denouncing those church members who did not attend all the meetings. I resented it at the time; I had a feeling that it was wrong, but I could not understand it. As I sat in the pew, my mental reply to the minister was this: 'Well, the question you ought to ask yourself is: Why do people not come? And perhaps if you examine that question thoroughly you may find the answer in yourself and not in the people.'

Now that was just a sort of non-Christian way of giving an answer. Since then, thank God, I think I have a little insight into these things, and that is why I never appeal to people to attend a place of worship. I do not think you can ever record against me a case in which I have chastised people for not attending services of public worship. I have never asked anybody to join this church or any other church where I have been minister.

Why not? It is because I believe the book of the Acts of the Apostles. I do not even put a 'test on the meeting' by asking people to come forward at the end. Again, why not? It is because I believe that there is a type of preaching, there is an action of the Spirit, that makes the congregation cry out, 'Men and brethren, what shall we do?' I do not understand this pressure brought to bear upon people to make them decide or to make them attend services. What I say is this: If you do not go gladly to Christian meetings, are you a Christian at all? These men and women in Acts 2 were born again and they manifested it by 'continuing stedfastly'. You did not have to round them up or keep watch on them and say accusingly, 'You were not here last meeting.' The Jerusalem Christians were there 'stedfastly', day by day, constantly; you could not keep them away.

That is how it was at the beginning, and that is how it has always been in every period of reformation and of revival. I could give you many illustrations from the great revivals. Think of two hundred years ago – the great evangelical Methodist awakening. The early Methodists were always coming together. They desired to meet together. And they did not want just the briefest possible diet of worship. They met every day, and would go on for hours. When they had finished their day's work, they would go to one another's houses and they would study the Bible and pray in little groups.

You see how far removed all this is from what has become so customary in many countries and from the common notion as to what Christianity is? People drag themselves reluctantly to a service on Sunday morning and hope, and pray, if they pray at all, that it will not be too long, particularly the sermon. I am told that there are certain churches now where the poor man who comes to preach is given a programme: 11 am – opening prayer; and then he will find at the end of his programme: 12 noon – benediction. He is not even given any choice, you see. He has to stop. The service must not be too long. Now again, can you fit that sort of thing into this book of Acts? Can you not see that to meet together was the greatest joy in these young Christians' lives? Their instinct was always to come together and you could not keep them apart. That is the expression of this new life.

The third principle which is shown here is that people of all types met together. That is a most important point. There is a modern idea that churchgoing only suits a certain type: the religious type, people with a religious complex. 'Quite simple,' says the psychologist. 'Of course, religious experiences only happen with a particular type.' And in their kindness of heart they are prepared to say they do not object if we want to do that sort of thing, as long as they are given liberty to do what they want to do.

But here, gathered in Jerusalem on this great day of Pentecost, were people from all parts of the world. 'There were dwelling at Jerusalem Jews, devout men, out of every nation under heaven . . . Parthians, and Medes, and Elamites, and the dwellers in Mesopotamia, and in Judaea, and Cappadocia, in Pontus, and Asia, Phrygia, and Pamphylia, in Egypt, and in the parts of Libya about Cyrene, and strangers of Rome, Jews and proselytes, Cretes and Arabians . . .' – there was never such a cosmopolitan gathering! And yet you see what happened under the influence of Peter's preaching in the power of the Holy Spirit? People out of all these different nations and groupings were united and wanted to continue steadfastly together.

In other words – and this is a most important and fundamental principle – this diversity is in many ways one of the most important proofs of the reality of the new birth, the fact of regeneration. It proves it like this. Here were people who, taken by nature, were all different from one another: different nationalities, different classes in society, some employers, some workers, some in professions, some doing more mechanical work. Not only that, there were men and women who differed tremendously in temperament and in intelligence. It is always interesting to notice how different the twelve disciples of our Lord were from one another – a man like John, for instance, and a man like Peter. And the apostle Paul was altogether different again. The great thing that we are told here and, indeed, everywhere in the New Testament, is that people of all backgrounds, temperaments and abilities come together and are made one. There is an extraordinary unity, which is deeper than all superficial divisions and distinctions, and this has continued in the history of the church throughout the centuries and right down to today. I repeat that to me this is an absolute proof of the reality of the new birth.

Look at the great illustration of this that is to be found in the first epistle to the Corinthians. The apostle Paul was writing to people to whom he could say, 'Ye see your calling, brethren, how that not many wise men after the flesh, not many mighty, not many noble, are called' (1 Cor. 1:26). It is clear that the majority of the members of the church at Corinth were not highly gifted people in an intellectual sense. They were not great philosophers; they were simple people. The world called them 'foolish', the philosophers certainly called them foolish, and yet the amazing and astonishing thing is that the apostle Paul, with one of the greatest brains that a man has ever had, was able to enjoy the most glorious fellowship with them.

Then in Paul's letter to the church at Rome we find the same thing. Most of the members of the church seem to have been slaves in Caesar's household, and yet the apostle could write to them like this: 'I long to see you, that I may impart unto you some spiritual gift, to the end ye may be established; that is, that I may be comforted together with you by the mutual faith both of you and me' (Rom. 1:11–12). Here was this colossus, a man who was not only a trained Pharisee, but was familiar with the Greek poets and literature, and probably knew a great deal about Roman law, and he could sit down among them, the slaves, ignorant people, who had none of his great erudition, and enjoy the most intimate fellowship with them. Why? Oh, there is only one answer – they had something in common, and that was nothing else but this rebirth.

It does not matter what you are by nature. That is why I have always said that a preacher of the gospel, unlike the medical doctor, never needs to know the details about his people. If you are a medical doctor, it is very important that you should know something about your patient. You want his history. You want to know what exactly is the trouble. You ask, 'Where is that pain?' So the sick person states his case, and you put your questions and get all the details. Then you say, 'I wonder whether this is hereditary?' So you want to know the family history. You cannot make a true diagnosis without going into these things very thoroughly. You ask about the father and mother. Are they still alive, or what did they die of? And sometimes you go back to the grandparents. Then you ask, 'Is this man working too hard? Is his illness caused by the stress of modern life? Is it the anxiety of his profession?' You must know all these things because you cannot make an accurate diagnosis without them.

But the work of a preacher is altogether different. None of those things matter at all. Here we are not so much interested in symptoms as in the disease. And we are concerned not with diseases but with *one* disease. There is only one disease and it is sin. It does not matter what a man is. It does not matter whether he has a giant intellect or whether he is an ignoramus. That does not make the slightest difference. I do not know you individually but I know that you are a sinner. You are a sinner because I am a sinner, because we are all sinners.

So I do not need to have a long history. I do not want to know about your father and mother because I know that they were also sinners. I know, 'There is none righteous, no, not one' (*Rom.* 3:10). And I know that all the divisions and the distinctions do not make the slightest difference. Intellect is not immune from immorality. Altruism is not immune from failures and weaknesses. Tell me all about yourself – it does not matter, you do not change the picture at all. 'One touch of nature makes the whole world kin.' That is why every nation, every colour, every conceivable temperament and personality, come down to a common denominator. Everyone needs the same thing, and they are given the same thing. They are all given the same life, and that new life expresses itself in them all. It is deeper than intellect, deeper than nationality, deeper than temperament, deeper than gifts and possessions. It controls the whole of a person's life and outlook.

The fourth principle concerns the reason why all these different people in Jerusalem came together. Why could no one keep them apart? Why did they delight to come? Well, it is all here before us, and the answer is perfectly simple. The world has the answer. It is explained in the proverb, 'Birds of a feather flock together.' That is true in the spiritual realm. In his letter to the church at Ephesus, the apostle Paul writes about 'the unity of the Spirit in the bond of peace' (*Eph.* 4:3), and Jude talks in his letter about 'the common salvation' (*Jude* 3).

In 1 Corinthians 1 we see the negative expression of this great principle. A Christian is not perfect immediately. It takes time to make us perfect, and none of us will be perfect in this world. But we are being perfected. The Christians in Corinth were born again. But the devil was busy. He had come in, and some foolish people who did not detect his hand were becoming his instruments and were causing divisions. So in chapter 1 of his letter, the apostle reprimanded the Corinthian Christians. He said in effect, 'Don't you realize that you are a church? Don't you realize that Christ, and he alone, was crucified for you? You are interested in Paul or Apollos or Cephas. Have you forgotten what it is to be a Christian and what it is that makes a Christian church?'

Why did these people in Jerusalem come together and continue steadfastly in the apostles' doctrine and fellowship, and breaking of bread and in prayers? The simple answer is that they had become members of the same family; they had the same life. They were born of the Spirit, and the life of God had entered into their souls. These people were drawn together as the members of a family are drawn together.

Now there is something about this that is almost mystical. It is not easy to analyse and define in words, but we say, do we not, 'Blood is thicker than water'? You may have disputes in your family, but if an outsider begins to attack, you are all immediately united! Blood is thicker than water – of course it is! Yes, and the life of God in the soul is thicker even than natural blood. Here is something, as I have shown you, that cuts even into family life. It brings one out of one family and another out of another, making them one, brethren and sisters together.

All this is but a manifestation of this new life that has come into a person's soul. Christian people are living in the same world as everybody else, but they have a different outlook; they see themselves differently. A man of the world thinks of this world only and about his money and his success, food, drink, clothing, sex, excitement, pleasure. That is his outlook, is it not? But that is entirely different from the Christian outlook. All Christians have the same fundamental view on life in this world and the whole state and history of the world. They also have the same view of death. They know that much more important than this world is the other world that they cannot see. They have to live in this world, of course. Some people foolishly thought that you could not be a Christian and live in the world, so they became monks and hermits and so on. But though Christians do not go out of the world, the things that used to interest them no longer attract them.

When you become a Christian, you start from the tremendous postulate that you are made in the image and likeness of God, and that you are going on to meet him, and that life is short and is passing. You must now think about this. Before, you tried not to think about it. You switched on the radio; you had a glass of whisky; you took a drug – anything not to think. But now you say, 'But I must think, it's madness not to. My life is moving on and I'm moving on, and there is God and eternity, there is judgment and my everlasting condition.' Your whole outlook is governed by that. And is it not quite inevitable that you should desire to spend your time with others who view things in this world in the same way? Of course you want to know more about these great facts and you want to talk about them. You know you are different from the other people and you cannot enter into their enjoyment as you used to. This is inevitable. It is because of life with a new outlook, a new understanding, a new orientation, if you like.

Not only that, you see that Christian people have all had exactly the same fundamental experience. Now I do not mean that all Christians have had the same type of experience in every single detail. That is not so. But they have had the same fundamental experience. People cannot be Christians without knowing that they have been awakened to these tremendous truths which I have been mentioning to you. They used to live that other worldly life and they knew that life of struggle. They knew what it was to be a failure and to be miserable, and to say, 'Oh, is there no way out of this? Can't I start afresh? Can't I live a new life?' And yet it all always ended in futility. But now they know that they have a new life. They have been set free. There is an essential difference in their lives. As I have said, they are not perfect, and they do not fully understand, but they know there is something in them and about them that was not there before. It varies in its dramatic intensity from case to case, but it is the common experience of all Christians. They are no longer hopeless, no longer left to themselves. They know Another. And that, as we have seen, leads to the same desires and the same interests.

This is expressed in many hymns:

Through the night of doubt and sorrow,
Onward goes the pilgrim band.

Why? Well, they are one, as the hymn goes on to say:

One the object of our journey,
One the faith which never tires.

S. Baring-Gould

The Christians in Jerusalem continued 'daily with one accord' because they had their eyes on something beyond this world and greater than this world.

Christians have come to evaluate this world as it is. They know it will never be perfect. They used to think it would be. Some of them may have been politicians for that reason, thinking that by Acts of Parliament you could change the world and change life and introduce and legislate for the kingdom of God. They have come to see you cannot do it. That does not of necessity mean that they cease to be politicians, but now they think of political action merely as that which restrains the manifestations of evil and makes life bearable.

Christians have the same hope set before them. They say, 'We are but strangers and pilgrims in this world. We used to think we had settled down in it and we tried our best to do so and we thought of nothing but this life and this world.' No longer. Christians are people who always know they are strangers, sojourners, travellers. They are on the road to eternity, to reality, to life that is life indeed, to glory everlasting! They have their eyes fixed on that; and all who are looking in the same direction inevitably come together – they are travelling together.

But, perhaps supremely, Christians rejoice in the same Saviour. This is what ultimately brings them together and makes them one. They are still different in their temperaments and in many other respects, but there is one thing in which they are always one, and that is in their attitude and their relationship to him. Christians say, 'I am who I am by the grace of God.' Nothing else. 'I was a miserable failure. I was blind. I was a fool. I was spiritually dead. I was defeated. But Christ, the Son of God, loved me, and gave himself for me. While I was yet an enemy and a rebel against God, even while I was speaking and working against him, while I was opposed to him with all the bitterness of my being, he loved me. He came into this world and took my sins upon himself. He bore my punishment. He died my death. He rose again, and there he is in heaven, seated at the right hand of God, ever living to make intercession for me. I have nothing to boast of.'

The apostle Paul ends 1 Corinthians 1 by saying, 'He that glorieth, let him glory in the Lord.' Why? Because, 'Of him are ye in Christ Jesus, who of God is made unto us wisdom, and right-eousness, and sanctification, and redemption.' Christians are those who have come to see that they are nothing, that they have nothing of which to boast. They used to boast, like everybody else. One was proud of his appearance, another of his great brain, another of his gift of writing, another of his gift of speech, or his wonderful singing voice; another was proud of his philosophical understanding; another of his political acumen. We boasted of our possessions. We were all proud. And the apostle Paul himself tells us he was like this before his conversion. But when men and women become Christians, all that is smashed. They say with Paul:

What things were gain to me, those I counted loss for Christ. Yea doubtless, and I count all things but loss for the excellency of the knowledge of Christ Jesus my Lord: for whom I have suffered the loss of all things, and do count them but dung [refuse], that I may win Christ, and be found in him, not having mine own righteousness, which is of the law, but that which is through the faith of Christ, the righteousness which is of God by faith (Phil. 3:7–9).

The Christian says: I'm nothing, a fool, a sinner, vile, rotten. 'In me (that is, in my flesh,) dwelleth no good thing' (*Rom.* 7:18). And everything I have will soon all be rotting away to nothing. So I am what I am by the grace of God in Jesus Christ. 'I live; yet not I, but Christ liveth in me: and the life which I now live in the flesh I live by the faith of the Son of God, who loved me, and gave himself for me' (*Gal.* 2:20).

Christian people are one because they are all like that, they are all saying the same thing. The divisions have gone and they are one: one in Christ, one in attributing to him the glory and the praise, one in saying that it is he alone who saves and has saved and will save. They all look to him, anxious to follow him, anxious to please him, resting their hope in him and in him alone. So they continue steadfastly in the apostles' doctrine about him, and in the apostles' fellowship round him, and in breaking of bread, in which they remind themselves of him, and in their prayers to him and the Father and the Holy Spirit.

Let me be more personal: Why do I stand in this pulpit Sunday by Sunday? Forgive me, I do not want to talk about myself, but I never entered the ministry to make money. I made much more money before I entered the ministry. The idea that we are here just to get people to give money is a travesty. No, I am here for one reason only, and it is to tell men and women about this Christ of God, this blessed Saviour, this new life which he gives which lasts not only in this world but through death and to eternity. That is the reason and it is the only reason. I am here and I preach this gospel in order that we may all prepare ourselves for that glory which is coming. 'Blessed are the pure in heart: for they shall see God' (*Matt.* 5:8). That is what I have my eye on – heaven and God. O, the glory! The purity! The holiness of it all!

And time is short. Time is hastening. It is passing. I want to prepare. 'Every man that hath this hope in him purifieth himself, even as he is pure' (*1 John* 3:3). There is not a moment to spare. That is why 'they continued stedfastly in the apostles' doctrine and fellowship, and in breaking of bread, and in prayers.' They had come to see that finally nothing matters in this world but just that, and they wanted to know everything they could in order to be ready and prepared for it.

A Christian is bound to come to that. How can you believe that you are a sinner, how can you believe in God, how can you believe in judgment, how can you believe in hell, how can you believe in the glory, and yet be content with just coming to church once on a Sunday, once a year, or just now and again, or not at all? How can you think that you are a good Christian though you do not go to church, because you are better than those hypocrites who do? It is just impossible. It is unnatural. It is not an expression of this new life. This life of God must express itself in the way that it did immediately after the day of Pentecost, in the way that it has continued to reveal itself in those who are truly Christian.

So how do you come out of these tests? It is as simple as that. I am not interested in your opinions, but I am asking you this: Do you have in you that which makes you desire the companionship of people who have their eyes on the Lord Jesus Christ and the glory everlasting? That is the test. Life shows itself and that is how Christian life, spiritual life, the life of God in the soul, has shown itself from the very beginning and must do so. Have you got this life? If you have not, tell God that you have not. Ask him for it and he will give it you. That is all you have to do. Repent, acknowledge and confess that you are dead and ask him to give you life anew. Ask him to do this glorious work of re-creation. Ask him to send something of that divine life into you. Ask him truly and he will do it for you. And then you will inevitably find yourself behaving as those first Christians immediately did on the day of Pentecost.

8

The Apostles' Doctrine

And with many other words did he testify and exhort, saying, Save your-selves from this untoward generation. Then they that gladly received his word were baptized: and the same day there were added unto them about three thousand souls. And they continued stedfastly in the apostles' doctrine and fellowship, and in breaking of bread, and in prayers (Acts 2:40–42).

We have seen that essentially a Christian is one who has been entirely changed and we are now considering the ways in which this new life, this new nature that Christians have received, manifests itself. Let me remind you again that I am holding this before you, not out of a theoretical or academic interest, but because I trust we shall all examine ourselves in the light this gives. The world needs Christian people today. Not only that, we are all moving forward. Our lives are advancing and life is uncertain. We do not know how long we have left in this world, any one of us, quite apart from war and bombs. Are we ready to meet death and eternity? That is why this subject is so vital. We may say we are Christians – very well, let us test ourselves in the light of what we are told about these people in Acts. Are we like them? Here are the first Christians. Do we conform to the pattern they set?

We have seen that these first believers showed their new life in certain ways. We saw, first, that they left the world and that, positively, they joined the apostles and the apostolic company.

In other words, they became members of the Christian church, which immediately became the biggest thing in their lives.

And the next question we must consider is this: What did they come together for? Here were these people who had come out of the world to join the group of people called disciples, and they formed the first church, but what is the Christian church for? What does she do? What does she provide? Do Christian people come together for socials, whist drives, dances, raffles, dramatic performances, lectures on politics, literature and sociology? You see the importance of a negative, do you not? There was nothing like that in the early church. It is not my object to denounce these things. But I do want to show how far removed they are from the Christian church. You can get all that in the world, and you can get it very much better there. The Christian church makes a fool of herself when she attempts these things – she does them so badly. If you want activities like that, then go and get them organized professionally.

But that is not the Christian church. It is a travesty. I do not want to defend Christendom or advocate any particular section of the church or any particular local church. I want to hold before you the pictures of the New Testament church. That is the only church I recognize. Those people did not come to the church to do things like that. And when true revival takes place, those are the first things to go out; people lose interest in them. A church which can only exist by resorting to things like that is utterly different from the New Testament church. No, 'They continued stedfastly in the apostles' doctrine [teaching] and fellowship, and in breaking of bread, and in prayers' – purely spiritual activities. And that is the pattern for the church at all times.

So let us look at this. First, doctrine. The apostles' teaching is put first in this list – that is why we must start with it, and it is very important that we should, because today there is real opposition to what we read here. The first thing these Christians desired was further teaching from the apostles. They coveted this with the whole of their being. And before we go any further, let us ask ourselves a simple question: Do we desire the apostles' doctrine? God grant that we may.

This longing for the apostles' doctrine tells us something tremendously important. It is that Christianity is not only an experience. Now I have been emphasizing that it is an experience and not merely an intellectual point of view. When men and women become Christians, they have undergone the profoundest change they can ever know; it is indeed a profound experience. But it is not only that and I must emphasize this because there are other agencies in the world that can give people experiences.

How do you tell the difference between becoming a Christian and some other experience, an emotional experience, or a change as the result of psychotherapy, or something like that? The teaching put out by the cults can produce a change. Adherents of a cult talk about their lives being transformed. How, then, do you tell the difference between an experience which is Christian and one which is not? There is only one answer and that is the *cause* of the experience. Christians experience change as the result of believing the truth about Jesus Christ. Two people may say, 'I'm very happy.' They may both say, 'I used to do that, but not any longer. I've been delivered from it all.' Now it does not follow that they are both Christians. How, then, do I know who is? And the only test, I repeat, is the source of the experience.

As we have seen, the people in Acts came together because they had had the same experience, but the thing that strikes us at once about them is that they had had the same experience because they had believed the same teaching, the same message. 'Then they that gladly received his word were baptized: and the same day there were added unto them about three thousand souls.' There would never have been an early church but for a particular teaching. So we are bound to emphasize that the teaching must come first because it was that which led to the conversions, the change. It was Peter's preaching, his teaching, his doctrine, that brought these people together. They 'gladly received his word' and were baptized. And we are told in verse 44, 'And all that believed were together.' What did they believe? The same teaching.

But let us ask a second question: Why did these people want this teaching? Why did they gather together every day in that part of the temple that was allowed to them and there listen to the exposition of truth from the lips of the apostles? This, too, is very important. We are living in an age when people are trying to say that we must scrap preaching and teaching and replace it by – oh, here is the word – *dialogue*. That just means two people talking together, but it sounds so much better as 'dialogue', does it not? Discussions! Questions and answers for about twenty-five minutes or so – as if that could ever lead to anything!

But it was not like that in the early church. The people continued steadfastly every single day. Why did they want this doctrine? There are many answers, so let me give you some of them. The apostle Peter later wrote a letter to a number of Christian people and this is what he said to them, 'As newborn babes, desire the sincere milk of the word, that ye may grow thereby' (*1 Pet.* 2:2). In other words, wanting to listen to the word is inevitable if men and women are born again and have become Christians. A babe does not understand but it has an instinct for milk. It wants it and it makes for it! Of course, this is a proof of the fact that this is a child and not an adult. It is alive and wants the mother's milk, and rightly so. It is exactly the same with the Christian. One simply cannot be a Christian and have no desire for a knowledge of this truth – it is impossible.

Let me put it in another way. Here were people who had suddenly heard something marvellous which they had not known before. This was the most astounding thing they had ever heard, and the preachers had said, 'There's more. I cannot tell it all to you now.' So the people came together; they were afraid of missing something. I do not understand some Christian people: they seem to want the minimum of teaching. But are you not sometimes afraid that something tremendous may happen in the house of God when you are not there? It is a wonderful thing to be in the house of God. It is a wonderful thing to be listening to the preaching of the gospel, because it is God's truth. Because the Holy Spirit is there, you never know what may happen. What if he should suddenly come in the glory of his power and you were not there? These people in Acts were taking no risks -- they wanted all they could get. They were afraid of missing something very precious. This is all instinctive in the Christian.

But, further, why did they want more and more of this teaching? Another answer is that they had become aware of their ignorance. I have already dealt with that, but let me put it in another way. Here were the people who had shouted, 'Away with him! Crucify him!' They had thought they knew all about Jesus of Nazareth. 'Who is this fellow?' they had said. 'This carpenter, this Nazarene, who is he to claim to be the Son of God and Saviour, this monstrous thing? Away with him! Crucify him! Let's get rid of him.' And they had thought they were clever, as people still think it is clever to deny Christianity and make fun of the message of the Christian church.

But suddenly they were awakened; they were 'pricked in their hearts'; they were convicted. And what they discovered was their appalling ignorance - that though they had thought they knew so much, they knew nothing. They had made the greatest blunder, the most tragic blunder, that men and women can ever make. They had been blind, but suddenly their eyes were opened.

You cannot become a Christian without being made humble. Our Lord himself said, 'Except ye be converted, and become as little children, ye shall not enter into the kingdom of heaven' (*Matt.* 18:3). 'Let no man deceive himself,' says the apostle Paul. 'If any man among you seemeth to be wise in this world, let him become a fool, that he may be wise' (*1 Cor.* 3:18). The first thing that happens to those who become Christians is that they are convicted of their ignorance, their darkness. And once they have been shown that, then they are terrified lest they should still be ignorant of certain things that are vital. So they say, 'I must listen to that. I want more and more and more. I don't want to be held in ignorance any longer. I want life.' So they long for the teaching.

Have you realized your ignorance about yourself? Any man or woman who thinks highly of himself or herself is just plain ignorant. How difficult it is for us to know ourselves! It is only this gospel that can dispel our ignorance. What do you know about God? What do you know about life? We talk so grandly and so glibly – what do we know? The gospel convicts us of ignorance, and those who know they are ignorant thirst and hunger for knowledge. They do not want to be held any longer in the thraldom, the darkness, of ignorance. So the Jerusalem Christians came together daily.

Then, thirdly, they wanted to understand more and more about this tremendous thing that had happened to them. The natural question to ask was: What is this? What has happened to me? They were newborn babes and they wanted to understand, to have some explanation. They had come into this new realm, this wonderful life, and it was quite natural and instinctive, was it not, to want to know more and more? When you have something really good, you want more of it. They said, 'This is only the beginning, we can see, let's hear more.' Like newborn babes, they wanted to grow and to develop.

But let me give you a still better reason. They wanted to learn more about truth in order that they might be able to help others. These were ordinary men and women like ourselves and they had fathers or mothers or husbands or wives or children. Their eyes had been opened. They had seen the peril of their position, the darkness of their existence, and they were in this new realm with all its wonder and glory, but their loved ones were still outside. And they were worried and troubled about that. They wanted to help them, but how could they? What did they have to say? It was no use saying, 'I've had a wonderful experience.' That would not help the other person who might well reply, 'What has happened to you? How did you get the experience?' And, just like newborn babes, they were not in a position to answer. So they desired the teaching, the instruction, the information that the apostles were giving in order that they might be able to help others.

This same Peter, writing in his first epistle, says, 'Be ready always to give an answer to every man that asketh you a reason of the hope that is in you' (*1 Pet.* 3:15). For instance, if somebody says to you, 'What were you doing last Sunday?' you might say, 'I went to church.'

'Ah,' comes the response, 'why do you do that?'

'Because,' you reply, 'I was brought up to go.'

'But I was not,' says the other.

'Well,' you say, 'I've not really thought much about this, but I've always gone, and there's something about it I like.'

'But,' continues the questioner, 'what is it? What do you do there? Why do you go? What's it all about?'

And if you cannot answer, what a poor Christian you are! What an opportunity you are missing! You see, Christians are men and women who *know*. They are taught why they are what they are, and they can tell others what they must do. These people in Acts cried out as Peter was preaching, 'Men and brethren, what shall we do?' And what would have been their position if Peter had turned to them and said, 'Well, I really don't know. I've had a wonderful experience myself but I don't quite know what it is.'

Or, 'I've been brought up in this way and this happens to be my temperament and I happen to like this sort of thing'! It would all have been useless. But Peter could give specific answers, and we must be able to do the same.

Your next-door neighbours may be in great trouble – their marriage may be breaking down, or they may be going through some sadness, bereavement, sorrow, or disappointment. Their lives may have been shattered and they do not know what to do or where to find help. The world laughs at them, the jazz goes on, the music is played, the television continues and they are left with their own misery and, oh, they are waiting for a word. The people in Jerusalem wanted to understand in order to help others and show them the way of salvation and deliverance. These are the reasons that made them continue steadfastly in the apostles' doctrine.

But come, let me take you to another aspect of this matter. There is a definite teaching – 'They continued stedfastly in the apostles' doctrine.' There is such a thing as apostolic doctrine. I am a preacher for one reason only and it is that I have believed the apostolic doctrine and teaching. I have no other teaching. I do not stand here to say what *I* think. I am simply repeating what I find here. I am expounding the Scriptures, the apostolic doctrine. But the importance of doing this is seriously questioned today. Indeed, it is not only controverted, but ridiculed and dismissed, and I must of necessity deal with this criticism.

Recently I was sent a copy of a little book called *Not So Much a Creed, More a Way of Life*[1], and this is what it says in the introduction:

Jesus taught very little theology. The four records of his life and message say nothing about the fall of man or of God's plan of salvation. He did not require from his disciples the acceptance of any creed. There is no hint of the need for any atonement for sin. He says plainly that forgiveness depends on repentance and on showing a forgiving spirit in one's dealings with others. He proclaims a new way of life, the way of righteousness, a righteousness that exceeds the righteousness of the scribes and Pharisees . . . As a way of life it has tremendous value and can contribute a great deal to the welfare of the world and the happiness of its people.

[1] By A. V. Fox, Union of Modern Free Churchmen, 1965. The title echoes that of a popular television programme of the time, *Not So Much a Programme, More a Way of Life*.

I hope to deal with that, God willing, in the next sermon. The writer continues:

Modern education in geology, in astronomy, in history and in simple logic has made the old beliefs incredible to most people today. It has created an attitude of mind which just cannot accept them as true. Does this mean the end of Christianity? Are we about to enter the post-Christian age?

And the author's answer to that question is that Christianity will die as a theology and rise again as a way of life'.

Now it would be very difficult to find summarized in smaller compass such a complete denial of what we are taught, not only in the second chapter of Acts, but in the whole of the New Testament. But some of you may agree with it. You may say, 'We don't want doctrine. We don't want teaching. We don't want theology. All we want is something to help us to get along.' But the answer to that is that nothing will help you to get along except this apostolic teaching! So it is my duty to disabuse your mind and to open your understanding.

First of all, the apostles are full of doctrine. Now according to this writer there should be no doctrine, so the apostles were wrong and contradicted the Lord Jesus Christ. Now there is only one answer to that: it was the Lord Jesus Christ who called these apostles. It was he who taught them. It was he who gave them the message and it was he who sent the Holy Spirit down upon them to enable them to preach. Now we see that in John 16 which seems to me to have been written almost deliberately to meet this very kind of objection. People say – and it sounds so wonderful! – 'Do not listen to that man Paul, do not listen to these apostles, listen to Jesus with his simple gospel. No theology there.' But listen to John 16:12: 'I have yet many things to say unto you, but ye cannot bear them now.'

It is, of course, perfectly right and true to say that there is less doctrinal teaching in the Gospels than in the epistles. But the Gospels themselves tell you that, and they tell you why. If you read the four Gospels, you will find that our Lord kept on refer-ring to his death and resurrection, and the disciples could never accept it. They stumbled over this teaching. Peter remonstrated with our Lord and said: Why are you talking about dying? This is impossible for you! The disciples never grasped the truth abou the resurrection. So when our Lord was crucified on the cross the were cast into the depth of despair.

What was the matter? The trouble was, as our Lord said, '. . . y cannot bear them now.' As our Lord talked about his death an resurrection, the disciples were blind; they were stunned; the could not receive it. But he continued, 'Howbeit when he, th Spirit of truth, is come, he will guide you into all truth: for he sha not speak of himself [from himself]; but whatsoever he shall hea that shall he speak: and he will shew you things to come. He sha glorify me' (*John* 16:13–14).

Not only that, we have still more powerful evidence. If you rea the last chapter of Luke's Gospel, you will find that after hi resurrection, our Lord gave instruction to his followers an disciples. They were utterly disconsolate and he said, 'O fools, an slow of heart to believe all that the prophets have spoken: ougl not Christ to have suffered these things, and to enter into hi glory? And beginning at Moses and all the prophets, h expounded unto them in all the scriptures the things concernin himself' (*Luke* 24:25-27). After his death and resurrection, h expounded it to them. He explained it, and they were now able t receive it. And when the Spirit came upon them, they were abl to understand still more.

So the statement in the booklet *Not So Much a Creed, More a Wa of Life* is altogether wrong. It says that our Lord taught us nothin about the fall of man. But did not he himself teach, 'Ye must b born again' (*John* 3:7)? Why must someone be born agair Because, 'That which is born of the flesh is flesh; and that which born of the Spirit is spirit' (*John* 3:6). Our Lord said, 'Ye are of you father the devil, and the lusts of your father ye will do' (*John* 8:44 He said, 'The Son of man is come to seek and to save that whic was lost' (*Luke* 19:10). 'Lost' – that is it! All this teaches the fall c man.

And then the author of that booklet said that our Lord did n teach us anything about the plan of salvation. Did he not? Rea the twelfth chapter of John's Gospel: 'The hour is come, that th Son of man should be glorified . . . what shall I say? Father, sav me from this hour' – no! – 'but for this cause came I unto this hou . . . And I, if I be lifted up from the earth, will draw all men unt ne' (*John* 12:23, 27, 32). That is his teaching. He said, 'As Moses lifted up the serpent in the wilderness, even so must the Son of man be lifted up: that whosoever believeth in him should not perish, but have eternal life' (*John* 3:14–15). Listen to him: 'For even the Son of man came not to be ministered unto, but to minister, and to give his life a ransom for many' (*Mark* 10:45). What is this? God's plan of salvation, God's atonement. 'No creed,' says this writer, and many with him. But this is pure creed; this is sheer doctrine.

And on one occasion when certain people had believed in him, he said, 'If ye continue in my word, then are ye my disciples indeed; and ye shall know the truth, and the truth shall make you free' (*John* 8:31–32). Read him in his high priestly prayer in John 7: 'I have given unto them the words which thou gavest me; and they have received them, and have known surely that I came out from thee, and they have believed that thou didst send me' (*John* 7:8).

In other words, even in the Gospels we are given teaching on all the most essential doctrines, but as our Lord said, he could not give it fully because the disciples were not yet in a position to receive it. As he told them about his coming death, they staggered, but as they looked back upon it in the light of the resurrection, they began to understand. The resurrection proves that he is the Son of God. And the Spirit made the meaning of his life and death yet clearer and gave his followers power to preach it and to proclaim it. That is the simple answer to this monstrous suggestion that twentieth-century man with his knowledge of geology and science and so on does not need doctrine. My dear friend, there is nothing new about rejection of the gospel. It was rejected in the first century. Modern knowledge has nothing to do with it. It is the blindness of sin that makes people write and say such things.

But there is infinitely more that I could put before you. 'They continued stedfastly in the apostles' doctrine' – and these apostles all preached the same doctrine, every one of them. Read the book of Acts right through: they continued to preach it. At times they seemed to differ, but then they would have a conference and they would agree. Read about that in Acts, chapters 11 and 15. They were all of one mind and one accord, and whatever the

differences, they settled them. They all believed the same truth
Indeed, we have specific statements to this effect. When the
apostle Paul was being questioned in Corinth as to whether he
was an apostle at all, this is how he answered: 'Moreover, breth
ren, I declare unto you the gospel which I preached unto you
which also ye have received, and wherein ye stand; by which also
ye are saved, if ye keep in memory what I preached unto you
unless ye have believed in vain' (1 Cor. 15:1–2). And then Paul
reminds his readers of the content of the gospel and goes on to
make this claim: 'I am the least of the apostles, that am not meet to
be called an apostle, because I persecuted the church of God. But
by the grace of God I am what I am: and his grace which was
bestowed upon me was not in vain; but I laboured more abun
dantly than they all: yet not I, but the grace of God which was
with me' (verses 9–10). They all preached the same message. Paul
explicitly says the same thing again in Galatians 1 and 2, and we
find the apostle Peter paying him tribute by referring to his
writings as 'scriptures' (2 Pet. 3:16).

Again, the apostle Paul says that the church is 'built upon the
foundation of the apostles and prophets' (Eph. 2:20) – it has no
other foundation. This is not a shifting foundation, 'Jesus Christ
himself being the chief corner stone' (verse 20). There is such a
thing, I emphasize this again, as an apostolic message, as the
apostles' doctrine, the apostles' teaching, the apostles' instruction

Then in the first centuries of the Christian church, the Fathers of
the church met together in conferences, in great councils. False
teaching had come in, and how did they evaluate it? They
assessed it in the light of apostolic doctrine and teaching. And so
they formed their creeds – the Apostles' Creed (which was not
actually written by the apostles but represented their teaching)
the Nicene Creed, the Athanasian Creed. All these great creeds of
the church are expressive of the unity of the doctrine. And when
we come to the great confessions of the Reformation period, we
find exactly the same thing, whether it be the Church of England'
Thirty-Nine Articles or the Westminster Confession of Faith. In all the
great essentials of Christian teaching they are unanimous.

So the point I am establishing is that the first believers in
Jerusalem came together to listen to a particular teaching. No
speculations, not one man getting up and saying, 'I maintain this,

and another saying, 'No, I think it is that. Modern knowledge has taught me this!' No, they listened to a positive message given by the risen Lord to the apostles. Did he not meet Saul of Tarsus on the road to Damascus? Did he not reveal himself to Saul? Did he not say, 'I have appeared unto thee . . . to make thee a minister and a witness' (*Acts* 26:16)? Did he not tell Saul what to say – the same message he had given to all the others?

What is this message, this teaching? Here is the vital question. 'They continued stedfastly in the apostles' teaching.' What did the apostles teach? Do you know the apostolic teaching? Have you believed it? Have you received it? Do you want to know more about it? Is it possible for me to tell you what Christian teaching is? Is it something vague and nebulous? Is it something that must change because we now know geology and other sciences? Is it different from what it was in the first century? No! The message is still the same. There is no other message.

And this message is summarized in many places in the New Testament. Peter had already given a summary of it by saying, 'Repent, and be baptized every one of you in the name of Jesus Christ for the remission of sins' (*Acts* 2:38). He had already explained the death on the cross to them:

Jesus of Nazareth, a man approved of God among you by miracles and wonders and signs, which God did by him in the midst of you, as ye yourselves also know: him, being delivered by the determinate counsel and foreknowledge of God, ye have taken, and by wicked hands have crucified and slain: whom God hath raised up (verses 22–24).

This apostolic teaching is summarized again in 1 Corinthians 15 and in 1 Thessalonians 1:9–10: '. . . How ye turned to God from idols to serve the living and true God; and to wait for his Son from heaven, whom he raised from the dead, even Jesus, which delivered us from the wrath to come.' That is apostolic preaching. That is Christian teaching. It starts with God. It does not start with modern man or with the latest knowledge. It does not start with biology or geology. It starts by saying, 'In the beginning, God' – the Creator of the whole universe and the Sustainer of the cosmos, God in his holy being, God in his righteousness, his glory, his everlasting light. God! And the world that he made and men and women that he made. People made in the image of God! Not snivelling creatures going through life just eating and drinking and indulging in sex as if they were animals in the farmyard. No, no; upright and righteous, a reflection of something of the divine glory itself. God! Man! The universe! And then the fall. Adam and Eve's rebellion against God, and sin and shame and havoc and misery and unhappiness and men and women in need of salvation, and the judgment of God upon it all. This is apostolic teaching.

But modern men and women do not like it: 'No, no,' they say, 'not so much a doctrine, more a way of life.' But you cannot have it! This is truth. This is God's message. And the Son of God is the proof of it. Why did he come into the world? Here is the answer, let me quote that verse again: 'God so loved the world, that he gave his only begotten Son, that whosoever believeth in him should not perish, but have everlasting life' (John 3:16). If people do not believe in God's Son, they will 'perish'. There is the judgment of God. John 3:16, they say, is the most wonderful verse in the Bible. Very well, if you say so, believe it! And it is God and man, and the fall and condemnation! And the only way of escape is Jesus Christ the Son of God, this blessed person who was born as a babe in Bethlehem: the incarnation. It is nothing but sheer doctrine that 'God sent forth his Son, made of a woman, made under the law, to redeem them that were under the law (*Gal.* 4:4-5). God was visiting and redeeming his people and the Son came. What for? Oh, to save us! How? By taking our sins upon himself, by bearing our punishment, by being smitten by the stripes we deserve, by dying in our stead. He 'bare our sins in his own body on the tree, that we, being dead to sins, should live unto righteousness' (*1 Pet.* 2:24). This is apostolic teaching.

And then came the gift of new life in the Spirit, the possibility of a new start. Not only are my sins forgiven, I am made a child of God. I have a new nature. I am born again. I am a new person. And the Spirit of God is in me enabling me and strengthening me, progressively sanctifying me. What for? Oh, to prepare me for the 'glory everlasting' that is awaiting me in Christ. That is the apostolic message. And that is what these people longed to hear more and more of. They knew they had new life, but, they said, 'We need more of it. We're in the world still and the world and the flesh and the devil are powerful and we are weak, tell us more of the teaching.'They wanted to know what it means to be 'in Christ' and 'Christ in you, the hope of glory' (*Col.* 1:27). They wanted to know more about this blessed Spirit who can change people and give them power. They wanted to know about the world that is to come, not this passing evil world, but that future world and its pleasures and its joys. And who could teach them all that but the apostles? And how did they know? Because Christ had revealed it unto them. So, 'They continued stedfastly in the apostles' doctrine and fellowship, and in breaking of bread, and in prayers.'

And these are the only things that matter. I am not an expert in politics. I do not know the future of this world. I do not know what is happening behind the scenes, so I do not waste your time by preaching politics to you. I am not here to get you to organize campaigns against this or that. I am here to tell you what has been delivered to me through these apostles, the only authority I have, and their message is that you and I and all humanity will have to stand before God in the judgment and that all of us, as we are by nature, cannot do this. 'The ungodly shall not stand in the judgment' (*Psa.* 1:5). You would be swept away like the chaff, as the psalmist puts it in Psalm 1, and this is what matters, whatever the political future may be. Whatever governments may come or go, we are living souls and we are facing God and eternity.

This is a passing world at best. We have all got to die and our time is short. Life is but a breath, a vapour, and the supreme question is, 'How should man be just with God?' (*Job* 9:2). How can I get forgiveness for my sins? How can I get new life and start living in a worthy manner? How can I lose the fear of death and the grave? How can I prepare for that eternity that is coming? And, thank God, the apostolic doctrine deals with those questions and it answers them. It is the only teaching that does so. The philosophers do not know. They can talk cleverly, but they cannot live so well, many of them. There is nothing under the sun that deals with our fundamental and essential problems and questions save this apostolic doctrine.

Oh, thank God for it! Thank God that it is plain. Thank God that it is clear. Thank God that it has been preached through the running centuries. Thank God that it is as true today as it was nineteen hundred years ago. Thank God it is the everlasting gospel.

There will never be another because this is about what God himself has done in his only begotten Son for our salvation.

My dear friend, have you believed? Have you received this apostolic doctrine? I can test you simply. If you have believed this and received it, you have new life, spiritual life, and that will show itself in this way: You will be hungering and thirsting for more. It will become the greatest interest of your life. You will still be interested in other books but you will find, as I find – and I say this to the glory of God – that there are many books I would like to read but I just do not have the time. I am too busy reading the Bible and books that help me understand it.

Now I am not criticizing the others. I like to read books on history. I like reading biography. I like reading about music. I like reading medicine, aspects of science, psychology, philosophy and so on. But my whole problem is to find the time. It is because I find life here, in this book. It moves my heart. It melts me. It fills me with righteousness. It strengthens my feeble will. I want this. And men and women who have spiritual life in them, the life of God in their souls, will be like newborn babes, desiring 'the sincere milk of the word' that they may grow (1 Pet. 2:2). If you do not have that desire, you are dead. I do not care whether you are a church member or not, if the Bible is still boring, if you find prayer difficult and a task, you are dead, and therefore you have one thing to do: Go to God, repent, confess your sin, tell him you realize you are dead, and ask him to give you life anew, to breathe his Spirit upon you and give you new life from among the dead.

He will not refuse you. I have his authority for saying this: 'Him that cometh unto me I will in no wise cast out' (John 6:37). Get hold of the water of life that he alone can give, that will be 'a well of water springing up into everlasting life' (John 4:14). Thank God, this is Christianity; this is God's way of salvation.

9

Doctrine First

Then they that gladly received his word were baptized: and the same day there were added unto them about three thousand souls. And they continued stedfastly in the apostles' doctrine and fellowship, and in breaking of bread, and in prayers (Acts 2:41–42).

The early Christians described in these verses desired, as we have seen, above everything else, to know more of this Christian teaching, the apostles' doctrine. This is the exact opposite of what is most popular at the present time. Modern men and women have a rooted objection to Christian doctrine, Christian dogma and Christian creeds. This is therefore a very serious matter.

There are people out in the world who dislike Christian doctrine, and in a sense I have no complaint at all against them. I would not expect them to like it. They would not be where they are if they did like it. You do not expect anything from the world except rejection of Christian teaching. There is nothing at all new about this. It was the world that rejected the Lord Jesus Christ and his teaching. It was the same world that rejected the teaching of these apostles. But what is new today – and this is what is alarming and tragic – is that the opposition to Christian doctrine is not confined to the world, but is at the very centre of the teaching of the church herself. The church is now speaking against Christian doctrine. She is saying that doctrine is not what is needed and that it is no longer of any value whatsoever.

Let me quote again from that little booklet called *Not So Much a Creed, More a Way of Life*,[1] in order that you may know exactly the kind of situation before us. 'A Christian church,' we are told, 'may still perform a useful service in teaching men the Christian way of life and in persuading and helping them to walk in this way.' Now the writer says that, after he has said something like this:

Throughout the ages Christianity has been taught as a theology, a body of beliefs about God and his dealings with mankind. It concerned the creation, the fall of man, the awful consequences of the fall. It concerned God's plan of salvation whereby he came down to earth as a man, was crucified, rose again from the dead and ascended into heaven in order to make possible the forgiveness of sins and the gift of eternal life to those who by faith accepted this amazing sacrifice of himself for the sins of the world. These are the topics about which the councils of the church disputed and about which they drew up the creeds.

Then comes the characteristic statement:

Modern education in geology, in astronomy, in history, and in simple logic, has made the old beliefs incredible to most people today. It has created an attitude of mind which just cannot accept them as true.

As if everybody until this generation had believed them all and there had never been any objection to Christian doctrine!

'Does this mean the end of Christianity?' asks the writer. 'Are we about to enter the post-Christian age?'

Well, in his kindness, he says the Christian church may still perform a useful service in teaching people the Christian way of life, and in persuading them and helping them to walk in this way.

We may rightly rejoice that the Christian spirit is very widely active outside Christian churches, but we must also recognise that it does not yet dominate the lives of most of us.

That is a typical example of this modern position.

Or again, I read in a recent book review: 'At a time when the role of the church in modern society seems dubious, and the survival of Christianity doubtful . . .' Then the reviewer goes on to deal with the book under consideration. The author of this book says:

[1] See p. 116

Doctrine First

It is harder for the modern man to believe in the Christian faith than it was for his forbears. Scientific and social revolution have produced the assumption that with knowledge and power men can make their own world. Life has become a do-it-yourself affair, and the sense of Providence has been weakened. Whereas man once prayed for rain, he now builds reservoirs.

I must preach on that last sentence sometime – not now. Only last summer there was trouble in certain cities and the water had to be turned off at a given hour because the water level in the reservoirs had gone so low. Work out that for yourselves!

Now those are quotations from secular papers, but I am even more concerned about 'Christian' papers which, while alarmed at the moral declension and the publication of a salacious magazine,[1] at the same time attack the apostolic teaching and laud men like Bishop Robinson[2] and Paul Tillich who are doing their utmost to deny the apostles' doctrine. Now this is very serious because it is of all attitudes the most hopeless. Shall I be misunderstood, I wonder, when I say this: I see much greater hope for the people of the world who are producing this magazine than for the Bishop of Woolwich and Tillich and others like them.

Why do I say a thing like that? Well, here, to me, is the greatest problem at the present time. It is that the Christian church is herself attacking the only doctrine and teaching that can deal with the moral situation, and yet it does not see that. The church is blinded: alarmed at the moral situation but attacking and denying the only message that can deal with it.

What is our answer, then, in terms of an exposition of this second chapter of the Acts of the Apostles? I shall not waste your time with all this nonsense about the 'modern man'. Fancy talking about geology and biology, as if it were our modern knowledge that made people deny the gospel and live a life of sin! I think it is a most interesting psychological problem, how people can write such utter nonsense. The denial of the truth is as old as the truth. But I let that pass.

[1] The magazine was *Penthouse*, which appeared at this time.
[2] John A. T. Robinson, the author of the book *Honest to God*.

Come to the second point. The astounding thing about these people is that they simply cannot see that it is their own attitude that in many ways has produced the moral problem about which they are so alarmed. Why has there been a declension in morals during the past years? There, surely, is the fundamental problem. And for me there is only one answer. It is not the two world wars, though I know that undoubtedly they have contributed. It is not the advance of knowledge. There are some of us who have had a little scientific training – perhaps more than these people who write so cleverly – but still believe this message.

No, I have no hesitation in saying that the main factor in the lowering of the moral tone and life of this country has been the loss of the authority of the Bible. And the institution that has been most responsible for the lowering of the authority of the Bible has been the Christian church herself. For the last hundred years or so, 'scholarship', as it is called, has been attacking the truth of the Bible. The Bible has been riddled with criticism – there is no authority here any longer. Modern theologians have simply put up their own suppositions, their own theories, and speculations. The church with her so-called higher criticism has undermined confidence in the Bible. It is said that we must not take it as an authoritative word from God, that it cannot be because we now know that the Bible is just a man-made compilation, like many other similar books.

Or let me put it in another way, a way which I find fascinating merely as a psychological study. During this present century in particular, there has been a great reaction against the old evangelical preaching, the old apostolic doctrine, and instead men have been preaching what was called, before the First World War, 'a social gospel'. Preachers used to say, 'That old gospel of individual personal salvation is no good, what we need is a social message.' So they gave ethical teaching and said that this was the only way to redeem society. But the interesting thing is that the more they have done that, and the less they have preached the apostolic doctrine, the more the immorality and the vice and the ethical problems have increased. They themselves have aggravated the problem at which they are so aghast.

But they do not see that. They do not read their Bibles, you see. They need go no further than the Old Testament to see that it was always when Israel turned her back upon God that she sank into immorality. She only returned to morality and the Ten Commandments when she was in the right relationship to God. Indeed, history proves the same thing. The most moral, the most productive, the most uplifting epochs and eras in the history of Britain have always been those that followed religious revivals and re-awakenings. The Elizabethan era followed the Reformation, and the Cromwellian period the Puritan influence. A religious newspaper talks about 'the morality to which we have been accustomed', but that morality came directly out of the Methodist or Evangelical Revival of the eighteenth century. Contemporary theologians cannot have it both ways. The morality to which we have been accustomed was the direct outcome of this preaching and teaching which they are attacking. Thus you see the tragic inconsistency.

But let me give you a third reason for rejecting this extraordinary view which dismisses the doctrine and simply puts up an ethical way of life, saying that only the teaching of Christ matters – that view is the ultimate and final denial of Christ. That was the whole trouble with the Pharisees and the Sadducees and the scribes. Our Lord once contrasted them with the tax-collectors and the harlots. He said, 'John came unto you in the way of righteousness, and ye believed him not: but the publicans and the harlots believed him: and ye, when ye had seen it, repented not afterward, that ye might believe him' (*Matt.* 21:32). In other words, our Lord always made this perfectly clear. 'There is more hope in the end,' he said in effect, 'for the publican, the sinner and the harlot, than there is for you Pharisees.'

So who is the Pharisee? The Pharisee is the person who is interested in the teaching of Christ but denies him at the most vital and essential points. What annoyed the Pharisees was when Christ told them that they were sinners. They were always pointing to the tax-collectors. So now religious people get excited when a prurient magazine is about to be produced, and they point at the editors. But Christ says: You are worse than those. You are self-righteous. You think you can save yourselves. You are satisfied with your morality. And when I say that I have come to die for you, and to save you, and that is the only way you can be saved, you reject me and hate me.

That is the final blasphemy, that is the ultimate denial of Christ. There is more hope in London tonight for hopeless drunkards, for prostitutes, for people in the very gutters of sin, there is more hope for them than for these people who say, 'All we want is the teaching of Jesus. We can imitate him and follow his example, and put ourselves right with God.' That, I say, is the final denial. But they are not aware of this. These people are like the late Lord Birkett, who was once a Methodist local preacher but gave that up. When he was interviewed on television and was asked, 'What is your position now?' he replied with a smile, 'I no longer believe the doctrine, but I still hold on to the ethic.' Poor man.

My last general point is that all this clever writing is to be rejected because of its utter futility. It does not work. It has nothing to give, nothing to offer. Indeed, it has no answer for the publishers of a salacious magazine who say, 'This is our view of life. You people say it's wrong but what right have you to say that? We think it's all right. This is what we think is interesting, this is what we think produces happiness in this world.'

'But you must not say that,' say these modern theologians, and when they are asked why not, they cannot say, 'Because the Bible says so.' Their only answer is, 'Because we say so.' But that is no answer. So their criticism is useless. The others have as much right to their personal opinion as these people who pick and choose from the Bible and reject the death of Christ and just emphasize his teaching.

Why, then, is it utterly futile to substitute ethics for doctrine? Why did these people in Acts continue steadfastly 'in the apostles' doctrine and fellowship, and in breaking of bread, and in prayers'? Why must we put doctrine first? Why is it wrong to say that doctrine does not matter, and it is a way of life that is needed – *Not So Much a Creed, More a Way of Life*? Why is this view to be rejected as of the devil himself? Here are my answers.

The first is that it has no authority. We are living in an age which is very similar to the time of the Judges in the Old Testament. That age is summarized in these words: 'In those days there was no king in Israel, but every man did that which was right in his own eyes' (*Judg.* 17:6), and that is what is happening today. There is no authority, no standard. 'You must not do that,' they say. And the others reply, 'Why not?' You see, if it is all just your opinion and mine, then you can do what you like; everything becomes entirely relative.

Now let me show you the terrible danger of this position. I am now going to quote to you out of the autobiography of Mr C. Day Lewis, one-time Professor of Poetry in the University of Oxford. He is not a Christian but this is what he says of his life in Oxford: 'Each proposition advanced by Plato or Aristotle, Hume or Berkeley, Spinoza or Kant, seemed irrefutable till I read the opposite viewpoint. It appeared that of everything that was true, the opposite was true.' This is what he learned at Oxford. Then he quotes from a cynical verse that was written by a friend of his:

> *In case you think my education wasted*
> *I hasten to explain,*
> *That having once been to Oxford*
> *You can never really again*
> *Believe anything that anyone says,*
> *And that, of course, is an asset*
> *In a world like this.*

But Day Lewis goes on to say that he did not find it an asset. He tells us he was in trouble. He was disturbed and distressed. He confesses: 'My mental confusion spread outward from the subject I was reading to the life around me, so that I found it difficult to make up my mind about anything at all.' He says, 'It produced a mental state of doubt, uncertainty, scepticism and confusion, that made positive action almost impossible. Extreme doubt,' he says, 'is like a thick fog.'

Now here is a man, an able man, who gets the best education that this country can provide, but see where it leaves him – he is uncertain about anything and everything. What can you believe? There is no authority, there is no sanction at all. One person's opinion is as good as another's. And not only that, these ideas are always changing. There was a time when everybody would agree in condemning sexual perversion, but not today – it is almost gloried in. That is public opinion with respect to morality. You never know. A view that is right today may be wrong tomorrow. You are never certain of anything and everything is moving and shifting. Where are you? What are you to do? There is no standard. What is the use of condemning this proposed magazine?

What authority have you got? Perhaps it will be all right to-morrow – perhaps the philosophers will all be on that side. You do not know, you have nothing on which you can rest.

No, no, there is only one standard, and that is the standard of God's law which is eternal and unchangeable. The Old Testament has faced the problems that the modern world faces. David and Solomon could teach many people who like to play with sin what sin really means – these snivelling people who sin vicariously in cinemas and look at pictures! The people of the Old Testament knew what sin was. They had been through all this before and they came to this conclusion – 'The fear of the Lord is the beginning of wisdom' (*Prov.* 9:10). No other beginning is of any value. You have to come here. It is eternal; it is absolute. Let philosophies come and go; let climates of opinion change; let winds of change blow in every sense – moral and ethical as well as political – here is the only thing that abides. Ultimately, there is no standard apart from the law of God, which is universal in its application.

And, of course, it was because it had God's law that the nation of Israel stood out in the ancient world. They were the most moral of all the nations for the one reason that their teaching was not all speculation and relativity. They had the law of God as it had been revealed to them and that accounted for their uniqueness. There, then, is my first reason for rejecting as the very plague itself this modern suggestion that we do not need the apostles' doctrine, that we simply need ethical teaching.

My second reason is that, not only does this view not give us any standard by which to live, but it does not give us any reason why we should live it. This is equally important. I have no standard, but why should I even be concerned? Why should ethical problems engage my attention? Why should I be troubled by the proposal to print this magazine and why should I be disturbed at the tendencies that are so evident before our eyes? No reason is given. No motive at all is offered as to why I should try to live a good life. And this question of motive is a very important one which I could illustrate in many other ways. It is even important industrially. I am not here to preach politics and I never do, but I think that it is a fallacy to assume that if a man belongs to a state-owned industry, he will work as well as if he were in a private company where there is the opportunity to earn more money. The profit motive is important. Why? Because of the biblical doctrine of man. You see, there is an idea that if you just hold the ideal before men and women they will all rise to it. But will they? Do they?

No, the appeal of the teaching which excludes doctrine and only preaches ethics is too narrow. It is only interested in human conduct and not in human beings themselves. It is only interested in time, and knows nothing about eternity. It is all too contingent; it is all too small. It is all due to the fact that it is based on an entirely false view of man.

Now the apostle Paul has put this in a vivid phrase in that great fifteenth chapter of his first epistle to the Corinthians where he deals with the doctrine of the resurrection. Nineteen hundred years ago, there were people in Corinth who were beginning to say that it did not matter whether or not you believed in the physical resurrection of Christ. They said that you could get a great advantage from his teaching, but you were not bound to believe that he literally rose in the body from the grave. The apostle wrote that tremendous chapter in order to refute that view, and he says: Be careful. 'Be not deceived: evil communications corrupt good manners' (*1 Cor.* 15:33). He means that once you begin to go astray in your doctrine you will very soon be going astray in your behaviour. You cannot divorce doctrine from behaviour. It is essential, he says, that we should hold on to this.

Today we need to remind men and women of Paul's warning. The present condition of society is the result of the rejection of doctrine. It is the inevitable result. And you will never deal with it until you come back to this so-called irrelevant and unnecessary doctrine.

When I speak of the importance of understanding the doctrine of man, I am thinking of things like this. Modern teaching has no conception whatsoever of the depth of sin in fallen human nature, and this is very surprising. Let me again give you a quotation from a secular writer, and I choose this deliberately: 'In the eighteenth and nineteenth centuries some, not all, emancipated thinkers' – You notice these phrases, 'eighteenth and nineteenth centuries', 'emancipated thinkers'? They were all slaves until the eighteenth century, remember! All people were stupid before the enlightenment of the eighteenth century and the great scientific advance of the nineteenth.

In the eighteenth and nineteenth centuries some emancipated thinkers developed an optimistic view of the nature of man; they saw him basically as a noble savage, an innocent, corrupted by society. This view still lives in the doctrines of Karl Marx, but the political experiences of this century have not encouraged such optimism.

How true!

In this century, also, scientific study has discovered much about the source of human emotion. This is beginning to explain, among other things, why our propensity for destructiveness is as great as the pessimism of theology had imagined.

This is tremendous!

But man's control of himself remains much less thoroughly explored than any other aspect of his situation.

What does all this mean? Let me translate it to you. The writer is saying that the thinkers at the end of the last century had a very optimistic view of man. They said: Man is a noble savage. He is a wonderful fellow, but his environment has always been against him. He has been corrupted by society, and therefore you need only to change society. Put that right and people will reveal their nobility. 'But,' says this writer, 'political experiences' – he is referring to the two world wars – 'have not encouraged such optimism.' I should think not!

Today it is even harder to be an optimist, is it not? One of the astounding things the writer says is, 'Scientific study has discovered much about the source of human emotion.' He calls it 'scientific study'. But he is wrong in his description. He is referring to the Freudian view of man, the study of all the things that govern and control our desires and our activities. He is referring to psychoanalysis and things like that, and he says, 'This is beginning to explain, among other things, why our propensity for destructiveness is as great as the pessimism of theology had imagined it to be.' You see, this author is saying that in a sense Freud has proved that the old theologians were right, that Christian doctrine has always been right in its pessimistic view of human nature. But these modern theologians have not learned that, even yet. They cannot see it. Two world wars have not convinced them. They say, 'We don't need your doctrine, we simply need ethical instruction.' Oh, how superficial all their writing is!

Why do they not examine themselves? Why do they not stand before a moral mirror? Why do they not listen to their own imaginations and thoughts? Why do they not face it all?

If they did face themselves, they would begin to say, with David, 'In sin did my mother conceive me' (*Psa.* 51:5). Oh, he says, 'Create in me a clean heart, O God; and renew a right spirit within me' (verse 10). My trouble, says David, is not that I do an occasional wrong thing, it is not that I committed adultery and then murder on top of it, the thing that troubles me is that I ever wanted to! My heart is unclean. It is vile. I am rotten – 'Purge me with hyssop' (verse 7). I need to be cleansed.

Or take the words of our Lord himself. He says, 'This is the condemnation, that light is come into the world, and men loved darkness rather than light, because their deeds were evil' (*John* 3:19). That is the trouble! It is not light we need, it is a nature that can love it, and hate the darkness, instead of vice versa.

Or, again, take the words of our Lord to those Jews whom he promised to set free. When they replied, 'We be Abraham's seed, and were never in bondage to any man: how sayest thou, Ye shall be made free?' Jesus answered, 'Verily, verily, I say unto you, Whosoever committeth sin is the servant of sin' (*John* 8:33–34). My dear friends, we are all slaves – slaves to sin and evil, slaves in thought, imagination and action. Consider that supreme piece of autobiography given us by the apostle Paul in Romans 7 – here is honesty for you. Here is a man facing the facts, not simply writing a beautiful article.

I know that in me (that is, in my flesh,) dwelleth no good thing: for to will is present with me; but how to perform that which is good I find not. For the good that I would I do not: but the evil which I would not, that I do. Now if I do that I would not, it is no more I that do it, but sin that dwelleth in me. I find then a law, that, when I would do good, evil is present with me. For I delight in the law of God after the inward man: but I see another law in my members, warring against the law of my mind, and bringing me into captivity to the law of sin which is in my members. O wretched man that I am! who shall deliver me from the body of this death? (Rom. 7:18–24).

These people do not believe that. That is apostolic doctrine. That is the doctrine of the fall, the doctrine of humanity in sin and evil.

These theologians do not realize the depth of sin in human nature. And in the same way, they do not realize the harm that worldly passions do to the soul. They never realize that, with the apostle Peter, we must say something like this: 'Dearly beloved, I beseech you as strangers and pilgrims, abstain from fleshly lusts, which war against the soul' (*1 Pet.* 2:11). That is why I must not do these things. Or, in the words of our blessed Lord himself, 'What is a man profited, if he shall gain the whole world, and lose his own soul?' (*Matt.* 16:26). But theologians today do not speak about the soul. This is teaching, you see; this is doctrine. This implies the fall, and the position of men and women in this fallen condition.

And then, you see, today the doctrine of the rebirth is altogether excluded. Read that great argument in Paul's epistle to the Ephesians. You must not walk any longer as the other Gentiles walk, he says. Do you not realize that you have been born again and you are God's dear children? 'Ye were sometimes darkness, but now are ye light in the Lord: walk as children of light' (*Eph.* 5:8). But these theologians have no such argument. Why? They do not believe the doctrine of the rebirth and regeneration.

And then, over and above all this, there is the teaching about judgment and our eternal destiny. They entirely exclude the great argument that is based upon the need to prepare ourselves for the glory that awaits us. Yet the apostle John, believing all the apostolic doctrine, says, 'Beloved, now are we the sons of God, and it doth not yet appear what we shall be: but we know that, when he shall appear, we shall be like him; for we shall see him as he is' (*1 John* 3:2). And then John says, 'Every man that hath this hope in him purifieth himself, even as he is pure' (verse 3). They reject that. This is what the Bishop of Woolwich will not have. This is what he says you must not believe. It is even doubtful, he says, whether God is personal at all. He is simply, as Tillich says, 'the ground of being', and there is no such thing as a final judgment. So the modern man says, 'Well, then, it doesn't matter very much what I do.'

But, says Paul, again in 1 Corinthians 15, 'If Christ be not raised, your faith is vain; ye are yet in your sins' (verse 17). If man does not rise, if there is not a judgment, let us eat, drink and be merry, for tomorrow we die. And that is what people are doing. Take away the apostolic doctrine and you take away my motives for holy living.

And they take from me the greatest argument of all for holy, ethical, moral living - my gratitude to the Son of God, who loved me, and gave himself for me. Let Isaac Watts put the argument for us:

> *When I survey the wondrous cross*
> *On which the Prince of Glory died,*
> *My richest gain I count but loss,*
> *And pour contempt on all my pride.*

Therefore,

> *Were the whole realm of nature mine,*
> *That were an offering far too small;*
> *Love so amazing, so divine,*
> *Demands my soul, my life, my all.*
>
> Isaac Watts

But this has been excluded. This teaching is not wanted. So I am given no reason for living a holy life.

And lastly, and most practical of all, I am offered no power to enable me to live this life. Let us take modern theologians on their own showing. They praise the Sermon on the Mount, Christ's ethical teaching. They say, 'There it is, that is the life you are to live.' And as we are told in the booklet, *Not So Much a Creed, More a Way of Life*, you can only appeal and exhort and show an example. What does that mean? Good advice! But is good advice any use to us? What would be your position if I had nothing to say to you except that you ought to give up sinning, that you ought to live a good life? Suppose I just left you at that? Is it easy to live a good life? Is it easy to resist temptation and sin? Put a reform programme before people, and the answer in the Old Testament is this: 'Can the Ethiopian change his skin, or the leopard his spots?' (*Jer.* 13:23). Listen to Solomon writing in the book of Ecclesiastes – a wise man, a worldly man with great experience. He says: I have come to this conclusion, 'That which is crooked cannot be made straight' (*Eccles.* 1:15). It cannot be done. Education cannot straighten out men and women, can it? Read the proceedings of the police courts and the divorce courts, and of any other court you like. No, no – 'That which is crooked cannot be made straight.' It is no use telling us to do things, we cannot.

These people talk beautifully, they write very well, but they leave me with no power, they give me no help. There is the

standard and I am left alone to live it, to imitate Christ! How can
I? Oh, no, it is all useless. These people know nothing about the
power of the devil. 'Ah,' they say, 'but that is apostolic doctrine.
People today cannot possibly believe in the devil. The apostles
believed in the devil, of course, but they lived nineteen hundred
years ago. We are modern men and women, we know biology, we
know geology, we don't believe in the devil.'

Don't you? Then in the name of God I ask you to explain your
world. Freud goes a good way but he does not go far enough. The
Bible says there is only one explanation of the state of the world,
and that is the power of the devil and the power of evil. But these
people do not know life; they do not know themselves. The world
is as it is because of the power of the devil. We are under the
dominion of Satan. 'The god of this world hath blinded the minds
of them which believe not,' wrote Paul (2 Cor. 4:4). The world is
enslaved; it is in bondage. The world is not free. Behind all that
psychoanalysis may reveal there is a malign power: 'The prince of
the power of the air, the spirit that now worketh in the children of
disobedience,' as Paul describes him in Ephesians 2:2. So what is
the use of good advice? The devil defeated every one of the greatest saints of the Old Testament – every one of them. He not only
defeated the first man and woman – Adam and Eve – when they
were perfect, but he has defeated all their progeny, the greatest
included. What is the value of good advice when you are fighting
the devil?

Very well, I do not know what you feel, but what I feel like saying
is this: Thank God for apostolic doctrine! Thank God for this teaching that the first Christians coveted and in which they desired to
be built up. What is it? It is this: 'I am not ashamed of the gospel of
Christ' – why not? – 'for it is the power of God unto salvation to
every one that believeth; to the Jew first, and also to the Greek' (Rom.
1:16). Here is the apostolic teaching, for which I thank God:

*The law of the Spirit of life in Christ Jesus hath made me free from the
law of sin and death. For what the law could not do, in that it was weak
through the flesh, God sending his own Son in the likeness of sinful flesh,
and for sin, condemned sin in the flesh: that the righteousness of the law
might be fulfilled in us, who walk not after the flesh, but after the Spirit*
(Rom. 8:2–4).

This means that the only hope for men and women is to get right with God. But how can I or anyone get right with God? I have broken his laws. I have defied him. I have laughed at him. I have denied him as a person and maintained that he is only 'the ground of being' or only 'goodness' or 'love'. How can I be reconciled with God?

There is only one answer: 'God was in Christ, reconciling the world unto himself, not imputing their trespasses unto them . . . He hath made him to be sin for us, who knew no sin; that we might be made the righteousness of God in him' (*2 Cor.* 5:19, 21). This is the only hope, this gospel, this apostolic teaching, this preaching that Christ, the Son of God, was crucified for our sins, was buried, rose the third day, ascended to heaven, and is seated at the right hand of God, sending down the Holy Spirit. It is the only hope!

How is the gospel message the only hope?

It is because it deals with our sins. It tells us that Christ has borne the punishment and we are forgiven. We are given a new heart, a new nature. We become the 'children of God'. We have new life within us. We now have a nature that loves the light and hates the darkness. We have the power of the Spirit of God within us. We have Christ, who says, 'I will never leave thee, nor forsake thee' (*Heb.* 13:5). There is a power in us, the power of God.

Paul puts it to the Corinthians in these tremendous words. Listen to the moral problem in Corinth. He says:

Know ye not that the unrighteous shall not inherit the kingdom of God? Be not deceived: neither fornicators, nor idolaters, nor adulterers, nor effeminate, nor abusers of themselves with mankind, nor thieves, nor covetous, nor drunkards, nor revilers, nor extortioners, shall inherit the kingdom of God. And such were some of you: but ye are washed, but ye are sanctified, but ye are justified in the name of the Lord Jesus, and by the Spirit of our God (1 Cor. 6:9–11).

In other words, it comes to what our Lord himself had said to those Pharisees: 'If the Son therefore shall make you free, ye shall be free indeed' (*John* 8:36).

'Ye,' says Paul to the Romans, 'were the servants [the slaves] of sin, but ye have obeyed from the heart that form of doctrine which was delivered you' (*Rom.* 6:17). That is the only thing that works, because it is the only thing that gives me any power. As we have seen, the problem men and women face is not knowing what is right, but being able to do it. 'To will is present with me; but how to perform that which is good I find not' (*Rom.* 7:18). But, thank God, the answer is in Christ:

> *He breaks the power of cancelled sin,*
> *He sets the prisoner free;*
> *His blood can make the foulest clean,*
> *His blood availed for me.*

Charles Wesley

Knowing him as the Son of God, I can turn to him and say:

> *I need Thee every hour, stay Thou near by;*
> *Temptations lose their power when Thou art nigh.*
>
> *I need Thee, O I need Thee! every hour I need Thee;*
> *O bless me now, my Saviour! I come to Thee.*

Annie Sherwood Hawks

Thank God for the apostles' doctrine! Here is a hope for the men who are going to produce *Penthouse.* Here is a hope for the vilest sinner. It is 'the power of God unto salvation' and it is to 'every one that believeth'. The gospel holds out as much hope to the most ignorant, besotted sinner in the slavery and the bondage of the devil, as it does to the greatest and the highest and the best. Thank God for the apostles' doctrine which tells us, 'He [God] hath visited and redeemed his people' (*Luke* 1:68).

Oh, is it clear to you? Is there anything more monstrous, more futile, more ridiculous, than to reject the apostles' doctrine and to say that the only need of men and women is to be shown the moral standard. Are you relying on the Son of God? Have you done what the apostle Peter told those people to do on that day of Pentecost at Jerusalem? Have you repented for your rejection of doctrine? Have you believed on the Lord Jesus Christ as the Son of God and the Saviour of your soul? Have you handed yourself, just as you are, to him, to be led, to be saved by him?

10

The Fellowship

Then they that gladly received his word were baptized: and the same day there were added unto them about three thousand souls. And they continued stedfastly in the apostles' doctrine and fellowship, and in breaking of bread, and in prayers. And fear came upon every soul: and many wonders and signs were done by the apostles. And all that believed were together, and had all things common; and sold their possessions and goods, and parted them to all men, as every man had need. And they, continuing daily with one accord in the temple, and breaking bread from house to house, did eat their meat with gladness and singleness of heart, praising God, and having favour with all the people. And the Lord added to the church daily such as should be saved (Acts 2:41–47).

According to many people who are worried about the state of the world, what we need is a new reformation. I agree with that, but the vital question is: What do you mean by 'reformation'? And in this series of sermons I am trying to show you that reformation does not mean scrapping the whole of the Bible and putting up your own ideas and theories. It means the exact opposite: it means returning to the Bible.

Now if we are going to use the term 'reformation', let us be honest. There was a great reformation in the sixteenth century, and there have been other reformations, but what were they? Well, every reformation that has ever happened in the life of the church, every reformation that has led to new life and power and vigour in the church, with a corresponding influence upon the lives of the people, has been based on a return to the New Testament. And it is because I am anxious to show that a return to the Bible is our only hope, that I am calling your attention to this whole subject. What we need is a reformation which is in line with all previous reformations. What we need is a restitution, a restoration, of the original, the primitive pattern. And this pattern, of course, is to be found in the pages of the New Testament and in particular here in this book of Acts.

This world of ours is an old world, with a long history, and if only modern people would read a little history, I think many of their foolish ideas and notions would soon be corrected. This idea that the problem of humanity is different today from what it has been in the past is, of all teachings, the most ludicrous. Different? Men and women are no different at all. They are still exactly what they have always been. The problem of the Roman Empire in its decadent days was nothing but the problem of the West today. Of course, it is expressed, perhaps, in a slightly different manner. The citizens of Rome went about in chariots then; they fly in aeroplanes now. But that is nothing. The question is: What do they go about doing? And when you come to analyse that, you find exactly the same thing: they had their feasts; they were interested in diets and in eating, drinking, dancing and sex. It is all there, even the perversions. The world today is exactly what it was in the first century, in the days when our Lord came, and when the apostle Paul and these other apostles were here: we see the same decadence, the same immorality, the same vice, the same hopelessness, the same fear.

And the only thing that has ever done any good in this world has been this message. We read in Acts that the members of the early church, and the preachers in particular, were referred to as 'These that have turned the world upside down' (Acts 17:6). Nothing made such an impact upon the Roman Empire as the Christian church. The Greeks had great philosophers, who, remember, had all lived, flourished and died before the Lord Jesus Christ was ever born – the best teaching had already been given. The Romans were experts in the art of government, and particularly local government. Even today the legal system of many countries is based upon Roman law. The Romans were famous for law, for order, for government, and they did everything they could to organize society and to improve the lot of men and women and to establish some kind of Utopia. Those ancients were very interested in Utopias. But they failed completely.

And then in that old world appeared this phenomenon called the Christian church. It all came out of the tremendous thing that happened on the day of Pentecost. These apostles, and others with them, who had been with Christ, were praying together in a room when suddenly the power of the Holy Spirit came upon them. It was not anything they did, it was not their organizing, it was not that they had decided months before to have a great campaign and to set up numerous sub-committees to plan how to do it. Not at all. In their utter helplessness and weakness they were just praying and waiting, and down came this tremendous power and they began to speak with authority. Three thousand people were saved in that one sermon which Peter gave. Then, 'The Lord added . . . daily such as should be saved' – and that was the church.

So what do we know about the church? Well, I have been holding it before you. The first thing we are told is that these people 'continued stedfastly together', first of all for 'the apostles' doctrine', and we have seen why they wanted that teaching.

Now we must look at this next reason for their coming together, and this is also vital for us: 'They continued stedfastly in the apostles' doctrine *and fellowship.*' I want to give you a picture of what the Christian church is, what a Christian society is, because, let me emphasize again, herein lies the only hope for the world. You read your newspapers – do you get any hope there? All right, be interested in politics, but will you find a solution to the moral problems of society there? You may perhaps solve industrial disagreements, though you may not even solve those if everybody is going to go on working less and less for more and more. That is how Rome went down. They all wanted to spend their time in their baths – and, of course, if you were very wealthy you had a golden bath! And so destruction went on, by all these steps and stages. That is how every empire has gone down, and that is how the West will go down. There is only one way of arresting all this, and that is this gospel. I am not preaching because I am a kind of agent of the government! I say all this because I am concerned about your individual soul. But at the same time I am showing you that this is not only true of the individual, it is true collectively. 'Where there is no vision, the people perish' (*Prov.* 29:18). 'Righteousness exalteth a nation' (*Prov.* 14:34). You cannot live on anything else.

Now, unfortunately, as we have seen, a false idea is current as to what the church is and what she is meant to be doing, but here in Acts we are given the true picture – this 'fellowship'. Remember again who these people were. They had rejected Christ and had said, 'Away with him! Crucify him!' But they had suddenly been convinced and convicted by the preaching of Peter, and three thousand had been added to the church. Here they were, going day by day to this company, to this fellowship, to hear the teaching. But what is 'fellowship'? This is a word that is much in fashion today, but I think that it is a word that is greatly abused. It is popular with supporters of what is called the 'ecumenical movement'. But, as I have been showing you, these people are not interested in doctrine. They say, 'Doctrine divides, therefore don't talk about it, we don't need it. What we need is fellowship.'

Today one comes across strange notions with regard to what constitutes fellowship. Fellowship means, as I shall show you, a very deep unity, and there is all the difference in the world between true unity and a coalition. It is a fallacy to say that when you have a coalition you have unity. You have not. The history of every political coalition proves that there was never any true unity, merely a temporary coming together. But that is not fellowship. You can persuade yourself that it is, but it is all on the surface. Deep down there is disunity; there is division.

The tragedy today is that people say, 'Oh, it doesn't matter what people believe as long as we all come together – Roman Catholics and Protestants, everybody. Differences don't matter, we're all one. Let's all be together – perhaps, even, those who belong to all the religions of the world. Let's have a great world congress. Let's amalgamate all religions.' The world laughs at that, and I think that for once the world is right. That is not Christianity. That is not fellowship and that is not unity.

People's ideas as to what constitutes fellowship can be quite pathetic. Some people think in purely social terms. This is an idea that is frequently found in the church, and I want to ridicule it because it has nothing to do with Christianity. People even think that fellowship just means having a cup of tea and a biscuit together. I have known others who think of fellowship in these terms: at the end of a service, or during a service, the minister says, 'Now you must all have fellowship with one another,' and he tells everyone to shake hands with the people sitting near them, and they all shake hands. Marvellous fellowship! Those are some people's ideas of fellowship – a superficial friendliness, a niceness, a joviality. In these ways that great word 'fellowship' has been degraded.

I remember an evangelical preacher speaking to me about a certain man who was not an evangelical at all but quite a notorious liberal, and this preacher said, 'You know, I find I have more fellowship with him than I do with many evangelicals.'

'Well,' I replied, 'it all depends upon what you mean by fellowship. If you mean that he is a nicer man than many evangelicals, I agree with you, but that is not fellowship.' That a man is pleasant and affable and kind does not mean you can have fellowship with him. You can pass the time of day with him, and there will be no disputes and quarrels perhaps, but that is not fellowship.

Furthermore, let me emphasize again that fellowship is not to be equated with institutionalism, and this, it seems to me, is the thing that is keeping so many outside the Christian church at the present time. They look at the church, and they see nothing but a great institution, a great organization. That is not only true of Roman Catholicism, it is true of Protestantism also. Look at either the modern Roman Catholic church or the modern Protestant church in Britain. Can you see it in the Acts of the Apostles? Can you see anybody in Acts corresponding to the Pope? Can you have fellowship with the Pope? Look at the protocol you have to go through before you can even see him. Look at people staring at him in the distance, considering it an honour just to kiss a ring on his finger. Is that fellowship?

No, that is why people are outside the church, and that is why they are not listening to Christianity. They look at that and they do not want it. And I am here to say that I do not want it either. Christianity is not a mere institution that all and sundry can use. In the name of God I say that I am getting rather tired of these statesmen and others who never darken the doors of a place of

AUTHENTIC CHRISTIANITY

worship while they are alive but who want Christian hymns at their funerals. I protest in the name of God! They say that we are hypocrites, but is not that sheer hypocrisy? Why do they want Christian hymns in their funeral services? Why do they not come and sing them when they are alive? The church is foolish enough to allow herself to be used, but that is not New Testament Christianity. No, no, it is here in Acts that we see true fellowship.

So what does it mean? Well, I have looked up the word and it means 'a deep association', 'a true communion', 'a close relationship of which the highest example is marriage'. It is a word that is sometimes used to denote 'partnership in business'. It is not just meeting occasionally in a church building, shaking hands at the end of a service or meeting and going home. That is not a church; no fellowship is involved in that. True fellowship is never anything superficial. It is deep. It is vital. It becomes the main thing in life. When people become Christians they become one. They enter into this community. They are in a family together. They are united by certain bonds that are indissoluble.

Now on one occasion our Lord himself put this very plainly. He had been speaking about the rich young ruler who 'went away grieved' because he could not submit to our Lord's demand to him to give away all his money to the poor. Then we read:

And Jesus looking upon them [his disciples] saith, With men it is impossible, but not with God: for with God all things are possible. Then Peter began to say unto him, Lo, we have left all, and have followed thee. And Jesus answered and said, Verily I say unto you, There is no man that hath left house, or brethren, or sisters, or father, or mother, or wife, or children, or lands, for my sake, and the gospel's, but he shall receive an hundredfold now in this time, houses, and brethren, and sisters, and mothers, and children, and lands, with persecutions; and in the world to come eternal life (Mark 10:27–30).

That is it! 'If you leave a human father or mother for my sake,' says Christ in effect, 'it is all right. You will have fathers and mothers, a hundredfold, in this present life; you will have a new family.' This is what is meant by fellowship. And this is only true of the Christian church.

So is it not time that we got back to this primitive pattern? Here is Christianity as it began in the ancient world – here we see this power, this church, this message that turned the world upside-down. And this has been repeated through the centuries. The story of the church is most extraordinary. I have often said that I know of nothing more instructive, next to the Bible, than church history. I know nothing more encouraging, nothing more exhilarating. What do you think the story of the church is? Do you think that it is a story that began here in Acts in infancy and gradually went on developing, continuing up, and up, and up? That is not it at all.

The story of the church is a story of ups and downs. The church, because men and women forget the primitive pattern, becomes a mere institution; she becomes dead. She may grow wealthy, she may gain great political power – the popes were tremendously powerful in the Middle Ages – but that has nothing to do with the church.

And how is it that there is a Christian church at all today? There is only one answer: it is because God in his mercy has looked down and has revived the church and has made her come back to the primitive pattern. This is true reformation. Do you want to know what the church is? Well, here it is in Acts 2. Look at these people. They met together every day to listen to the apostles' doctrine, to have fellowship with the apostles, to break bread with them, to pray with them. This phenomenon began to spread and people were amazed. There was a dynamic, there was a power, there was something living, and people said, 'What is this? I wish I could have it.'

Have you ever read the story of the church that used to meet in the catacombs in Rome? The believers were persecuted so severely that they could not meet anywhere else. But they met together in those burial places underground. These were little people, quite unimportant people. There were few great people among them. But they met together. There in the catacombs they engaged in this fellowship; and the power spread. That is the great story of the church. Alas, in the name of God, do not look at things as you see them today! Look back to this great history, and then you will see what a church is.

But when you look at those dark Middle Ages with Roman Catholicism ruling in pomp and power, and the Pope a great prince, manipulating kings and rulers, you may say, 'That's the church!' No, it is not! That is the 'great harlot'; that is the devil's counterfeit. It has nothing to do with Christianity.

So where was the church in those times? It was to be found among a very simple little people in the north of Italy – people known as the *Waldensians*. They met together in one another's houses. Sometimes they were not even allowed to do that, and then they would meet in caves away up in the hills and in the mountains. But they came together, those little groups. That was the church. Or there were the followers of John Hus, in what later became Czechoslovakia, or the followers of John Wycliffe in England: and all this well before the Protestant Reformation. That is the church, not a great institution but these little people believing the truth, knowing the Lord, having their lives changed, holding on to the teaching, and praying together.

And then we come to the Protestant Reformation itself, and immediately we again find the people meeting together in these little companies. Come along down the centuries: we find the church among the Puritans, and we meet it in the wonderful story of the Scottish Covenanters. Read these things and you will see what the church is, what Christianity is.

Usually the Covenanters had to meet away up in the mountains somewhere. I remember once visiting a place called the Communion Stones in the south of Scotland not far from Dumfries – one of the most thrilling places I think I have ever visited. You had to go off the main roads, up the secondary roads, and you came to a farm lane and you landed up in a farmyard. Then you had to walk up the side of a hill. There was a little break in the hills and just round the corner you saw a kind of natural meeting-place, almost a little amphitheatre, where there was a big stone. This was where the Scottish Christians in the seventeenth century used to meet together on Sunday afternoons for a Communion service. A man or two would be posted in the gap in the hills to see if the English soldiers were coming to arrest them. These were little, unknown people but they had the grace of God in their hearts. They were risking life and limb to meet in this way, but their lives had been transformed and they were ready to meet their God.

So this is the picture of the church; this is what is meant by fellowship. And, according to the New Testament, one of the best

ests we can ever apply to ourselves to know whether or not we
are Christians is just this test of fellowship. Would you like to
know whether you are a Christian? That is the most important
thing you can ever know. You cannot live truly and you certainly
cannot die truly unless you are a Christian. But how do you
know? Here is John's answer: 'We know that we have passed from
death unto life, because we love the brethren' (1 John 3:14).

What does John mean? Oh, he means that we like the fellowship
of Christians. The moment those three thousand were converted,
they joined the fellowship. Nothing could keep them away. Love
for the brethren had become one of the biggest and deepest things
in their lives. It had become more important to them even than the
sweetest earthly ties. When people become Christians they want
to spend all their time with other Christians, and they become
concerned about them. The proof of Christianity is that it changes
people, it gives them a new birth, and they belong to a new
family. And this new family bond is deeper than natural or social
or national ties. They are drawn together. They cannot keep apart
from one another.

So if you want to know for certain whether you are a Christian
at this moment, I can give you the test. Would you sooner spend
time with the humblest people who are Christians than with the
greatest who are not? It is as simple as that. It is not, ultimately, a
test of what you believe with your mind. We can believe things
with our minds without their affecting our hearts and our wills.
Here is the thorough test – love of the brethren. It is that you feel
something about the humblest and the lowliest because they are
Christians which you never feel about the greatest and the most
exalted if they are not.

Did you notice this: 'And all that believed were together, and
had all things common; and sold their possessions and goods, and
parted them to all men, as every man had need'? Some people
think that that is a sort of primitive Communism. But that is a
misunderstanding of what the text really says. It does not mean
that they all sold everything and put it into a common pool. The
meaning of the Greek is that the believers so loved one another
that none of them was allowed to suffer, and if one of them was in
a condition of penury, the other who had a superabundance was
prepared to sell some of his possessions and goods in order to

help his weaker brother. In other words, though they still held on to their possessions, they said this: We are all prepared to live for one another as the need arises. As men and women are prepared to do something for members of their own families who are in trouble, so Christians are prepared to help their brothers and sisters in Christ. There is a oneness, there is a unity, and, I repeat, this is the test – 'We know that we have passed from death unto life, because we love the brethren.'

What is it that makes this fellowship possible? There are, it seems to me, three main matters, and I shall just note them. What makes this possible, of course, is identity of nature. This is the result of the new birth. You do not argue about these things, you know them. The apostle Paul, in his second epistle to the Corinthians, says, 'Be ye not unequally yoked together with unbelievers' – why not? – 'for what fellowship hath righteousness with unrighteousness?' (2 Cor. 6:14). It is as simple as that. There can be no fellowship, no real community of interest, between righteousness and unrighteousness. Then Paul goes on: 'What communion' – the same word – 'hath light with darkness?' It is impossible. You cannot mix light with darkness. 'And what concord hath Christ with Belial? or what part hath he that believeth with an infidel? And what agreement hath the temple of God with idols?' – none at all! – 'for ye are the temple of the living God; as God hath said, I will dwell in them, and walk in them; and I will be their God, and they shall be my people' (verses 14–16).

So that is the first reason for fellowship. We have the same nature within us, we are sharers of the same life, and the moment you detect that life in another you have fellowship with that person. This is a wonderful thing! It has been my privilege as minister of Westminster Chapel for nearly twenty-seven years to have had many experiences of this fellowship, particularly during the war.[1] There were troops stationed in Britain from Canada, from America, from Holland, from Norway – from almost every part of the world. Here were these men and women for a while in London. They would come to the service and at the end they would come to see me. I had never seen them before but, you know, I knew them. I knew them and they knew me. We had

[1] The Second World War

never seen one another before, we had never spoken before, but you recognize a brother, you know at once, you belong together immediately. It does not matter what the colour is, it does not matter what the clothing is; nothing matters. It is instinctive. You speak the same language. You have fellowship. That is how it begins, but it does not stop there.

Then another thing that produces fellowship is the common teaching. The apostle Jude talks about 'the common salvation' (*Jude* 3). There is only one salvation and it is 'the common salvation'. I have had people from the South Sea Islands in my vestry, and we knew at once that we were brethren. How? Because we were sharing the same salvation. We had a fundamental agreement about basic things. We agreed about God; we agreed about ourselves in sin; we agreed about the blessed Saviour; we agreed about the new life. We were one and we knew one another. Though we did not agree about everything, there was a fundamental agreement. Without this, it is impossible to have fellowship. You may be speaking different human languages, but where the gospel is concerned, you speak the same language.

And then I would also emphasize a sense of trust and freedom. If there is any doubt, you do not have fellowship. There must be mutual trust and understanding so that you can speak freely. You open your heart, the other person does exactly the same, and you are enjoying fellowship, this freedom. An exchange is going on and it is wonderful. It is like a family at its very best.

Those characteristics, then, are the basis of the fellowship and they work themselves out like this: 'They continued stedfastly in the apostles' doctrine and fellowship.' These new believers had the same outlook and the same interests. The thing that had become all-important was this new life which they had received. The day before – no, no, that was something else. The day before they may have been interested in a thousand and one questions. Possibly these Jews, as most of them were, were chiefly interested in political questions – how to throw off the Roman yoke, how to get rid of injustices. Now I am not arguing against that. There is nothing wrong in that. You can still be – and, indeed, it is your duty to be – interested in politics. God has ordained government to keep evil and sin within bounds in this evil world; you must be interested. But politics is not the main interest of the Christian. No,

it is this new life! And this is why they came together to the
fellowship. They wanted to know more and more about it. They
had never heard it until that day, and now that they had it, they
knew that it was wonderful and that it had changed everything.

In many ways, one of the best summaries in the whole of the
New Testament of this new outlook is given by Peter – the same
Peter who preached on the day of Pentecost. He writes:

*Dearly beloved, I beseech you as strangers and pilgrims, abstain from
fleshly lusts, which war against the soul; having your conversation
honest among the Gentiles: that, whereas they speak against you as evil-
doers, they may by your good works, which they shall behold, glorify God
in the day of visitation* (1 Pet. 2:11–12).

'Look here,' says Peter in effect, 'because you are Christians you
know that you are strangers and pilgrims in this world.' And this
is one of the first things that the Christian realizes. The great
ambition of everybody else is to settle down in the world. 'This is
the only world,' they say, 'and the thing to do is to make the best
of it. Don't think of death, it will come soon enough. Don't worry
about these things. Live for the moment. Have a good time.' But
when men and women become Christians they realize that they
are nothing but strangers and pilgrims in this world. They are
only journeymen, only just passing through, and they say, 'I must
not give myself to it because this is Vanity Fair. It will be gone
tomorrow and I'll be gone – what then?' They say with Paul, 'Our
conversation is in heaven' (*Phil.* 3:20).

The Christian's whole outlook on this world and its life is
revolutionized. Once Christians lived for it; they were of it. But no
longer. They have been separated. Peter keeps on using these
great phrases: 'Ye are a chosen generation, a royal priesthood, an
holy nation, a peculiar people; that ye should shew forth the
praises of him who hath called you out of darkness into his
marvellous light' (*1 Pet.* 2:9). You were in the dark and you had
friendships and fellowship, as it were, with the people in the dark,
but you have been brought out into the light and you want the
people of the light. You realize that you are a new person, that you
do not belong to this darkness any longer. You are in a new realm.
Or again, as Peter says, 'Which in time past were not a people, but
are now the people of God' (*1 Pet.* 2:10). You were just a rebel,

rresponsible, not understanding, not knowing, living like an animal. But you have been brought out of that. And naturally people who are aware of this come together, they belong together. You cannot live in a no-man's land spiritually. That does not mean you are perfect, nor that you may not occasionally fall into sin, but you do not live there.

But that is the negative and I do not want to leave it there. Put positively, these people met together not only because they no longer belonged to the darkness, but because they realized the dignity and the value of their new life. Listen to Peter again: 'Ye are a chosen generation, a royal priesthood, an holy nation, a peculiar people [a people for God's own special possession].' That is what you have become as the result of your new birth. As the result of the operation of the Holy Spirit upon you, you have new life in you and it is the royal life. You are a child of God. You belong to the household of God. You are a member of the royal family.

So, realizing that, you want to spend your time with the members of the royal family. You have a sense of dignity that you never had before. And you do not take this great name and this great family that you now belong to into the realm of darkness. No, no, you have been promoted; you have been honoured; you realize who you are. You cannot demean or disgrace your new life. You want to be in this other realm for its purity, its glory, its wonder and its unusual honour. That is how Peter writes to unknown Christian people.

The last thing Peter mentions is this: Why have you been made 'a chosen generation' and 'a royal priesthood'? Here is the answer: 'That ye should shew forth the praises [the excellencies] of him who hath called you out of darkness into his marvellous light.' This is most important. Why am I preaching about the church? Why am I anxious that we should have a true idea of the church and the Christian message? My ultimate answer is the glory of God and the souls of men and women. I am here to tell you about God, and I am here to tell you about God because I know you have a soul within you which you have not known about and which you have ignored. I can see you living for this present evil world and for darkness and sin. And I know that if you die like that you will go on spending eternity like that, only the misery will be much greater than it is now, and the suffering and the realization of your folly, when there is no time to change and you can do nothing about it. That is why I preach.

But I want to tell you that you can be made a child of God. You can become a member of this 'chosen generation'. You can become one of the priests in this kingdom. You can become a member of this 'holy nation'. You can become a person who is the special object of God's care and love. He will count the very hairs of your head. He will give you a new life, new power, new strength. This is possible for you. It is possible for you to die as a noble man or woman and enter into your eternal inheritance.

One of the main reasons why the first believers in Jerusalem constantly attended the fellowship was because they said: This marvellous thing has happened to us, but what about our relatives? What about our friends? What about our neighbours? They don't know. We want to tell them but we are ignorant. We must learn. We must listen to this apostolic teaching and spend our time with these apostles. We want to ask questions. We want help and advice. We want to learn how to 'tell forth his praises'. The Jerusalem Christians said: We are one. We are partners, God's emissaries, God's agents. The world is miserable. It is dying in sin and men and women are defeated and don't know about this. Let us show them. Let us demonstrate that there is another type of life.

These Christians in Jerusalem were doing what the apostle Paul exhorts the Philippians to do, and this is what God, I think, is calling us all to do at this present time: 'Do all things without murmurings and disputings: that ye may be blameless and harmless, the sons of God, without rebuke, in the midst of a crooked and perverse nation, among whom ye shine as lights in the world [in the heavens]; holding forth the word of life' (*Phil.* 2:14–16). These people said: We are like lights in the heavens and we must shine brightly. Men and women are in darkness. They do not know where they are, nor where they are going. Let us tell them. Let us show them together.

That is the church! Not some pompous institution which is ever ready to sell itself to great men. No, no, it is simple, unknown people. But they are the people of God, and their desire is not to be men-pleasers, not to be court chaplains, as it were, but to show forth his praises who has called them out of darkness into his marvellous light. Is this true of you? Do you delight in this sort of fellowship? Do you want to know more of these things? Are you worried and troubled that perhaps you have been missing some wonderful programme on the television while you have been considering these things? These are the questions that tell us whether or not we are Christians. What comes first? What are we living for? What are we relying on? How do we face life? How are we going to face death? How are we going to face God? These are the supreme questions.

What else matters? Are you burdened about the state of your country? Are you merely annoyed at the increase in sin or is your heart full of sorrow for poor men and women who are its victims? Are you merely annoyed with these poor young people, or do you feel sorry for them because they do not know any better, because they have never heard about God and Christ and the possibility of being children of God? Are you just irritated by them, or does your heart bleed for them? Do you want to show them this 'marvellous light'? Do you want to hold before them the word of life? People come together in fellowship in order that they might shine the more brightly and show this evil generation to which they belong that there is a way of which they know nothing, the way of God, the way of Christ, the way of the life of God in the soul, the way of eternal salvation.

'We know that we have passed from death unto life, because we love the brethren.' Is the Bible the most important book in the world for you? Do the children of God come first before everybody else, no matter who? May God give us honesty as we examine ourselves. That is Christianity. That is the church. That is the life which is life indeed. That is the way to live. It is the only teaching which can prepare us to die gloriously.

Do you belong to the 'fellowship'? If you do, thank God; if you do not, go and tell him. Tell him you feel you are outside. Tell him you do not understand these things, that they are strange to you. Tell him that you would like to know. Ask him to enlighten you with his Spirit and he will. If you are honest, if you really want this life, ask him and he will give it you. And once you have it, oh, then you will love the brethren and you will covet the fellowship above everything else on earth.

11

The Breaking of Bread

*Then they that gladly received his word were baptized: and the same day
there were added unto them about three thousand souls. And they
continued stedfastly in the apostles' doctrine and fellowship, and in
breaking of bread, and in prayers* (Acts 2:41–42).

As we have been considering the book of Acts, we have
constantly emphasized that there is only one thing that has
ever affected profoundly the life of this world, and that is the
message of the Christian church. That is not merely my opinion,
but is the verdict of history. History will testify that the most
civilizing force that the world has ever known has been the
Christian church. Most of the things of which we boast today
came originally through the medium of the Christian church. She
began to look after and to help those who were in need and
suffering. Hospitals, for instance, came directly through the minis-
trations of the church, and in the nineteenth century most
government legislation that brought liberty to men and women
was initiated by people who had become Christians.

So in order to discover what the Christian church really is, we
are now looking at the second chapter of Acts and we have seen
that those early Christians continued steadfastly in the apostles'
teaching and in the fellowship of the believers. Now we must
consider the next phrase: they continued steadfastly 'in breaking
of bread'. Here, again, is a characteristic of the Christian church
and we shall, of course, not only be looking at this in a detached,
theoretical manner, we shall incidentally be examining ourselves.

These people wanted to be together, constantly listening to this teaching, in the fellowship of similar people – and in breaking of bread. Are we like that? This is how Christianity began. Here is the authentic thing.

You see, you can hold Christian ideas, but that does not prove you are a Christian. As we have seen, Christianity is more than a notion; it is in the heart, changing a person radically and completely so that there is a thirst for teaching and for fellowship. And there is also a desire to come together for the breaking of bread.

I have already shown you that what we are told here in Acts about doctrine and fellowship is the direct opposite of what is being taught at the present time, and this is equally true of the breaking of bread. Popular teaching today says that because of our modern knowledge, we do not need the historical teaching and practices of the church. So I do want you to see the relevance of these verses in Acts to all this modern talk which is enticing so many people.

The first comment I have to make is that there is nothing new about the fact that men and women do not believe in God. We are being told that this is the hallmark of modernity, but have you ever read the fourteenth Psalm? This is the first verse: 'The fool hath said in his heart, There is no God.' That was probably written by David about 1000 BC, nearly three thousand years ago. So this idea that modern people are somehow different is quite wrong. There have been atheists throughout the centuries.

Secondly, modern men and women do not say that they believe there is no God because they are modern or because of their learning, they say it because they are fools. This is the sort of thing that people never seem to understand. 'The *fool* hath said in his heart, There is no God.' They are ignorant; they are blinded by what they see from 'seeing him who is invisible' (*Heb.* 11:27). They think they are clever, but they do not even explain their world. They leave more unexplained than explained. They are fools. So atheism has nothing at all to do with modernity; it has nothing at all to do with learning. You can find any man standing on a street corner who will tell you that there is no God. Does he say it because he is a great philosopher? No; 'The fool hath said in his heart, There is no God.'

The answer to all this talk is that the greatest need of modern men and women is, as at all times in the past, to know the gracious God and to be blessed by him. All their troubles arise from the fact that they are ignorant of God. That is the whole cause of all the trouble in life, between individuals, between groups, between classes and between nations. So we must not look for something new, for some further scientific discovery, or wait for a book that may come out next week with some new insight. No, no! As we have seen, we must look back to Acts chapter 2. And here we read of the 'breaking of bread', eating bread and drinking wine: the Communion service! This is something the church began to do at once and has continued to do throughout the running centuries.

If you read the New Testament right through, you will find that the first Christians did something like this: they would meet together in one another's houses – they did not have church buildings at the beginning. They would have a meal together and then at the end they would do this peculiar thing. One of them would take a loaf and he would break it into pieces and hand it round to the company. Then he would pour wine into a cup and he would take of it and pass it, too, round to the company. Now our Lord himself had done this very thing with his disciples just before his death. This is what we read:

And he said unto them, With desire I have desired to eat this passover with you before I suffer: for I say unto you, I will not any more eat thereof, until it be fulfilled in the kingdom of God. And he took the cup, and gave thanks, and said, Take this, and divide it among yourselves: for I say unto you, I will not drink of the fruit of the vine, until the kingdom of God shall come. And he took bread, and gave thanks, and brake it, and gave unto them, saying, This is my body which is given for you: this do in remembrance of me. Likewise also the cup after supper, saying, This cup is the new testament in my blood, which is shed for you (Luke 22:15–20).

Why did the first Christians break bread together, and why should we? The first and chief reason was that our Lord commanded it: 'This do ye,' he said, 'as oft as ye drink it, in remembrance of me' (*1 Cor.* 11:25). He gave this solemn charge just before his death, on the very night in which he was betrayed.

This is most important. These early believers in Christ did not decide to do this: he told them to do it. The apostle Paul, who came later into the church, wrote, 'I have received of the Lord that which also I delivered unto you' (*1 Cor.* 11:23). He had been taught by the risen Lord himself. Paul, you remember, had been a persecutor of Christians after these early days in the book of Acts. As Saul of Tarsus, he militantly persecuted and tried to destroy the Christian church, but he was converted on the road to Damascus, and the Lord appeared to him and gave him a commission. Paul constantly says: This is not my idea – 'I have received of the Lord that which also I delivered unto you.' The Lord revealed this ordinance to Paul, as he had revealed it to the other apostles immediately before his death.

So the Lord's Supper was not just the idea of the apostles, not something conjured up by the church, but it was a solemn command of the Lord. Why did he command them to keep it? And here is a most significant thing. I believe he gave this command in order to preserve the doctrine. This, you see, is an enactment of the doctrine, it is a kind of display of the truth, and our Lord wanted to preserve the truth throughout the centuries until the end of the Christian era.

What a wonderful thing this has been! This table with its bread and wine has often been a terrible condemnation of the pulpit. Men have entered pulpits and said that Jesus was only a man, that he was nothing more than a moral exemplar and a good teacher. They have said that his death was the death of a pacifist, that it was a great tragedy and that we must imitate his spirit and live in the same way. They have preached like that in pulpits and then they have gone down to the Communion table, and there has been no connection between their preaching and the message of that Communion service. The Communion table, the broken bread and the poured out wine, has been preaching a message.

And so, because of men and their fallibility – and we are all fallible – the Lord took a step to preserve the truth, the doctrine. And if you want to know how to test modern teaching and modern preaching, here is your test: What relationship does it bear to the bread and the wine? Does it lead to that? Is the Communion service a demonstration of the message that has been preached? If it is not, the message has been false. Here is the

Lord's own command and he has commanded it in order to preserve the teaching.

But I believe he also commanded it in order to preserve the unity of the church. The apostle Paul, in his letter to the church at Corinth, where there were so many divisions, says, 'The cup of blessing which we bless, is it not the communion of the blood of Christ? The bread which we break, is it not the communion of the body of Christ? For we being many are one bread, and one body, for we are all partakers of that one bread' (1 Cor. 10:16–17). There is no better way of preserving this fellowship that we have already considered, this 'unity of the Spirit in the bond of peace' (Eph. 4:3), than to come to the Communion table.

The members of the church in Corinth were split. Some boasted 'We're followers of Paul.'

'No, no,' said others, 'Apollos is the man. Much more philosophical.'

Yet again, others said that they were supporters of Cephas. So they were divided into parties. But Paul said, 'Is Christ divided? was Paul crucified for you?' (1 Cor. 1:13). No, when you come to this table you must forget all about Paul, Apollos, Cephas, myself, anybody else who has ever preached, and you must see only Christ. At this table you preserve the unity – one loaf, one bread, one communion, one Christ. He was crucified. Nobody else.

Unity is preserved at this table in another way, too. There is nothing that so humbles us as to come to this table. When you think something of yourself, you tend to divide from others, but when you come to this table, you are humbled. You think of him and of what he did and endured, and you say with Isaac Watts:

> When I survey the wondrous cross
> On which the Prince of glory died,
> My richest gain I count but loss,
> And pour contempt on all my pride.
>
> Forbid it, Lord, that I should boast,
> Save in the death of Christ my God.
>   Isaac Watts

When men and women truly come to the Communion table they are humbled, and they are one as they all look together to him.

The Breaking of Bread

Secondly, the disciples kept the Lord's Supper in order that they might remember him and all that he represented. This do,' he said, 'as oft as ye drink it, in remembrance of me.' So these people came together. And so we, too, come to that table to remember the gracious God who has done this for us. It is here we find him.

What is it we remember? Oh, it is the action of God! Here we are in this old sinful world, and there is only one message of hope, there is only one word of cheer. It is this: 'God so loved the world, that he gave his only begotten Son . . .' (*John* 3:16). Here is the message of the New Testament, this is Christian salvation. It is not that I go out and find a needy neighbour, not that I try to philosophize or use my scientific knowledge in an attempt to arrive at some understanding. No, no! Look back! It has happened! The great thing is done! 'God sent forth his Son, made of a woman, made under the law, to redeem them that were under the law' (*Gal.* 4:4–5).

'This do in remembrance of me,' Jesus said. Christianity is not just some sentimental feeling. No, it is a great declaration that Jesus of Nazareth is the Son of God, and that God has sent him, his only Son, into the world to do something about this predicament of ours in which we are so defeated and helpless. So the Communion service reminds us of his person - and we must always start with that: 'In the beginning was the Word, and the Word was with God, and the Word was God . . . And the Word was made flesh, and dwelt among us' (*John* 1:1,14). And if that is not at the very centre of the message, whatever it may call itself, it is not Christian. The whole essence of Christianity is that God is loving and kind and compassionate; and, while humanity in its folly had turned its back upon him and said there was no God, he sent his only Son into the world. This Communion service reminds us that salvation is possible in him and through him alone.

This, then, is what the church has been looking back to ever since, and this is the Christian message to the modern world. If you look for help to anything the world can do in the present or the future, you will suffer a sad disillusionment. The world has always been promising us something better, but it never gives it us. Men and women have always been optimistic: 'Hope springs eternal in the human breast.' But hope in the world is made to look very silly by history, is it not? Every generation has thought that it alone has understanding and knowledge and truth, and it has derided the past; it alone is right. But then the next generation comes and dismisses the previous one.

So listen to the message of the bread and wine. It tells you: Look back! It has happened! 'The great transaction's done.' The one thing that can help us has taken place. The Son of God is the only Saviour! 'There is none other name under heaven given among men, whereby we must be saved' (*Acts* 4:12). It is the exact contradiction of all that is so popular today.

So the first believers joined in the breaking of bread because our Lord had commanded them and because they wanted to remember him. But, thirdly, and in particular, the apostle Paul says, 'For as often as ye eat this bread, and drink this cup, ye do shew the Lord's death till he come' (*1 Cor.* 10:26). Paul says that these first believers were declaring the Lord's death.

This means a number of things. First, they were not hiding the Lord's death. They were not ashamed of it and they did not regard it as the greatest disaster that had ever taken place. Now the Gospels tell us very honestly that when our Lord was crucified all his followers were utterly cast down. They said: The end has come. We had thought that he was going to lead us through, but he has been killed.

The disciples were entirely without hope. Then our Lord suddenly appeared among them and explained what he had done. He reprimanded them for their blindness and gave them the full knowledge which they were lacking. So they were no longer ashamed or disappointed. They no longer thought that his death should be kept out of sight. Indeed, they now took up the opposite position. They broke the bread together in order to declare his death, in order to proclaim it. Indeed, the apostle Paul goes as far as to say that when he first went to preach in Corinth, 'I determined not to know any thing among you, save Jesus Christ and him crucified' (*1 Cor.* 2:2). He also told the Galatians, 'Jesus Christ hath been evidently set forth, crucified among you' (*Gal.* 3:1). This means that Paul had placarded him. He had, so to speak, put up a poster proclaiming 'Christ crucified'.

Paul tells the Galatians this: 'God forbid that I should glory, save in the cross of our Lord Jesus Christ, by whom the world is crucified unto me, and I unto the world' (*Gal.* 6:14). Paul's preaching was not about our Lord's teaching, nor about his example. It was about his death. It is the death of Christ that matters. This is what we announce as the only hope for the world.

Why? Because it is by his death, and by that alone, that we are saved. This is the rub. This is what the modern man or woman objects to. But this is the Christian teaching. The breaking of the bread announces that the only way of salvation is not by his teaching, not by his example, not by his encouragement, but through the broken body and the shed blood of the Son of God.

Why is this? Now here we come to the very heart of our gospel, and this is what the breaking of bread proclaims. The whole trouble with men and women, as we have seen, is their alienation from God. This is God's world, whether people like it or not, and as long as they do not recognize that, they will be 'kicking against the pricks', they will be hitting their heads against a wall, they will be like the foolish sea vainly dashing itself against the rocks. If they fight against God, they will always be thrown back in defeat, disaster and despair. Their greatest need is to know God and to be reconciled to him and to receive his blessing.

Why do they not receive it? The answer is because God is holy, just and righteous. God has told us this plainly in the Old Testament. It is the great message of the prophets – the whole Bible proclaims it. But in their folly men and women have rebelled against him. They have broken the communion. They have incurred the displeasure of God, and God's wrath is upon them. If you want to understand the modern world, here is the answer: 'The wrath of God is revealed from heaven against all ungodliness and unrighteousness of men, who hold the truth in unrighteousness' (*Rom*.1:18). This is the whole trouble. We are sinners, under the condemnation and wrath of God.

What can we do about it? We can do nothing. 'How should man be just with God?' (*Job* 9:2). Will it avail if I say to God, 'I'm sorry for what I've done'? No, it is not enough. Will it do if I say to God, 'I'm not going to sin any more but I'm going to live to serve you'? But you cannot do that. You have tried, have you not? We have all tried, but we cannot succeed.

> *Not the labours of my hands*
> *Can fulfil Thy law's demands;*
> *Could my zeal no respite know,*

Could my tears for ever flow,
All for sin could not atone:
Thou must save, and Thou alone.

Augustus Toplady

No matter how hard we try, we cannot save ourselves. But the wonderful message is that our Lord was made the Sin-Bearer. He himself said, 'The Son of man came not to be ministered unto, but to minister, and to give his life a ransom for many' (*Matt.* 20:28). We are told, 'When the time was come . . . he stedfastly set his face to go to Jerusalem' (*Luke* 9:51). Then we see him in the Garden of Gethsemane, shrinking against this terrible thing that was going to happen. He was going to be smitten, stricken of God, and lose his Father's face. That was the one thing he did not desire, so he said three times, 'Abba, Father, all things are possible unto thee; take away this cup from me: nevertheless not what I will, but what thou wilt' (*Mark* 14:36). And then he went like a lamb to the slaughter.

The Bible is full of this: 'God was in Christ, reconciling the world unto himself; not imputing their trespasses unto them . . . For he hath made him to be sin for us, who knew no sin; that we might be made the righteousness of God in him' (2 *Cor.* 5:19,21). Or again, Paul says, 'For what the law could not do, in that it was weak through the flesh, God sending his own Son in the likeness of sinful flesh, and for sin, condemned sin in the flesh: that the righteousness of the law might be fulfilled in us, who walk not after the flesh, but after the Spirit' (*Rom.* 8:3-4). These are the proclamations! 'Whom God hath set forth to be a propitiation through faith in his blood, to declare his righteousness for the remission of sins' (*Rom.* 3:25). These are the great declarations: 'That he [God] might be just, and the justifier of him which believeth in Jesus' (*Rom.* 3:26).

All the New Testament writers say it. Listen to John: 'If any man sin, we have an advocate with the Father, Jesus Christ the righteous: and he is the propitiation for our sins: and not for ours only, but also for the sins of the whole world' (1 *John* 2:1-2). All this means that God has laid our sins on his Son, and has smitten him. He has punished our sins in him. He has broken his body. He has shed his blood. That is why we break the bread and drink the wine. The bread stands for the broken body; the poured out wine stands for the poured out blood.

The Breaking of Bread

Oh, says Peter, I must come in on this: 'Who his own self bare our sins in his own body on the tree, that we, being dead to sins, should live unto righteousness: by whose stripes ye were healed' (1 Pet. 2:24). Let me remind you, says Peter again: 'Ye were not redeemed with corruptible things, as silver and gold, from your vain conversation received by tradition from your fathers; but with the precious blood of Christ, as of a lamb without blemish and without spot' (1 Pet. 1:18–19).

The early church continued steadfastly breaking bread to declare his death; to declare that this is God's way of forgiveness; to declare that a just God cannot pretend that he has not seen our sins. He cannot just wink at them and say, 'All right, I will forget them.' He cannot! He is holy. He is righteous. And he must punish sin, as he says he will, and he has done it in his Son. That is why we, too, break the bread and drink the wine. We are declaring that because Christ has suffered and died for us, God has forgiven us and blotted out our sins and washed our guilt away.

The first Christians did not stop at that, of course. They also wanted to remind themselves of what had been made possible for them as the result of our Lord's death. So the apostle Paul, repeating the words of our Lord, says: 'This cup is the new testament [the new covenant] in my blood' (1 Cor. 11:25). Oh, the trouble with the world is that it does not know these things. New covenant! God has made a new agreement with men and women in Christ, and he has ratified it by the shed blood of Christ. In the Old Testament, when agreements were made they were always ratified by the blood of a sacrificed animal. Every agreement God has ever made with his people has always been ratified with blood.

It is a sort of seal and stamp. This blood of Christ, says the apostle, represented by the wine in the cup, is the blood of the new covenant. In the Bible we can read many descriptions of this new covenant, but perhaps the best summary is in the eighth chapter of the epistle to the Hebrews:

Behold, the days come, saith the Lord, when I will make a new covenant with the house of Israel and with the house of Judah: not according to the covenant that I made with their fathers in the day when I took them by the hand to lead them out of the land of Egypt; because they continued not in my covenant, and I regarded them not, saith the Lord. For this is the covenant that I will make with the house of Israel . . .

Do you know about it? Listen, defeated modern men and women, defeated by sin, afraid of life, afraid of the future, afraid of death, afraid of the judgment – here is the new covenant in Christ:

I will put my laws into their mind, and write them in their hearts: and I will be to them a God, and they shall be to me a people: and they shall not teach every man his neighbour, and every man his brother, saying, Know the Lord: for all shall know me, from the least to the greatest. For I will be merciful to their unrighteousness, and their sins and their iniquities will I remember no more (Heb. 8:8–12).

You may be the blackest sinner in the world, you may have lived a life of sin until now, but I am able to tell you that there is a new agreement for you, the new covenant. If you believe that Christ, the Son of God, has borne your punishment and has died for your sins, then God tells you, 'Their sins and their iniquities will I remember no more.' They will be gone, wiped out, washed away, never to be seen again. Not only that, he will tell you that he is your God and you will begin to know him. He will tell you that he has adopted you into his family, that you have become his child.

Then he will give you new life. He will give you new power and he will work in you by his Holy Spirit. He will give you understanding of his word. He will give you an entirely new outlook upon the whole of life. You will be like a new person in a new universe, all because you have believed that. You will enter into the terms of this blessed new covenant, and you will be able to face death, the judgment and eternity in an entirely new manner.

'Declare the Lord's death!' That is what he has done by his death. His blood is on the covenant. God is offering you this, for nothing. Simply believe!

> *Only believe, and thou shalt see*
> *That Christ is all in all to thee.*
> J. S. B. Monsell

They met together to break the bread to declare his death and all that it meant.

The final thing the apostle Paul mentions is this: 'For as often as ye eat this bread, and drink this cup, ye do shew the Lord's death *till he come.'* Do not forget this! They were remembering the one who died, but who rose again and ascended into heaven. They reminded themselves that he is seated on the right hand of God, that he has not forgotten the world because he has gone back to the glory, but is looking at it. He is watching it. He is waiting until his enemies shall be made his footstool. He is governing all things. He said, 'All power is given unto me' (*Matt.* 28:18). And he is looking down upon his people. He is still a High Priest who is sympathetic towards us: 'In all points tempted like as we are, yet without sin' (*Heb.* 4:15).

So when we pray to God – I hope to expound this next – we know that he is there, and he 'ever liveth to make intercession' for his people (*Heb.* 7:25). He is your advocate, and you know that he will continue like this until an appointed day when he will again come back into this world, oh, as a mighty Conqueror in all his blessed glory, riding the clouds of heaven, surrounded by his holy angels. And he will come to judge the world in righteousness. He will destroy sin and evil, the devil and hell and all that has ever been opposed to him, and will set up his glorious kingdom of righteousness, of holiness and of peace – 'new heavens and a new earth, wherein dwelleth righteousness' (*2 Pet.* 3:13)

And this is what is so wonderful. Look at these simple people meeting together there in the early church in one another's houses, breaking bread, declaring the Lord's death till he come. Many of them were slaves, very ordinary people having a hard time and being persecuted and maligned, sick in body, perhaps, and some sick in mind, even, and here they were, going through this weary, evil world, with the world and the flesh and the devil against them. But they broke the bread, and they remembered, not only what he had done but what he was going to do. They lifted up their heads. They said: We are destined for glory. We are the children of God. We are joint heirs with Christ. We have an 'inheritance incorruptible, and undefiled, and that fadeth not away, reserved in heaven' (*1 Pet.* 1:4) What does it matter though men kill us, though they revile us, though the whole world be destroyed, there is an inheritance that can never be moved. It is ours. It will be there until he comes. Then he will take us to be with himself, and we will spend our eternity with him in his glorious presence.

So they continued steadfastly in the breaking of bread, to remember him, to declare his death, to declare his coming again. And, of course, the final thing is that they did it in order to praise him and in order to thank him. As I remember these things, as I take that broken bread and drink that wine, I know that my sins are forgiven. I know that God so loved me that he sent his only Son into this world to bear the punishment of my sins - 'The Son of God, who loved me, and gave himself for me' (*Gal.* 2:20). I declare that, I know that, so I end by thanking him and giving myself to him.

> *Were the whole realm of nature mine,*
> *That were an offering far too small;*
> *Love so amazing, so divine,*
> *Demands my soul, my life, my all.*
>
> Isaac Watts

And those who really believe will go on proclaiming this, reminding themselves of it, thanking God for it. You will not have to persuade them to come to the Communion table. You will not have to discipline them to come – you will not be able to keep them away. Above all, they will want to offer themselves and all they are and have as a thank-offering to him who gave himself for them. They will react, in other words, as that great Christian man Count Zinzendorf did when, looking at that picture of the crucified Christ, he heard the message: 'I have done this for you; what have you done for me?'

So do you come to the breaking of bread as the first Christians came? Do you delight in coming? Does it move you? Does it thrill you? Do you find it the most wonderful thing? If so, you are a Christian, as they were. If not, have you a right to call yourself a Christian at all? This is what Christians have always done. They do not come mechanically. They do not think it is a miracle worked by a priest – all that has been added on.

No, here it is in its stark simplicity, this wonderful good news that God's own Son has taken our sins upon himself, has paid the penalty and has endured even unto death, that his body was broken, his blood was shed. And when we believe, the one thing we want to do is to praise and thank him and to tell everybody about him.

12

Prayer

Then they that gladly received his word were baptized: and the same day there were added unto them about three thousand souls. And they continued stedfastly in the apostles' doctrine and fellowship, and in breaking of bread, and in prayers (Acts 2:41–42).

We all realize, I am sure, that we are in a vast world, a world that seems to be expanding almost from week to week. We have listened to the scientists, and read their articles and reports. We realize we are in this great universe which we cannot comprehend and we begin to feel lonely and lost and isolated. We are in a world of change, a world where we see everything decaying and dying. We see difficulties, bloodshed, war and endless troubles. And we are aware of problems within ourselves and in our relationships. We have tried to battle against these, and have struggled to solve the problems. Having failed, we turn to this message of the Christian gospel. Here, still in this world, the church issues a challenge, saying: Here is the answer. Here alone is the answer because it is God's answer. If that is true, then there is nothing more important than that we should know what this message is.

Now all the problems that we face – war, nuclear weapons and so on – are not certainties, but possibilities. There may be a third world war – God forbid! But on the other hand, there may not be. We are not sure of it. The same is true of the use of nuclear weapons. These are possibilities and it is right that we should prepare for them. But if it is right to prepare for possibilities, how much more is it to prepare for certainties. The one absolute certainty is that we are all going out of this life, every one of us. We may go out as the result of a war, and of the use of bombs, but whether they are used or not, whether there is a war or not, we all have to face the ultimate.

That is why I say that this problem is more urgent than any other. We not only face that unavoidable certainty of death, we also face something which is uncertain. What is that? It is the moment of death. We do not know that.

'Ah,' you say, 'but I'm young.'

But what has age got to do with it? Young people, just as much as older people, are subject to the ravages of some of these horrible diseases: viruses are no respecters of age. Youth gives no guarantee that we are going to live a certain number of years. No, 'In the midst of life we are in death.' And therefore there is only one sensible thing to do – to prepare for it, to be ready for it. That is why I say that this message of the gospel has first priority.

But the gospel not only helps us to face that inevitable fact of death, this, and this alone, enables us to live while we are in this world. First, we must prepare for death, because it may come at any moment, and because we can do nothing afterwards about it, but, having settled that, we then face how to live until we get there. And my challenge again is that nothing enables us to live as we should but the message of this gospel.

So we are looking at the book of Acts in order that we should know exactly what this gospel is and what the church is to preach, and what the church herself is. And here, in this second chapter, we are given an account of her great characteristics. We have considered the apostles' teaching; the fellowship of these people, the saints, separated from the world; and the breaking of bread and drinking of wine in the Communion service. And now we come to consider prayer. Here, again, we see one of the marks of the early church, and as we read the story of the Christian church throughout the subsequent centuries, we find that prayer has always been a characteristic of true Christians and of the true church. So here is something that is vital for us.

Let me start by making some general remarks. The first is that the order in which these things are put is very important. We do not read, 'They continued stedfastly in the prayers, and in break-ing of bread, and in the fellowship and in the apostles' doctrine.' No, no, it is the other way round. Now this is not an accident. These writings are inspired. The subjects were put in this order by Luke the historian, and they must never be put in any other order. This is the divine order, and, whether we like it or not, we must recognize it.

You notice what comes first – the apostles' teaching. That decides everything else. The nature of the fellowship is deter-mined by the doctrine. If the world saw an extreme Conservative and an extreme Socialist on the same platform claiming to belong to the same party, the world would think it was the joke of the century. But that is the sort of thing you see in the Christian church today. If you put fellowship before teaching, that is what you get. No, no, you must start with the teaching. The teaching controls the fellowship. The fellowship is of those who have kindred minds, who believe the same things.

And then when we come to the breaking of bread, as we saw, it is not that we try to work up some feelings, but we know exactly what we are doing because of the teaching. The teaching tells us the meaning of the broken bread and of the poured out wine. And without that, it means nothing. Have we not all had some exper-ience of that? For years I went along to Communion services with no idea of what was happening or what was meant to happen. I saw some older people weeping as they took the bread and wine, and I tried to weep, but I could not because I did not understand it. It was a mere ceremony without any real content. You do not understand the Lord's Supper unless you start with the apostolic teaching. And it is exactly the same in this whole matter of the prayers.

I emphasize that we must hold on to the order in which these subjects come in Acts because once more this is so different from the popular teaching in modern journals and books. Men and women are being told something different, and they are ready to believe it because it is said in the name of the church. But the church must always be under the judgment of the Word, the Bible. The church can become, and during the centuries it has often been, a synagogue of Satan. But I am here to hold before you the New Testament pattern: here we see the only true church.

Now what is this contrast to which I am referring? Let me illustrate this. I had the unfortunate, almost tragic, experience recently of listening to the story of a young minister, a young man in his first pastorate, who told me that he had been asked to resign by his deacons. When I asked him why this had happened, he told me the reasons that they had given him. One of them was that he still believed in prayer meetings and in holding a Bible exposition on a week night. They said that this was all wrong, and that he must come up to date. Prayer meetings, they said, were no longer contemporary. They asked him to leave the church because he still believed in prayer meetings!

Those deacons said they belonged to the church, yet the early church 'continued stedfastly . . . in prayers' – every day! This poor young man only had a prayer meeting one night a week, and because he was determined to hold on to it they asked him to go. 'Prayer meetings?' they said. 'The modern man doesn't understand them. They're old-fashioned, out-of-date. If you want week night meetings, let them be socials. Let there be something that appeals to modern people, not prayers or Bible exposition.'

Or take another way in which this account in Acts is in striking contrast to what is taught so often at the present time. We are constantly being told something like this: The greatest tragedy in the world is a divided church. We must come together. So don't start talking about doctrine, because if you do we shall be divided. But there is one thing we can do. We may not be able to agree about doctrine, but we can always pray together.' Is that not it? 'The thing to start with is prayer,' they say, 'because there we are all one.'

But according to this teaching, you cannot. That is putting prayer first, instead of last. That is starting with prayer, hoping that eventually you will arrive at agreement about doctrine. But in the early church they prayed together because they were agreed in the doctrine. The doctrine leads to the prayers. The modern idea entirely reverses the biblical teaching. And that is why it is failing and why it will always fail. If you depart from God's order in the Scripture, you will not be blessed. Here was the infant church, filled and thrilling with the power of the Spirit, and this is what she did. Men and women today in their cleverness, with modern ideas and organization, are reversing the order. They will not succeed. They cannot.

Prayer

And my last general remark is that, as we have seen with all the other characteristics of the church, prayer is a thorough test of our profession of Christianity. One of the dangers always besetting us is to be content with an intellectual belief. There are many people with an intellectual belief in Christianity who are not Christians. How do you tell whether or not men and women are true Christians? There is no better test than this: to look at the place of prayer in their lives. Someone may say, 'I believe this, that and the other' – how do you know whether that person is genuine? This is the test: Does it all come into practice in prayer?

Prayer is the best test of an individual and it is also the best test of a church. A church can be flourishing: she can be successful in terms of organizations, she can be tremendously active and appear to be prosperous; but if you want to know whether she is a real church or not, examine the amount of prayer that takes place. Prayer is the inevitable conclusion of a true doctrine. The first Christians started with the apostles' teaching, and it led to – prayer!

So I ask you this: How much do you pray? What evidence is there of prayer in your life? This is the way to discover where we are. It is easy to talk. It is, in a sense, easy to preach. Any preacher will tell you that it is easier to preach than it is to pray. But these converts, these early members of the Christian church, continued steadfastly in the prayers of the Christian community.

Let me go on to ask a second question: What does prayer mean? 'You're saying,' says someone, 'that one of the best tests of our faith is how much we pray, but what do you mean by prayer?'

That is a very good question and we are given the answer in the New Testament very plainly and clearly. First, let me tell you what prayer is not. Prayer does not just mean 'saying your prayers'. So many people get on their knees, hurry though a few phrases, and think they have prayed. Now I am not saying that you should not say the Lord's Prayer any more, but what I am saying is that you can get on your knees and rush through the Lord's Prayer and utter every word correctly without having prayed at all.

'Oh, yes,' says someone, 'I don't claim I'm a hundred per cent perfect, but I've always said my prayers, of course. In my very worst days I always said my prayers.'

'Said my prayers.' This phrase comes up constantly. I remember reading a man's account of his visit to a great city and he said he felt weary and tired. 'Then,' he said, 'I suddenly saw a cathedral. I turned into it and said a prayer and I felt better.' 'Said a prayer!' But that is not praying.

Then there are others who think that prayer means reading prayers – prayers from a liturgy, perhaps. I grant that it is possible to pray with printed, written prayers, but if you merely read them, that does not mean that you are praying. You can gallop through them and gabble them – that is not prayer. Merely to go through a form of words is not of necessity prayer; it depends how you do it. That can be as useless as just 'saying our prayers'.

Then there are others who seem to think that praying means that you just relax in a comfortable chair and start listening to God. But I want to show you that that is not prayer either.

So what is prayer? Well, it is shown to us very plainly in many places in this book. The people in Acts did not come together to read written prayers, they did not have any. No, they were filled with the Spirit, and they prayed extempore and they prayed willingly, freely, one after another. The difficulty was to keep order among them.

There are some illustrations in the book of Acts itself which tell us very plainly the meaning of prayer. Let me take you to one example in the fourth chapter. The apostles Peter and John had been arrested and arraigned before the court. The court had decided this time to set them at liberty, but on condition that they did no more preaching and performed no more miracles in the name of Jesus Christ. This was very serious. The authorities were deciding to exterminate the Christian church. These Jewish leaders were trying to put an end to the Christian church almost before she was born. She has always had to fight and here she was fighting for her very life.

So what did the first believers do? Well, we are told that, 'Being let go, they [Peter and John] went to their own company, and reported all that the chief priests and elders had said unto them. And when they' – that is to say, the church – 'heard that' – what did they do? – 'they lifted up their voice to God with one accord, and said . . .' (*Acts* 4:23–24). In other words, they prayed.

What is prayer? Listen:

Prayer

Lord, thou art God, which hast made heaven, and earth, and the sea, and all that in them is: who by the mouth of thy servant David hast said, Why did the heathen rage, and the people imagine vain things? The kings of the earth stood up, and the rulers were gathered together against the Lord, and against his Christ. For of a truth against thy holy child Jesus, whom thou hast anointed, both Herod, and Pontius Pilate, with the Gentiles, and the people of Israel, were gathered together, for to do whatsoever thy hand and thy counsel determined before to be done. And now, Lord, behold their threatenings: and grant unto thy servants, that with all boldness they may speak thy word, by stretching forth thine hand to heal; and that signs and wonders may be done by the name of thy holy child Jesus (Acts 4:24–30).

That is prayer!

The apostle Paul gives us another wonderful definition of what prayer means in his epistle to the Philippians: 'Be careful [over-anxious] for nothing; but in every thing by prayer and supplication with thanksgiving let your requests be made known unto God. And the peace of God, which passeth all understanding, shall keep your hearts and minds through Christ Jesus' (*Phil.* 4:6–7). And, again, we read in Hebrews:

Having therefore, brethren, boldness to enter into the holiest by the blood of Jesus, by a new and living way, which he hath consecrated for us, through the veil, that is to say, his flesh; and having an high priest over the house of God; let us draw near with a true heart in full assurance of faith, having our hearts sprinkled from an evil conscience, and our bodies washed with pure water (Heb. 10:19–23).

And what follows next? 'Let us hold fast the profession of our faith without wavering' – that is, to the apostles' teaching!

What a subject prayer is! People talk so lightly and glibly about it. They say, 'There are great fundamental doctrinal differences between Roman Catholics and Protestants, but we can at least pray together.' Can we? Do you know what prayer means? The writer to the Hebrews says that it means 'to enter into the holiest'. He was writing to Jews who had become Christians and he was using an illustration out of their Old Testament Scriptures concerning the old way in which they had worshipped. The children of Israel had a tabernacle and later a temple and these buildings were divided into different areas. There was a large outer court-yard which anybody was allowed to enter, including the Gentiles, then there was a court where Jewish women could go. Further in, there was a special courtyard for Jewish men, and then a court-yard where only priests could go to offer sacrifices. Inside the temple building was 'the holy place', which priests alone were allowed to enter to burn incense. Finally, there was a veil, and on the other side of that curtain was the place that was called 'the holiest of all'. Into that only one man was ever allowed to go, and then only once a year, and that man was the great high priest him-self. He alone went in there. Why? It was because God dwelt there. It was where God met the people.

And prayer means that you and I go into the presence of God, and that we have communion with God. We do not just go on our knees and offer up some pious hopes and fears and aspirations and our own thoughts. No, we are going to have communion with the living God! We are entering into his very presence. The first thing about prayer is that we realize that.

Then, as those New Testament prayers that I quoted to you illus-trate so plainly, when we pray we do not immediately start with our problem or what we want or need. No, we start by worship-ping God and by adoring him. Take the Lord's Prayer – how perfectly that puts it. 'Our Father which art in heaven, hallowed be thy name. Thy kingdom come. Thy will be done on earth, as it is in heaven.' This is adoration! This is worship! This is praise! Watch our Lord, the Son of God, praying, and listen to him. This is how he prays: 'Holy Father' (*John* 17:11)! This is not 'saying a prayer', not just 'offering a prayer'. No, no! 'Holy Father'! This is what prayer means.

And it is exactly the same thing in that passage from Acts 4. Here are people in dire straits and yet this is how they pray: 'Lord, thou art God, which hast made heaven, and earth, and the sea, and all that in them is.'

Then there is thanksgiving. If we realize who God is and what he has done, thanksgiving will have a very prominent part in our prayer. How often have you thanked God? How often have you thanked him for life? How often have you thanked him for health and strength, for food and clothing and all the blessings of this life? This is prayer. Thanksgiving!

And then you come to your supplication. You do not start here. You are not self-centred. You are not just wanting something from God. Oh no! You realize the greatness and the glory and the privilege – the everlasting God is listening to you! You are having fellowship. So you end with your requests and your petitions; you, 'Let your requests be made known unto God' (*Phil.* 4:6). That is prayer.

And you do all that with confidence and assurance. The author of Hebrews writes, 'Having therefore, brethren, boldness' – assurance, confidence – 'to enter into the holiest by the blood of Jesus . . . Let us draw near . . . in full assurance of faith' (*Heb.* 10:19, 22). You do not kneel down and wonder whether there is a God and whether you have a right to pray and whether he is listening, and spend the time arguing with yourself and your doubt. No, you go 'with boldness' into the holiest 'by the blood of Jesus', and you go 'in full assurance of faith'. That is what these people were doing. We see it in chapter 4, but they had been doing it ever since they were converted on the day of Pentecost. This and this alone is prayer.

But let me ask another question. Why did they pray like this? And this is where the test that I have mentioned comes in so clearly. Why did they not just go on listening to the teaching and the preaching of the apostles? Why not go on enjoying the fellowship and have the Communion service? Why pray? Here is a test of where you and I are. We may be brought up in a church and in religion. We may have been made church members at a given age – I do not care how. You may have been christened when a child, baptized when you were older, but that does not make you a Christian. No, here is the test: Do you realize the need of prayer?

Why did they pray? It was because they realized their need. When people become Christians – I have already shown you this – they are humbled. That is what had happened to these people when they were 'pricked in their hearts'. Before that point, they had stood in confidence. The crowd is always confident – 'Away with him! Crucify him!' They knew all about it. But under this preaching, they were brought low and saw what fools they had been. How blind! How ignorant! How dull! Pitting their little minds against God, crucifying the very Son of God himself and the Saviour of the world. They realized that they knew nothing. They were humbled, and no one can be a Christian without being humbled. 'Except ye be converted, and become as little children,' said our Lord, 'ye shall not enter into the kingdom of heaven' (*Matt.* 18:3). Listen to him in his beatitudes: 'Blessed are the poor in spirit' (*Matt.* 5:3).

That humility is the exact opposite of modern self-confident men and women who stand on their own feet and know what they are doing. They do not pray. Why not? They do not need any help – they can do it all themselves! That is why prayer is such a test of our profession of Christianity. When people are born again they realize their ignorance and are afraid of it. They realize their own unworthiness, their own uncleanness. We read, again in Hebrews, 'Seeing then that we have a great high priest, that is passed into the heavens, Jesus the Son of God, let us hold fast our profession [of faith]. For we have not an high priest which cannot be touched with the feeling of our infirmities; but was in all points tempted like as we are, yet without sin. Let us therefore come boldly unto the throne of grace' – what for? He answers – 'that we may *obtain mercy*, and find grace to help in time of need' (*Heb.* 4:14–16).

Christians realize their need of mercy and forgiveness. They know that they are sinners, that they are failures; they feel unclean. They know themselves as nobody else can. It is only Christians who know themselves, all the others are fooling themselves. They think they know, but what do they know? What do you know about life? What do you know about yourself? What do you know about God? What do you know about death? What do you know about eternity? You know nothing! We are ignorant, but it is only the Christian who comes to see that.

'I don't like your doctrine,' says someone. ' "Vile and full of sin I am." – I'm not! I don't say that when I go and look for a new job. I'm all right. I'm not perfect, but I'm all right.'

Are you? Oh, if you feel you are all right, you do not pray. But these people had been brought to see their desperate need of mercy and forgiveness and cleansing.

Another reason why the first Christians prayed was that they realized their need for help and strength: 'Grace to help in time of need' (*Heb.* 4:16). When they are young, non-Christians often think they can waltz through life. But this is impossible, even they discover that. They soon begin to tire and then to limp and then they need all sorts of crutches, spiritual and moral, to help them, and still they fail. Life is a tremendous business and it is a battle: the world, the flesh and the devil are all against us. It is not easy to keep straight and to keep pure and clean in this world. The hoardings, the papers, the television screen, all shout enticements. Books and all the clever people are against us, and oh, life is hard! We realize our own weakness and helplessness and our need 'to find grace to help in time of need'.

That is why these early Christians prayed. That is why Christians always pray. They realize that apart from God, they are undone. Christ said, 'Without me ye can do nothing' (*John* 15:5). And the men and women who have become Christians realize that. They know how they are defeated so constantly. 'What a lie that is!' we say to ourselves, until we become Christians. We do not face our own failures. We are not honest, we are liars, we 'cook the books'. But when we become Christians we face the facts and the truth. We know we need to be washed, to be cleansed, to be purified, to be renewed, to be given strength and power. We need someone greater than ourselves to hold us by the hand, to lead us on and to empower us to do the things that we are called upon to do in spite of all these obstacles and enemies.

But I have kept back to the end my greatest reason for praying. It is that anyone who has ever had any knowledge at all of God likes to talk to him. The little child likes to talk to his father. You like to talk to people who have been good to you and whom you love. And Christians, who are people who have discovered all that God in his love has done for them, like to talk to him, and like to keep in touch with him. That is our phrase, is it not? We 'keep in touch' with important people, with those who can benefit us, with those we like. Multiply that by infinity, and that is why Christians like to pray. And so they say:

> *A sovereign Protector I have,*
>   *Unseen, yet for ever at hand,*
> *Unchangeably faithful to save,*
>   *Almighty to rule and command.*
> *He smiles, and my comforts abound;*
>   *His grace like the dew shall descend,*
> *And walls of salvation surround*
>   *The soul He delights to defend.*

Inspirer and Hearer of prayer,
  Thou Shepherd and Guardian of Thine,
My all to Thy covenant care
  I sleeping and waking resign.
If Thou art my Shield and my Sun,
  The night is no darkness to me;
And, fast as my moments roll on,
  They bring me but nearer to Thee.

Augustus Toplady

So Christians draw near to God in prayer. These are the expressions used in the Bible about praying – 'drawing near to God', 'approaching God', 'entering into his presence'. 'Nearer, my God, to Thee, nearer to Thee!' wrote S. F. Adams. And that is what Christians desire. So they pray.

Do you pray? The test of Christianity is not the ability to talk cleverly, it is not being able to give your opinions on politics and the latest newspaper headlines. No, no! The test is: Do you hunger and thirst for him? Do you want to know him? Are you seeking his face because he is God, the 'Inspirer and Hearer of prayer'?

Someone may say, 'That sounds wonderful, but I don't know anything about it. I've never done that, and I would like to. How can I pray? How can anyone pray?'

That is a most important question, and that is why I have been saying that all this modern talk which says, 'We can at least pray together' – as if prayer were the easiest thing in the world – is so wrong. Prayer is the most difficult thing in the world. We need instruction, and, thank God, the apostles' teaching gives us the instruction. That is why you must start with the apostles' teaching.

There is also very good teaching about prayer in the Old Testament. Have you sometimes wondered what is the point of all those details about the construction of the tabernacle and the temple, all those measurements, all those descriptions of the curtains and the decorations, all the information about the burnt offerings and the meal offerings and the sacrifices? There is a simple answer. It was to teach people how to approach God. That is all. By means of the ceremonies and the symbols they were taught how to get into contact with God and how to maintain that

ontact. They were travelling through a wilderness, and in a
wilderness it is important to have your eyes on him and know
him, and know that he is with you. So here they were taught how
to pray. That is the meaning of the Old Testament ritual.

And it teaches us the very thing I have already mentioned, that
God has to be approached in a certain, given manner. Job knew
the problem: 'Oh that I knew where I might find him!' (*Job* 23:3).
Have you ever felt that? If you have not, you know nothing about
Christianity. To know God! To be able to take myself and all my
problems to him, knowing that he is there and that he is listening.
How can one pray? Here is the problem of the centuries, and the
problem is inevitable, is it not? It is because of the holiness of God!
'God is not a man,' says Numbers 23:19. It is difficult enough to
approach certain people in this world, and the greater they are, the
more difficult it is to get an audience with them. But oh, here we
are approaching the everlasting and eternal God! 'God is light,
and in him is no darkness at all' (*1 John* 1:5). We are going into the
holiest of all, where everything is light and purity and glory.

God's holiness and glory were depicted in that old ceremonial.
In that holiest of all there was what was called the *shekinah glory*.
There was a kind of light, an indescribable light, that never was on
land nor sea. What was it? It was the hem of God's garment, it was
some effulgence of the eternal glory. The *shekinah*! 'There shall no
man see me, and live,' said God to Moses (*Exod.* 33:20), but that is
just a reflection. That is where you are going to pray!

> *Immortal, invisible, God only wise,*
> *In light inaccessible hid from our eyes,*
> *Most blessed, most glorious, the Ancient of Days,*
> *Pavilioned in splendour and girded with praise.*
> Walter Chalmers Smith

Have you ever thought of yourself standing before God? This is
where the problem of prayer arises. You do not rush in and 'say a
prayer'. You do not say, 'At least we can pray.' Prayer means
going into his presence. But, 'Who shall ascend into the hill of the
Lord? or who shall stand in his holy place?' (*Psa.* 24:3). The
trouble with most people is that they have never seen the problem
involved in prayer. They do not even see the difficulties.

And then, having realized something about God, we realize all this truth about ourselves – our sinfulness, our uncleanness. David realized it. He was in trouble. He had committed terrible sins. But he turned back to God. He could not go anywhere else. This is what proves that David was a child of God. He had committed adultery and then murder but he had to go back to God, for nobody else could help him. He was in an agony of soul. He did not know what to do with himself. He knew that God was the only one who could help him. But how could he go to God? He said, 'Thou desirest truth in the inward parts' (*Psa.* 51:6). He knew that he was unclean. 'I was shapen in iniquity,' he said, 'and in sin did my mother conceive me' (*Psa.* 51:5). How can such creatures pray to God? Not only the sins we have committed, but our inherent vileness and rottenness make us unfit to pray. That is why people sin. The cause of the trouble is not the evil things outside, but the corruption within that responds to the evil, that desires it, and is pleased by it.

So what do I need when I pray? God is in his heaven, and in all his everlasting glory, and here am I on earth, small, finite, vanishing, feeble, lacking understanding, perverted, polluted – a vile foul creature! How can I approach God? Job gives his answer, 'Neither is there any daysman betwixt us' (*Job* 9:33). Oh, that there were somebody who could come between us, and take my hand and his hand and bring us together! A 'daysman'! Or, to use the New Testament term, we need a mediator. If we could only find somebody who could, at one and the same time, understand us and sympathize with us and yet be capable of standing in God's holy presence and know him also.

Or look at it in another way. Here am I on earth and God is in heaven: Is there a way from earth to heaven? Is there a way from man to God? Is there a way from sin to holiness? I consult the maps of the universe and the philosophers; they do not know. 'Canst thou by searching find out God?' (*Job* 11:7) 'The world by wisdom knew not God' (*1 Cor.* 1:21). There is no way; it is a blank, a wilderness. I can never find God. I am cast back in utter defeat and despair. I can but cry out:

Eternal Light! Eternal Light!
How pure the soul must be,

Prayer

When, placed within Thy searching sight,
It shrinks not, but with calm delight
  Can live and look on Thee.

The spirits that surround Thy throne
  May bear the burning bliss;
But that is surely theirs alone,
Since they have never, never known
  A fallen world like this.

O how shall I, whose native sphere
  Is dark, whose mind is dim,
Before the Ineffable appear,
And on my naked spirit bear
  The uncreated beam?

Thomas Binney

How can I? I cannot! I am left. I shrivel to nothing, eternally in punishment because of my sin and iniquity and vileness. That is what is involved in prayer. When you realize who God is and what you are, you realize that left to yourself prayer is utterly impossible.

But my privilege is to tell you that there is a solution to the problem, there is an answer to all our questions: 'Having therefore, brethren, boldness to enter into the holiest by the blood of Jesus, by a new and living way, which he hath consecrated for us, through the veil, that is to say, his flesh' (*Heb*. 10:19). We are living in an age of new motorways, direct routes, and the message of the gospel is that there is a new road, a 'new and living way' which has been planned by God and made and opened by the Son of God. It is a road, a wonderful road. It has a solid foundation. It will last for all eternity. And it is made of – what? It is made of the broken body of the Son of God. There is the road, that is its foundation – 'through the veil, that is to say, his flesh'.

That is the whole message of the New Testament. That is what Peter preached on the day of Pentecost – that the Jesus whom they had hounded to death is none other than the Christ of God. They had crucified their own Saviour and Redeemer! 'But,' Peter said in effect, 'you did it in ignorance. Nevertheless, in spite of you, God was making a way from human beings to himself, from earth to heaven, from sin to salvation.'

There is only one way whereby we can ever enter into the presence of God and that is through Jesus Christ and him crucified. 'Through him,' says Paul to the Ephesians, 'we both have access by one Spirit unto the Father' (*Eph.* 2:18). You cannot find God by yourself. And these people in Acts had discovered this. The apostles' doctrine, the apostles' teaching, had taught them this very thing. He is the daysman that Job had longed for. Paul says, 'There is one God, and one mediator between God and men, the man Christ Jesus; who gave himself a ransom for all' (*1 Tim.* 2:5-6).

That is how those first believers prayed, and that is how anybody can pray. But you cannot do it unless you believe the teaching. You do not just come to God, you go 'through Christ', 'for the sake of Christ', 'in the name of Christ'. I have already quoted the first part of Thomas Binney's great hymn. Now let him complete his own statement:

> *There is a way for man to rise*
> *To that sublime abode;*
> *An offering and a sacrifice,*
> *A Holy Spirit's energies,*
> *An Advocate with God.*
>
> *These, these prepare us for the sight*
> *Of holiness above;*
> *The sons of ignorance and night*
> *May dwell in the eternal light*
> *Through the eternal love!*

That is the way to pray. It is the only way to pray. We pray in the name of Christ, knowing that he has died for us, and is risen, pleading at the right hand of God for us, an 'advocate with the Father' (*1 John* 2:1). So when you get on your knees you go with boldness into the holiest of all. The devil will say, 'Who are you? Remember you did this. Remember you thought that. Remember that sin of forty years ago.' He will hurl it at you. But you can stand and face him and say, through the Lord Jesus Christ:

Prayer

Be Thou my shield and hiding-place
That, sheltered near Thy side,
I may my fierce accuser face,
And tell him Thou hast died.
Philip Doddridge

And that silences even the devil and all the accusing voices of conscience and of hell.

Just as you are, you can go into the holiest of all by the blood of Jesus, and you can worship and adore the glorious Father. You can thank him for his grace in Christ. You can thank him for opening your eyes, for giving you a new life, for washing away your sins, for strength and power, and for the 'blessed hope' that awaits you in the glory everlasting. And the moment you believe and see these things, why, you want to go on doing this. So, 'They continued stedfastly' – day by day – 'in the apostles' doctrine and fellowship [of the apostles and the others], and in breaking of bread, and in prayers.'

13

Gladness

And they, continuing daily with one accord in the temple, and breaking bread from house to house, did eat their meat with gladness and singleness of heart, praising God, and having favour with all the people. And the Lord added to the church daily such as should be saved (Acts 2:46–47).

People often forget that it is an old world in which we live. They talk as if the world had only come into being in this century, and as if men and women were some new creatures with new powers and faculties and new problems. All that, of course, is sheer nonsense. Humanity is very old indeed, and the great story of civilization, the history of the human race, is, in a sense, nothing but the story of the endeavours of men and women to solve their problems. Nobody has ever wanted to be miserable. People have always sought for happiness. They have done everything possible to find it. The inventiveness and the genius of the human race have almost been exhausted in this effort to find peace and rest and happiness and joy. This great quest has sometimes been called 'the quest for the quiet heart'. But today, perhaps more than ever before, it is evident that the quest has not led to a successful outcome. People of the world are still searching and asking: How can we find happiness? And the answer is still eluding them.

Gladness

But the early Christians knew that they had found happiness. Seeing the truth and believing it, they had left the world and joined the church. We have been considering aspects of the life of the early church, and now I want to show you this further characteristic – gladness and rejoicing. 'They did eat their meat with gladness and singleness of heart, praising God . . .' I would reiterate that I am holding before you the picture of the early church not merely that we may have a correct view of Christianity and of the church, but more importantly, that we may test ourselves. The question we ask ourselves in all these instances is: Am I like that?

So now we come to this extraordinary description of these Christians in Acts – gladness! Praise of God! Joy has always been a characteristic of the church in every period of reformation and revival. The Roman Catholic Church, whatever you may think of her, recognizes this. Its theologians have tests which they apply to any man or women whose name has been proposed for canon–ization, and one of the marks that they look for is joy. Someone may have been very learned, but that is not enough. There must have been this element of rejoicing and gladness in a person's life before he or she can be made a saint.

But this again is something that does not feature in the average person's idea of the church. The Christian faith is regarded as something that spoils life. People's notion of Christianity is that it is nothing but a kind of moral striving and effort and endeavour. The Christian church, they say, is always against everything. It is always protesting. It is against drink; it is against smoking; it is against war. If you listen to the church, they say, you always find she is negative. Christianity puts forward a philosophy which gets us to 'scorn delights and live laborious days'. The average person's notion is that Christians live narrow, cramped, miserable little lives, mainly characterized by what they do *not* do, that they are people who just know enough about God to make them miserable, people who seem to find no enjoyment whatsoever in what they do. Christianity has put some kind of a brake upon their lives. It stands between them and a full, free, joyous and happy life.

Why do most adolescents turn against Christianity? Is not this the simple answer? They say, 'When I was a child, I was compelled to go to Sunday School. Now I'm grown up, no more of that!' They are going out to enjoy themselves, to live life with a capital 'L', a life of freedom and emancipation, of true happiness.

The idea has become current that with a stern, iron will Christians force themselves to fulfil duties which they believe to be somehow right, and they are afraid, perhaps, if they do not do them, and so they trudge wearily through this world, missing so much. That is why people are outside the church. They have turned their backs upon it, claiming to have found happiness in doing so.

And that, again, is the exact opposite of what we find here in Acts. Here is the account of the early church: 'They . . . did eat their meat with gladness and singleness of heart, praising God, and having favour with all the people.' And that is the picture given of the Christian church throughout the whole of the New Testament. I defy you to find anywhere a more joyful letter than Paul's epistle to the Philippians. The apostle cannot contain himself. At the beginning of chapter 3 he writes, 'Rejoice in the Lord,' and he repeats that exhortation in chapter 4: 'Rejoice in the Lord alway: and again I say, Rejoice.' This is Christianity, and that was the life of the early Christians.

I have often said that Acts is a most stimulating and exhilarating book. You can feel this joy pulsing through the life of the people. It is one of the happiest books in the world. The apostle Peter later wrote to a number of Christian people whom he did not even know. They were 'strangers scattered throughout Pontus, Galatia, Cappadocia, Asia, and Bithynia' (1 Pet. 1:1). Writing of their relationship to the Lord Jesus Christ, he says, 'Whom having not seen, ye love; in whom, though now ye see him not, yet believing, ye rejoice with joy unspeakable and full of glory' (1 Pet. 1:9).That is the authentic picture. That is how it began and that is the characteristic of the church in all times of reformation and revival. This dull institution with which we have become familiar, which is called in on great state occasions, this is not the New Testament church. It is a travesty of the truth to think of Christianity as a grievous task and heavy burden, leading to a mournful, apologetic way of life. Indeed, I want to try to show you that there is nothing else in the world that can really make us happy and give us joy but this message.

Gladness

Let us look, then, at the nature of the joy and the gladness which these people had. Again, it is something that is dealt with many times in the New Testament; this is where we find what Christianity really is. Do you think that Christianity would ever have turned the world upside-down if it were as negative as people represent it? Of course not! What conquered the ancient world was this joy, this gladness, this verve, this indestructible quality in the life of these people, and this is the greatest need in the world today.

As we look at the nature of this joy, we must be careful. The modern world is abusing most of the things that are sacred; it is even abusing language. The world has never talked more about love than it does today, but it does not know anything about it. So often, what it calls love is lust! People who pass through the divorce courts say that they have 'fallen in love', but they have never opened their eyes upon love. They are completely ignorant of it. All these glorious terms are abased and abused.

So we must be careful when we talk about joy and gladness. The world thinks it is expert in this subject, does it not? Can you not see it shouting at you on the television? What a wonderful life this is! Look at the cheeriness of the pub! Look at the happiness, the abandon and freedom, and the jokes about the church. So we must define our terms, and they are defined here for us.

Now when we come to talk about 'gladness and singleness of heart' as we find it here, we must take it in its context. This is what we read: 'They continued stedfastly in the apostles' doctrine and fellowship, and in breaking of bread, and in prayers.' Then: 'And fear came upon every soul: and many wonders and signs were done by the apostles.' So in defining joy and gladness we must remember that other element – fear. What fear? Oh, the fear of God! The Holy Spirit had descended, the mighty power of God had been made manifest, and when men and women feel just a touch of the power of God, they are filled with fear.

There are many examples in the Bible of the fear of God. Once, the apostle Peter and some of the other disciples had been out fishing all night without catching anything. The next morning, our Lord said, 'Launch out into the deep, and let down your nets . . .' (*Luke* 5:4). And they did, and immediately they caught so many fish that their net broke. Then do you remember what happened?

Peter fell down before Jesus and said, 'Depart from me; for I am a sinful man, O Lord' (verse 8). Our Lord had not said a word to Peter. He had not reprimanded him. He had not condemned him for his sinful life. No, all he had done was work a miracle. He had manifested his divine power. And when you feel the touch of the power of God, when you feel awe before a holy God, you are alarmed and frightened, you feel so small.

Now this is something that is little known at the present time. I am reminded of the word of an old Puritan who lived three hundred years ago. He said, 'I never find myself in the presence of death but that I always bow my head in the presence of his majesty.' What a tremendous thing the touch of God is! The birth of a child; the death of a soul. God – the Maker and the Creator! When death comes, it is God acting. And have you not felt the awe, the presence of the power of God in a chamber of death?

And that is what people felt here in Jerusalem. The Holy Spirit had come down. These disciples were filled with power – the power of God. 'And fear came upon every soul' (Acts 2:43). Yes, but that is not inconsistent with joy and gladness. It is here that we have the secret of our definition of those words in a Christian sense. It is so different from the joy and the gladness that the world talks about.

The world's so-called joy and gladness is artificial. It is synthetic. It is not true. That is the trouble with that joy. And thank God for opening our eyes to see through it. What does the joy of the world depend upon? Well, it always depends upon some sort of make-believe. It is artificial, an artefact. The world cannot find joy without drugs of some sort. That is why all the drinking goes on – for many people it is the only way they can be happy. You must get your higher centres knocked out before you can be happy, says the world. It does not put it like that, but that is its philosophy. People who cannot be happy unless they drink are confessing that they are miserable souls. Drink! Drugs! Society life! Expensive clothes! Dinners! Entertainment! All this has to be kept going, and you know the amount of money that is being spent. People object to paying a little more for milk, but not for pleasure. We must have it! We are so miserable otherwise.

And, of course, the result of that is that the world's happiness is superficial. It is only something that enables you to forget your troubles for the moment – simply some kind of soporific, as it were, a tranquillizer. It takes the edge off your anxiety, but does not take it away.

Yet the world lives on this pleasure-seeking, pouring money out on it, keeping it going. And it always has an excess, a kind of riot, about it. The element of fear is never there. That is why the apostle Paul says in Ephesians 5:18: 'Be not drunk with wine, wherein is excess' – which means riot – 'but be filled with the Spirit.' He is contrasting two forms of joy. The joy of the world, he says, has a lack of control, a wildness about it, which you regret afterwards.

But, of course, the final trouble about the joy that the world has to give is that it is invariably dependent upon circumstances. This is what reveals to us the real tragedy of life without Christ and without the Christian message. I am almost alarmed when I meet certain people because they appear to be so happy. I have known them, husband and wife, living a life of happiness together, but the joy has been entirely dependent upon their relationship to one another and not to Christ. And I have known that if one partner is taken, the other will be left devastated and desolate. Even at its very best and highest, the joy that the world gives is a contingent joy.

And so much of the joy of the world vanishes if you do not have money. If you cannot afford to buy your pleasures, then you have no pleasure, and you are not happy. You sit sulking in a corner, envious of those who are enjoying themselves and wishing that you were. But joy that demands health and wealth and the presence of other people is not real joy. Analyse it, and I think you will have to agree.

But Christian joy is a deep joy, a pure and a holy joy. The Bible calls it 'joy in the Holy Ghost' (*Rom*. 14:17). This is a joy that includes the element of fear. The world, of course, says that you cannot mix fear and joy. But you can. This is the only true joy. There is a control; there is a depth; there is a holiness. It is a joy that comes from God. It is a part, a foretaste, of the very glory of God and of heaven which he shares with those who are in Christ Jesus.

I have reminded you that the apostle Peter talks of a joy which is 'unspeakable and full of glory'. He means that it is such a wonderful joy that language is inadequate to describe it. Do you know anything about a joy that is so amazing that you cannot find words to express it? That is the joy which these people had, a joy that is full of glory, and unalloyed purity.

Furthermore, this joy is independent of circumstances. As we have seen, it is easy to be happy when the sun is shining and everything is going well, when we have our pockets full of money and our family around us. That is marvellous! But what if we lost it all, where would we be then? And when you have lost your money, the world can be cruel and cold. It does not want you. The world only wants cheerful people. When you need its help most of all, it has nothing to give you, and it turns its back upon you. The only joy worth talking about, the joy that we should surely be seeking, is the joy which is independent of circumstances. That is what was so wonderful about this joy that these first Christians had. After they became Christians, they were persecuted and mal-treated, but they still had this joy.

In the book of Acts there are some wonderful pictures of this joy in the midst of persecution. Let me give you just one of them. The apostle Paul and a companion of his called Silas visited that very town of Philippi to which the apostle later wrote that joyful letter from which I have quoted. When Paul and Silas arrived in Philippi, they preached the gospel by the river, at a place where people were in the habit of meeting to pray. A poor demon-possessed girl who, we are told, 'had a spirit of divination', began to follow Paul and Silas, calling out, 'These men are the servants of the most high God, which shew unto us the way of salvation' (*Acts* 16:17). This went on for many days. So Paul and Silas cast the evil spirit out of the girl. Her masters, who had made money out of her, therefore went to the authorities and said that Paul and Silas were law-breakers who were turning everything upside-down. So the magistrates arrested them. Though Paul and Silas were perfectly innocent, and had not even had a trial, they were scourged, that is, their backs were beaten with whips and with cords, and scarified – a most painful punishment. Then they were thrown into the very innermost prison and their feet were fastened in the stocks.

What effect did that have upon Paul and Silas? This is what we are told: 'And at midnight Paul and Silas prayed, and sang praises unto God: and the prisoners heard them' (verse 25). Something remarkable was happening in that prison. Two lots of people were there: Paul and Silas, servants of Christ, members of the church, and the prisoners, the unbelievers, the godless, the men of the world who were in prison, cursing fate, unable to sleep at night, even at midnight, because they were so unhappy, wondering how they had ever got there and how they could get out. They were typical of those who have no joy apart from that which the world supplies.

But here, in the midst of such adversity, Paul and Silas were singing praises to God, 'and the prisoners heard them,' and they were amazed, and so was the keeper of the prison. This is a joy that is not dependent upon circumstances. Why, says the apostle Paul to the Romans, 'We . . . rejoice in hope of the glory of God. And not only so, but we glory in tribulations also' (*Rom.* 5:2–3). When everything goes against us, we are still rejoicing.

Later, when he was again in prison, Paul wrote to those Philippians, 'I have learned, in whatsoever state I am, therewith to be content. I know both how to be abased, and I know how to abound . . . I can do all things through Christ which strengtheneth me' (*Phil.* 4:11–13). He knew what it was to be on trial, with people saying, 'We'll come and stand by you,' only to disappear at the critical moment (see 2 Timothy 4:16–17). He stood, and went on rejoicing – rejoicing in tribulations! His joy was independent of circumstances. Everything could go against him but he still went on rejoicing.

Now that alone is true joy. We shall all eventually be in a position in which most of the things on which we rely in this world will be taken away from us. Here is the great test of life: How will you stand up to loss and calamity? How will you face death? Can you rejoice then? The world, of course, cannot meet the test; it cannot face it. On their deathbeds people do not call for drink; they do not want that funny programme on the radio. When you are bereaved and sorrowing, you do not turn to things like that, do you? Of course not – they mock you. And your boon companions, where are they? They are of no value to you. It is a terrible thing when a soul is left alone, going out of life and out of the world alone, absolutely alone. Can you rejoice then? Will you know gladness in that position? Here is the test. Now these people did. This is what Christianity offers. This is the nature of its joy and gladness.

So what is the explanation of such joy and gladness? Can we all obtain this? The message is – we can. We must just do what these people did. They 'gladly received his word' (verse 41) – the preaching of Peter. When they cried to him, saying, 'Men and brethren, what shall we do?', Peter said to them, 'Repent, and be baptized every one of you in the name of Jesus Christ for the remission of sins, and ye shall receive the gift of the Holy Ghost. That is all you have to do. You must realize that the so-called joy and gladness of the world is a wretched counterfeit – tinsel. That realization is repentance. You confess that to God, and you go to him and ask him for mercy and pardon and forgiveness. Though you are unworthy of it, you believe his word of love. You embrace it and cast yourself upon it. These people did that and that is the explanation of their wonderful joy and happiness.

The secret – and I suppose, if you look at these things from the standpoint of thought and philosophy, that is the best way to put it – is to understand that happiness is the consequence of something else. The world makes the very great mistake of putting happiness as its goal, and therefore it never finds it. Happiness is never meant to be a goal. Our Lord put it in one memorable phrase: 'Blessed [happy] are they which do hunger and thirst' – not after happiness but – 'after righteousness: for they shall be filled' (*Matt.* 5:6).

Why, then, were these three thousand people so happy? It was because they had heard Peter's sermon and had believed it. And it was because day by day they had listened to the apostles' teaching and had known fellowship, breaking of bread and prayer. This is the experience of every Christian. Christians are glad and rejoicing because of the deliverance that they have received from what they once were. They have been delivered from appalling ignorance about God and about themselves.

Still more vital, Christians have been delivered from danger. Those first Christians were 'pricked in their heart'. They had suddenly seen themselves under the wrath of God. They had seen that men and women are not animals but are creatures made in the image and likeness of God, that they are responsible beings who will have to stand before their Maker and give an account of the life lived in the body in this world. They had seen that nothing was facing them but a hell of misery and wretchedness and suffering, everlasting destruction from the presence of God. As they had listened to Peter, they had felt it. They had seen the enormity of their rejection of Christ and they wondered whether they could ever be forgiven. But now they had found that they could be delivered from condemnation and from the wrath to come.

And anyone who knows anything about that is happy. Such a person is like a man who has been suffering from some incurable disease and has gone the rounds of all the doctors but is still going from bad to worse and is at the point of despair. Suddenly he reads in a paper one morning that a drug has been discovered that can cure his illness, and he gets it and he is cured. Need I tell you that that man is happy, that he is glad, that he rejoices? Of course he does!

Or the new Christian is like a drowning man in the ocean who has exhausted all his efforts. He sees the end has come and he has abandoned himself in his utter hopelessness. Suddenly a hand from somewhere grips him and pulls him out. Can you imagine that man's feelings when he is lying in the boat of this friend who suddenly appeared and rescued him?

Multiply both of these by infinity and that is the gladness and the joy of a person who becomes a Christian. Oh, what the Christian has been delivered from!

But look at these new Christians in the present – they find themselves in a new life – and how different it is! They have new life in them. You cannot explain life, you just know you have it. They know they are new men and women. They know that God is their Father. They now have a new understanding of the whole of life. And we have already looked at something of what that means. Nothing is more wonderful than to be delivered from dependence upon the world and its ways. Have you seen people, even in some of the highest and greatest professions, ready to cut one another's throats, filled with jealousy and envy? This attitude is to be found throughout industry. It is in the professions. It is in the highest academic circles. What a wretched miserable life it is, this 'rat race', as it is rightly called – such people are a race of rats.

It is glorious to be delivered from that worldly ambition, that hollow, worldly success. Success is all right, but if you live for it and make it the object of your life, it is wretched, it is slavery. But this new life delivers men and women from all that. Now they belong to a new society, and a new kingdom - the kingdom of the redeemed. 'Where the Spirit of the Lord is,' says the apostle Paul, 'there is liberty' (2 Cor. 3:17). They are free. They are independent of the world and circumstances and chance and accident.

And above all, Christians see the plan of God, the plan of the ages, the purposes of God at work in the world. They see the wholeness of life: 'They see life steadily, they see it whole.' And that is thrilling. 'This is the victory that overcometh the world, even our faith' (1 John 5:4).

But still more glorious and wonderful is the view which these people have of the future. Ah, here's the rub – the future. This is the problem of the human race, is it not? You may be so happy at this moment, but you never know what is going to happen tomorrow. There is always a fly in the ointment, is there not? Am I being depressing? No, I am being realistic.

But you say you are the one who is being realistic. Very well, let us accept that. Are you going to rest upon the joy you have now? But what if . . . ? What if! What may happen at any moment? You do not know. Think of the uncertainty of life – 'The slings and arrows of outrageous fortune'! Here is the trouble, and that is why men and women are not really happy. Everywhere there is a spirit of fear. 'What if another war is coming? What if all I have built up is going to be shattered? What if all my castles come crashing to the ground? What have I got then? Where am I?' Oh, there is no rest nor peace!

'Stop thinking,' says the world. 'Drug yourself in some shape or form. That is the only way to be happy.' But that is simply to fool yourself. Here we see people who have a gladness and a joy that enables them to face the future, no matter what may come. Christians do not expect too much of this world. They know that our Lord has said, 'In the world ye shall have tribulation' (John 16:33). And he said, 'Ye shall hear of wars and rumours of wars' (Matt. 24:6).

They know that this is an evil, sinful world, that while it is like that, it will be a place of unhappiness. All sorrow and death itself comes as the result of sin. Death would never have entered the world but for sin.

Gladness

So Christians do not expect too much. They are ready to meet life. They are prepared for every eventuality. They see the wholeness of life and know that they will never be left alone again. There is someone who will always be with them. There is one who has said, 'I will never leave thee, nor forsake thee' (*Heb.* 13:5). Never! So they are ready to face the remainder of their lives. They no longer depend upon the life of this world but upon the life of God in the soul.

And death? Well, it must come. But they are no longer afraid of it because they know that the sting has been taken out of it. 'The sting of death is sin; and the strength of sin is the law' (*1 Cor.* 15:56). That is why people are afraid of death. They have this awful feeling that the gospel may be true after all, and that after death there is a judgment. The law of God condemns us. That is the sting! But, says Paul, writing to the Corinthians, in that great chapter on the resurrection, 'O death, where is thy sting? O grave, where is thy victory? The sting of death is sin; and the strength of sin is the law. But thanks be to God, which giveth us the victory' (*1 Cor.* 15:55–57). Christ is risen! He has vanquished death and the grave! 'For to me to live is Christ, and to die is gain . . . having a desire to depart, and to be with Christ; which is far better' (*Phil.* 1:21, 23).

That is why these people in Acts were glad, that is why they were filled with a spirit of rejoicing. They saw through life, they saw through death, and beyond death. They had been given a glimpse of the glory that awaited them. The apostle Paul, writing to comfort the Romans, says, 'I reckon that the sufferings of this present time are not worthy to be compared with the glory which shall be revealed in us' (*Rom.* 8:18). Oh, this sight of glory! Or again, he says, 'Our conversation is in heaven; from whence also we look for the Saviour, the Lord Jesus Christ; who shall change our vile body, that it may be fashioned like unto his glorious body, according to the working whereby he is able even to subdue all things unto himself' (*Phil.* 3:20-21).

This is what fills men and women with gladness and joy and rejoicing. 'If our earthly house of this tabernacle were dissolved, we have a building of God, an house not made with hands, eternal in the heavens' (*2 Cor.* 5:1). Let the bombs fall, let war come, let disease and pestilence ravage the lands, let me die –

what is it? Translation! To be with him! This old body of mine, the body of my humiliation, the body of infirmity, the body of disease, the body of death, transfigured, changed, glorified, made like the body of Christ's resurrection, and I, in this new, glorified body, ushered into his blessed presence to spend my eternity with him. It is because they knew things like that that these people were filled with gladness.

That is what this gospel does. It enables you to say with the great apostle, 'I am persuaded, that neither death, nor life, nor angels, nor principalities, nor powers, nor things present, nor things to come, nor height, nor depth, nor any other creature, shall be able to separate us from the love of God, which is in Christ Jesus our Lord' (*Rom.* 8:38–39). My soul is in his keeping. I am a child of God, and the work that he has begun in me he will continue until the day of Christ. There is a glory awaiting us which nothing can destroy, let the world do its worst, let hell be let loose, let the evil one make his final fling – as he will. He cannot touch us, he cannot affect the children of God. He cannot do anything, finally, to those who have gladly received the word of this gospel.

That is it. Here is a view of life that is ready for everything, that can never be disappointed, can never be put to shame. It is the life of God in the soul! So I end with those ringing, glorious words, again of the apostle Paul, who, looking out upon the great problems and trials and tribulations of life was able to say:

Our light affliction, which is but for a moment, worketh for us a far more exceeding and eternal weight of glory; while we look not at the things which are seen, but at the things which are not seen: for the things which are seen are temporal; but the things which are not seen are eternal (2 Cor. 4:17–18).

Beloved friends, 'Set your affection on things above, not on things on the earth' (*Col.* 3:2), and then, like these first Christians, you will be filled with a spirit of gladness, and you will spend your days in praising the God who has delivered you out of the kingdom of darkness, and translated you into the kingdom of his dear Son.

14

Singleness of Heart

And they, continuing daily with one accord in the temple, and breaking bread from house to house, did eat their meat with gladness and singleness of heart, praising God, and having favour with all the people. And the Lord added to the church daily such as should be saved (Acts 2:46–47).

The central error of modern thinking, surely, is that today men and women imagine that they have the right to decide for themselves, anew and afresh, what Christianity is, what the church is, and what her message is. Now this is not only presumption, it is unutterable folly, because we are dealing here with something that is historical. Today is Palm Sunday. Why do people call it Palm Sunday? It is because it is connected with certain facts of history. The message of the gospel is not a philosophy, it is not just a teaching amid many other teachings. As we have seen, it is based upon facts: the fact of Palm Sunday, the fact that this person, Jesus of Nazareth, rode on the foal of an ass and the people crowded round him, shouting, 'Hosanna!' And then the fact of the trial and the scourging and the death upon the cross on Good Friday and the tomb, followed by the resurrection.

These are facts of history and the church came into being as the result. So if we really want to know what Christianity is and what the Christian church is, then in common honesty, there is, I repeat, only one thing to do, and that is to go back to the record.

So we have been considering the account in Acts 2 of these early Christians. The words and expressions used here were not chosen at random. They were inspired by the Holy Spirit himself. And we have here the marks and characteristics of the true Christian. The moment men and women become Christians, these are the ways in which they show it. And we come now to one of the most interesting: 'They did eat their meat', not only with gladness, but also 'with singleness of heart'.

This most important statement means, first and foremost, that these Jerusalem Christians were all of one mind, that they were experiencing a wonderful unity. 'Singleness of heart'! Their hearts, as it were, were melted into one another. It is a description, then, of the company, the society, of these believing people looked at in general. Our Lord had prayed that his disciples might be one, even as he and his Father were one (*John* 17:21), and here they were giving expression to this oneness. They had different temperaments, different backgrounds, different upbringings. They differed in almost every conceivable way, yet they were all melted into one in this extraordinary unity.

Now the New Testament constantly emphasizes that great truth. The apostle Paul was particularly proud of it. He was called to be the apostle to the Gentiles. Though he had been a narrow and rabid Jew in his old life, he now said, 'There is neither Greek nor Jew, circumcision nor uncircumcision, Barbarian, Scythian, bond nor free: but Christ is all and in all' (*Col.* 3:11). All are one in Christ Jesus, and it is amazing. The Christian church, when she functions truly as the church, is the greatest phenomenon that the world has ever known. It is the only thing that ever can unite people.

The world is disunited. We see groups and classes and divisions. But in the true church, all are one. 'Singleness of heart' – melted into one in Christ Jesus. This is astounding. Here, in Acts, we are given a picture of what the world will eventually be like when Christ comes back to reign, having conquered all his enemies, to set up his glorious kingdom. Singleness of heart! A day is coming when wars shall cease. But this will not be as the result of human organizations. They will never come to anything: 'Ye shall hear of wars and rumours of wars' (*Matt.* 24:6). Politicians and foolish idealists constantly claim that they will produce a state in which there will be no war. They never will. But Christ will put an end to war when he returns. He will reign from shore to shore, and there shall be 'peace . . . as a river' and 'righteousness as the waves of the sea' (*Isa.* 48:18) over the whole universe and cosmos. What we see here in Acts in embryo, will be world-wide.

But the question that arises is: Why were they thus manifesting this great unity? And the answer is that they showed this singleness of heart because each one of them separately had a single heart. Each one had been made a unit, had been unified. This is one of the most remarkable things about the gospel and it is one of the greatest characteristics of the Christian life. Our Lord said, 'The light of the body is the eye: if therefore thine eye be single, thy whole body shall be full of light. But if thine eye be evil, thy whole body shall be full of darkness' (*Matt.* 5:22–23). There is this same expression – 'if thine eye be single'. What does our Lord mean by that?

It is a great principle that when men and women believe the Christian gospel, the main effect it has upon them is to unify their life, to make them 'single'. Men and women apart from Christ and outside the life of God, have double vision. They do not see things properly. They do not see them unified. They do not see them steadily and as a whole. What Christianity does is get rid of the complications and produce an essential simplicity.

I can show you in general as well as in particular that the effect of Christianity is always to simplify, to make single. We see it in the history of the Christian church. Here is a lyrical picture of the church at the beginning. The believers went at first to the temple because they had been brought up to do so and it was available for them to have their meetings. But that was supplemented by their meeting together in one another's houses – 'breaking bread from house to house' – and we read in the epistles about 'the church that is in their [Priscilla and Aquila's] house' (*Rom.* 16:5), and so on. That is primitive Christianity. We, of course, inevitably tend to think of the church as some great institution with buildings and people dressed up in robes, and pomp and ceremony and processions. How different it has all become from what you find here in the second chapter of Acts.

How has the church ever developed into an institution? There is only one answer – people have done all that. They always make everything complicated. That is one of the tragedies of the hour, is it not? We have great problems, but in trying to solve them, we create fresh problems. Have you not noticed how government is becoming increasingly complicated? I am old enough to see the extraordinary development in complexity. Someone sets up one office, then has to set up another to look after that one, and another to look after the second, and so we get a bureaucracy and do not know where we are.

And that has happened in the life of the Christian church. The whole thing has become almost unrecognizable in terms of what we read in this second chapter of Acts. At the end of the Middle Ages, we see the Roman Catholic Church – such pomp and ceremony, with the Pope claiming political as well as religious power, and the Vatican becoming a state. True Christianity had almost become lost and the people simply went one to this priest and one to another. No one knew God, nobody had assurance of salvation. Everybody was relying upon payments of money for favours and blessings. The whole thing had become so involved and complicated that ordinary people had no idea what Christianity meant.

And then came the Protestant Reformation. What did that do? It went back to the New Testament, back to the Acts of the Apostles, and Christianity immediately became much simpler. And Puritanism took this further, saying that even the Reformation had not gone far enough, that it had carried too much of Rome with it. Puritanism asked: Where in the New Testament do you find all these other things? No, no, they must go. That was Puritanism purifying, making Christianity single. And the great Evangelical Awakening of two hundred years ago did exactly the same thing.

The gospel always gets rid of complications. It says that God's way is the way of singleness of heart, the single eye. Complications are man's doing; simplicity ever characterizes the true gospel.

But look at this in the case of the individual. The unbeliever's life is a complicated life. Sin always introduces complications. This is all to be seen in Genesis 3. What a delightful, simple life Adam and Eve were living before they fell and rebelled against God. The Garden of Eden was called Paradise. There was no need of government there. There was no need of all this great machinery to deal with problems and difficulties – they were non-existent.

When the man and woman lived life as they were meant to live it, in correspondence with God, it was essentially simple. But the moment they sinned, they were in trouble. They had sinned against God and now when they heard the voice of God, they had to run and hide. They did not know what to do. They could not face God. They needed protection. Already the complications had come.

Then, because of their sin, they were driven out of the Garden, and had to earn their bread by the sweat of their brow. We read about Cain starting to build cities. This was the beginning of civilization with all its complications. Sin makes life complicated and difficult because it divides up our lives into sections. We no longer have a unifying principle. Do you not see that in life today? Human beings are the most contradictory creatures on the face of the earth, on one side, brilliant in their achievements, and on the other, so often despicable in their living. Mastering the elements, they are unable to master themselves. They arrive at knowledge and understanding of great mysteries away up in the heavens, but often live like beasts and worse. What is the matter? There are warring elements and factions within them.

Now we have all found this out from experience. The apostle Paul expresses this problem perfectly in Romans 7 where he talks of this duality that is in us: 'To will is present with me; but how to perform that which is good I find not' (*Rom.* 7:18). 'For I delight in the law of God after the inward man: but I see another law in my members, warring against the law of my mind' (verses 22–23). That seventh chapter of Romans is the most profound psychological analysis of man without God and without Christ that has ever been written.

Paul says in effect, 'I am at least two "I's". There is an "I" that wants this; there is the other "I" that wants that.' And he seems to be outside both of them. He looks on at these warring elements in his personality and he does not know what to do, so he cries out in despair, 'O wretched man that I am! who shall deliver me?' (verse 24). Now that is the effect of sin – complications, divisions, warring elements. But the moment people believe the gospel, singleness comes in – 'singleness of heart'. Order is brought into the life. A principle is introduced which governs everything. Life is made whole.

The psalmist looked forward in prophecy and he, too, saw something of this. You will find it in Psalm 84:5. The King James Version renders these words: 'In whose heart are the ways of them' but a better translation is: 'In whose heart are ways'. When men and women become Christians, a 'way' is put into their lives. There is a unifying principle, a singleness enters and the complications begin to disappear. That is what happened to all these people in Acts 2.

This is something that is given to us by the Lord Jesus Christ. He came to do it. He said, 'I am come that they might have life, and that they might have it more abundantly' (*John* 10:10). 'As people are,' he said in effect, 'they are only existing. They do not know what life is. They are nothing but a conglomeration of factions. They do not know what it is to live. They do not have a unified view of life and a life which is itself unified. I have come that they might have it.'

So how does our Lord do this? How does the Christian life become simple and single? First of all, this principle is introduced into the mind. The first thing people discover when they become Christians is that there is only one thing that finally and ultimately matters, and that is their soul. Look at the world today. Look at the thinking people. Read the more intelligent journals and the books that come out dealing with the problems of society. I do not want to say a word against them, these are absolutely essential. Government and order are ordained of God. 'The powers that be are ordained of God' (*Rom.* 13:1). But let us make no mistake here: they were never ordained by God to solve the problem, but only to keep the problem within limits. And they cannot even do that. Today's problems can only be solved by the message of the gospel, which tells us that there is only one thing to examine, only one thing to investigate.

Now the trouble with people who are not Christians is that they begin to examine this problem piecemeal. One says, 'I must examine that.' Another says, 'No, it is this.' There they are, setting up commissions of enquiry, sub-committees and more sub-committees. But they never arrive even at an understanding of the problem, quite apart from a solution. And this is where the gospel is so different from every other teaching. It comes immediately to the centre and says, 'There is only one thing that matters, it is your soul.' I have often quoted that sentence of Shakespeare which is the perfect introduction to the gospel at this point:

> *The fault, dear Brutus, is not in our stars,*
> *But in ourselves, that we are underlings.*
> William Shakespeare: *Julius Caesar*

And what is it that is wrong in me? It is that I have not realized the soul. Here is the key and the centre of everything.

The story about our Lord in the house of Martha and Mary illustrates this well. We read that our Lord went to a village where *. . . a certain woman named Martha received him into her house. And she had a sister called Mary, which also sat at Jesus' feet, and heard his word. But Martha was cumbered about much serving, and came to him, and said, Lord, dost thou not care that my sister hath left me to serve alone? bid her therefore that she help me. And Jesus answered and said unto her . . .*

And here is the essence of the gospel and this is what he says to any troubled, unhappy, defeated soul:

Martha, Martha, thou art careful and troubled about many things: but one thing is needful: and Mary hath chosen that good part, which shall not be taken away from her (Luke 10:38–42).

'Martha,' our Lord said, in effect, 'the trouble with you is that you are distracted, you are trying to do this and that. You have invited me into your house, but now you are concerned about giving me a meal instead of listening to what I have to say. Martha, you are divided up. Mary has the single idea. One thing is needful, and one thing only.'

Our Lord was constantly saying this. Listen to him on another occasion: 'What shall it profit a man, if he shall gain the whole world, and lose his own soul?' (*Mark* 8:36). This is the tragedy of the twentieth century, the age of encyclopaedias. What knowledgeable people we are! How ignorant our forefathers were! They did not know what we know. Look at all our vast scientific knowledge, our learning, our books, and the lectures on the television and radio – what amazing people we are with all the information we possess!

Why do we fail, then? What is the matter with us? And that is the answer: What shall it profit a man if he gain the whole world of knowledge and wealth and everything else, and lose his own soul? Our Lord emphasized this from the beginning, there in the Sermon on the Mount. He says, 'Enter ye in at the strait gate: for wide is the gate, and broad is the way, that leadeth to destruction, and many there be which go in thereat' (*Matt.* 7:13).

Now there Jesus is not only talking about morals, but about thought also. If you want to know a 'single-eyed' life, if you want this essential simplicity that characterized Christianity, you must start with the mind and in this way you enter in at the narrow gate.

This means, in the first instance, that, as our Lord says, 'Except ye be converted, and become as little children, ye shall not enter into the kingdom of heaven' (*Matt.* 18:3). Or, as the apostle Paul puts it: 'Ye see your calling, brethren, how that not many wise men after the flesh, not many mighty, not many noble are called' (*1 Cor.* 1:26). If you want to learn how to live, says Christ, come to the strait – the narrow – gate. This means recognizing that nothing matters but the soul. Forget all your learning, all the lore of the centuries and all that you regard as wonderful will not help you. You can be brilliant in philosophy, wonderful in music and in art and in many other respects, but what is the condition of your soul?

And that is what happened to the people listening to Peter on the day of Pentecost. Oh, they had their interests and they talked about them, but as they listened to Peter they had come to the realization that there is only one thing that matters. They said, 'What does it matter what I think about the Roman government or about my wealth or learning? When I am on my deathbed, nothing will matter to me except God and myself and the relationship between us.' That is the way in which our Lord simplifies everything and produces this singleness of heart.

And this is still the truth. The world is busy with its learning but there is still only one fundamental question that we need to face, and it is: How can I stand before God? The world and its kingdoms are passing away: 'Change and decay in all around I see.' Every day I get a day older and I know that the time is inevitably coming when I shall be alone with God. So the gospel simplifies the problem, does it not? It tells us that all the teeming problems in the world have arisen directly because men and women have lost the face of God, and are sinners in his sight, and under condemnation. Do you know that it all comes to that? Alcoholics Anonymous meetings, marriage guidance councils – so many groups are being set up to deal with this and that problem, but if men and women were only right with God, we would not need one of them. All the problems would be solved because they all stem from this evil that is in humanity as a result of its wrong relationship to God. That is why the gospel talks about singleness of eye and singleness of heart – this great principle of unification.

Now these people in Acts had come to that. But, thank God, it does not stop at merely isolating the one question that matters. Christians have not only been given to see the one problem that confronts them, they have also found the one and only answer, and this is what, if I may say so, I rejoice in at times more than in anything else. Christians are people who are no longer seeking; they are people who have found. They are no longer swayed by different views and ideas and schools of thought. They are no longer waiting on tiptoe for a book that is to be published next week which they are assured by the publishers will be of great help. No, they say, 'I've got it. I've already found it.'

Christians have found the answer: it is in this one blessed person, Jesus Christ. There is no other answer. The seeking and the questing and the striving and the searching have come to an end. They know that Christ is the Son of God. He is the one who brings us to God. And we have already seen how Christ brings us to God by himself taking the punishment for the sin that separates us from a holy God.

Have you discovered this? Have you got singleness of mind, or are you still looking, searching, reading about other religions, reading about this or that latest cult? Come to Christ! Did he not say, 'I am the light of the world: he that followeth me shall not walk in darkness, but shall have the light of life' (*John* 8:12)? So, 'Repent, and be baptized in the name of the Lord Jesus Christ.' You will have an answer. You will have a singleness of mind and of understanding, and this knowledge will be a central controlling principle in your whole outlook upon life. What a wonderful thing it is to have a view of life that can take in all the contingencies, to have all your questions really answered, to have the singleness that comes to the mind of a believer in the Lord Jesus Christ.

But this same singleness affects the heart, also: 'With gladness and singleness of heart'. Here is an end to the old restlessness, and lack of peace. What a terrible thing that is. We have all known this, have we not? You remember that famous, often quoted statement of Augustine – and it can never be repeated too frequently – 'Thou hast made us for thyself, and our hearts are restless until they find their rest in thee'? The whole universe cannot satisfy us. We can have wealth in abundance, we can have possessions, and learning, they will not give peace and rest of heart. Listen to a hymn translated by John Wesley, a hymn by Tersteegen:

> Thou hidden Love of God, whose height,
>   Whose depth unfathomed, no man knows,
> I see from far Thy beauteous light,
>   Inly I sigh for Thy repose;
> My heart is pained, nor can it be
> At rest, till it finds rest in Thee.
>
> 'Tis mercy all, that Thou hast brought
>   My mind to seek her peace in Thee;
> Yet, while I seek but find Thee not,
>   No peace my wandering soul shall see;
> O when shall all my wanderings end,
> And all my steps to Thee-ward tend?

Gerhard Tersteegen

Have you not known something about that restlessness? The world cannot satisfy us. Why not? Because 'God has put eternity in the heart of man' (*Eccles.* 3:11, RV). Thank God, human beings are too big and too great to be satisfied by anything in this world. That is why those sociologists and others who say that people will be happy if they are given good houses, are insulting human nature. You cannot be satisfied with a house. Everyone deserves a decent house, but you can have a mansion and be miserable, and the heart is restless, longing, yearning for something that ever eludes it. The whole world is looking for the quiet heart, the rest, the peace that the world can neither give nor ever take away when it is truly given by Christ.

But when men and women come to Christ, the restlessness goes. Listen to Philip Doddridge expressing it from his own experience:

Singleness of Heart

Now rest, my long-divided heart,
Fixed on this blissful centre, rest:
With ashes who would grudge to part,
When called on angels' bread to feast?

Philip Doddridge

This is what had happened to these early Christians. It all went away – that old restlessness, that feeling that they wanted something else, that there is always a fly in the ointment, that there is no final satisfaction, no real peace. Now they were no longer divided within themselves as to what they ultimately wanted. Now they had peace because they had singleness of heart.

Our Lord has expounded that so fully in the Sermon on the Mount that I have nothing to do but to quote him. He said, 'Ye cannot serve God and mammon' (*Matt.* 6:24). That is the whole trouble with most people, with all people, indeed, who are not in Christ – the divided heart. They feel that they must serve God, and yet they want to serve mammon. And here they are worrying, saying: 'What shall we eat? or, What shall we drink? or, Wherewithal shall we be clothed? (*Matt.* 6:31). What will happen tomorrow?

So your heart is divided and distracted and you cannot sleep and you have to take more sleeping pills, and then you need a stimulus to enable you to live the next day. You are all divided. You are a mass of contradictions and you do not know what you want. You think you want to travel: you feel new sights and scenes are what you need. But you travel the universe and still your heart is as restless as it was before you left home. It is because the heart is lusting after various things. It is divided in itself. It does not know what it needs. So there is this conflict: God and mammon; heaven and earth; time and eternity. Which shall I live for? We do not know which is most important. All that is done away with in Christ.

Furthermore, the heart is restless and divided because of self. The ultimate cause of all this heart restlessness is self. I set myself up, and that means doing somebody else down. There is conflict, jealousy, envy, despising, hating, ambition, desire – what a terrible business it is! And then the heart is divided against itself. But the moment men and women come to Christ, they get a single heart. It all happens in Christ, and they are able to say:

Object of my first desire,
Jesus crucified for me.

Augustus Toplady

Charles Wesley says the same thing. Here was a man like ourselves who knew all about the restlessness and the division and the conflict and the seeking and the searching for a heart at rest and peace and a firm ground on which to place his feet. This went on for years but at last, in a very simple way, he just believed this message and was able to say:

Thou, O Christ, art all I want;
More than all in Thee I find.

Charles Wesley

And he meant what he said. It is all there. Everything is in Christ. There is nothing further that we can desire. He will satisfy your every need, whatever your need may be. In Christ we are 'Ransomed, healed, restored, forgiven'. He is with you in every respect and in every circumstance.

Once men and women really know Christ and his salvation, they are given a final satisfaction. Let the world rob them, or mock them, let the world spit upon them as it spat upon their Master, it makes no difference.

Man may trouble and distress me,
'Twill but drive me to Thy breast.
Life with trials hard may press me,
Heaven will bring me sweeter rest.

Francis Lyte

The world may rob them of everything, but Christ remains. So the apostle Paul was able to say, 'I am persuaded, that neither death, nor life, nor angels, nor principalities, nor powers, nor things present, nor things to come, nor height, nor depth, nor any other creature, shall be able to separate us from the love of God, which is in Christ Jesus our Lord' (*Rom.* 8:38–39).

Again, when he was an old man in prison in Rome, Paul heard a rumour that the emperor Nero had decided to put him to death at any time. How did Paul write about it all to the Philippians? He said: It's all right. Don't be worried about me, 'For to me to live is

Christ' (*Phil.* 1:21). Christ is life to me. He is as much life to me in this prison cell as he was when I was free, out and about, travelling across continents preaching his glorious gospel. 'To me to live is Christ, and to die is gain . . . having a desire to depart, and to be with Christ; which is far better' (*Phil.* 1:21,23). 'They did eat their meat with gladness and singleness of heart.' Christ was there in their thoughts and giving them full and complete satisfaction.

Finally, the need for singleness applies also in the realm of the will. What is our aim? What is our motive? What is our object and purpose in life? There are millions of people who are unhappy because they have the wrong aims to get on and cut great figures, to leave their names on the pages of history. But, 'Uneasy lies the head that wears the crown,' said Shakespeare. There is nothing that so troubles a man or woman as worldly ambition, muddle and confusion in the realm of motives and ideas.

But the moment someone believes in Christ, that person has singleness in the will as well as in the mind and heart. Each Christian has one great desire. It is, 'That I may know him, and the power of his resurrection, and the fellowship of his sufferings, being made conformable unto his death; if by any means I might attain unto the resurrection of the dead' (*Phil.* 3:10–11). That was the apostle Paul's sole ambition – 'That I may know him'. And anyone who knows anything about him gets consumed by this great passion.

Count Zinzendorf saw it. He said, 'I have one passion; it is he; it is he alone.' Oh, to know him who is life indeed, who so loved me that he came from heaven and suffered all that he suffered in this world, even the death on the cross, that I might live! Oh, that I might know him and live to his glory! Once you are imbued with this ambition, the whole of your life is revolutionized in that it becomes simple. Listen to Tersteegen again, as translated by John Wesley:

> *Is there as thing beneath the sun*
> *That strives with Thee my heart to share?*
> *Ah! tear it hence, and reign alone*
> *And govern every motion there;*
> *Then shall my heart from earth be free,*
> *When it has found its all in Thee.*

Gerhard Tersteegen

> *Take my will, and make it Thine,*
> *It shall be no longer mine.*
>
> Francis Ridley Havergal

That is the prayer of Christian men and women. They have singleness in the realm of the will. They have one idea, one desire, one motive, and that is to live to his praise who has died for them and opened the gateway of heaven to them. The whole of life becomes simple; the programme becomes a simple one. John Wesley said, 'I have become a man of one book,' and in a sense that is true of every Christian. Have you discovered that all the books in the world cannot help you unless you know this? This one aim will bring you to one book. It will bring you to one person, to one death, to one resurrection, to one hope, all in Christ Jesus. Here is the explanation of the singleness of heart of the Christian. This tells us why Christians are able to say,

> *O for a heart to praise my God,*
> *A heart from sin set free,*
> *A heart that always feels Thy blood*
> *So freely shed for me.*
>
> Charles Wesley

So there remains one question: Have you got this singleness in your mind, in your heart and in your will? The world knows nothing about it. The world is typified by Martha – cumbered, distracted, rushing about, fussing, and missing everything. The Lord of glory is there, and there she is, busy. He has not come to eat, he has come to teach. Come, have you sat at his feet as Mary did? Is this your prayer?

> *O that I could for ever sit*
> *Like Mary at the Master's feet.*
> *Be this my happy choice.*
> *My only care, delight and bliss*
> *My joy, my heaven on earth be this,*
> *To hear the Bridegroom's voice.*
>
> Charles Wesley

It really comes to that. Are you rushing about madly, intellectually, emotionally and in the realm of the will, seeking satisfactions which you never find, seeking knowledge you cannot attain to, divided and distracted and weary and tired? Listen to the invitation of this blessed gospel. Emulate the example of the people who 'gladly received the word' as preached on the day of Pentecost by the apostle Peter. Listen to the Lord's words spoken to Martha: 'One thing is needful', and one only.

So stop rushing about, stop reading, stop arguing. Take your seat with Mary at the Master's feet. Listen to him and he will say to you, 'Come unto me, all ye that labour and are heavy laden, and will give you rest. Take my yoke upon you, and learn of me . . . and ye shall find rest unto your souls' (*Matt.* 11:28–29).

15

Praising God

And they, continuing daily with one accord in the temple, and breaking bread from house to house, did eat their meat with gladness and singleness of heart, praising God, and having favour with all the people. And the Lord added to the church daily such as should be saved (Acts 2:46–47).

We come now to a further characteristic of the early Christians. They spent their time listening to the apostles' teaching, and in fellowship, in breaking of bread, in prayer, with rejoicing and gladness, all of one mind, with singleness of heart but, above everything else, in praising God. That is the church. That is Christianity. They did it every day. I am afraid it is true to say that many people who are in various churches today are paying their one annual visit to the church.[1] There is a record attendance on Easter Sunday. But these people met every day. Again we see how the Christian church, as the result of human faithlessness has turned itself into something that often bears no relationship to what we find in the New Testament. But we are not interested in Christendom, nor just in great institutions, with their pomp, ceremony and ritual and the coldness that so often accompanies that. That is not Christianity, that is pagan religion. Pagan religion is always sad; it is always solemn; it is always afraid. We are interested in the authentic thing – early Christianity, the sort of Christianity which has reappeared in every period of revival and

[1] This sermon was preached on Easter Sunday, 1965.

eformation. And the great characteristic of this kind of church is: praise of God.

Now to be a Christian means to know that my sins are forgiven, o know God as my Father, to have new life within me, no longer o be afraid of death, to look forward to the glory that awaits the hildren of God. And one of the best ways of testing whether or 10t I am truly a Christian is to ask: Do I praise God?

All the other tests we have looked at are important. Christians re very anxious to have the apostles' doctrine, and those who are 10t keen to understand the teaching of the Bible may be good, noral people, but they are not Christians. Yes, but it is possible for eople to be interested even in this teaching and not be Christians. They may be interested in the teaching of the Bible without it ever ouching their hearts. They can take it up as a hobby, and many 1ave done that. Many did that in the nineteenth century, and believe we are experiencing a reaction against that kind of ntellectual Christianity that never changed a life, and never rought happiness and joy and peace.

Then the early Christians continued steadfastly in the apostles' ellowship - the 'goodly fellowship of the apostles'. But the mere act that some may enjoy the fellowship of God's people does not of necessity prove that they are Christians. The devil can counterfeit most of these things. He has done so many a time. It is the same with attendance at the Communion service. There are eople who go to the Communion service, people who go to what hey call 'mass', and think that somehow that puts them right with God. But that is pure magic. The fact that they go to mass does not rove they are Christians. The fact that they take Communion in a non-conformist chapel does not prove they are Christians, either. Many people do it because it is the thing to do, and have never understood what it means.

The same is true even of prayer. And I will go further. I have emphasized gladness, but the devil can even counterfeit that. There are cults which can make people happy. It is true that Christian Science can make people happy. And, as I have often pointed out, whisky can do that also. The fact that a thing makes you happy does not prove it is right. There are drugs that can make you happy. So the mere fact that people can say they are now very happy, does not prove they are Christians.

No, there is only one thing that I know of that the devil cannot counterfeit. That is praising God. The devil never does that. Never! The devil has never made anyone praise God. He can counterfeit a belief in God, but that is very different. The apostle James tells us in his epistle, 'The devils also believe, and tremble' (*James* 2:19). Exactly. The devil persuades people that they believe in God. If it suits his purpose, he can transform himself into an angel of light and encourage people to believe in God and to be religious. He is doing that to large numbers today. He can give you a counterfeit intellectual interest in God and in God's people, a counterfeit interest in Communion services, a counterfeit interest in prayer, a counterfeit joy and gladness. But he has never made anybody praise God. Why? Because he hates God.

That is why praise of God is perhaps the ultimate test of any profession of the Christian faith. Are you praising God? I am not asking you whether you believe in him, or whether you try to worship him, or whether you try to say your prayers. I am not asking whether you make requests to God. I am asking you one thing only: Do you praise him? These people in Jerusalem did, and praise has always been the outstanding characteristic of the Christian church when she really has been functioning as the Christian church. A mournful Christianity is a contradiction in terms. God's people are meant to be praising people, and that is why we call our hymn books *Christian Praise*.

So if you have not praised God, there is only one reason for it: you are just not a Christian. Many people say they believe in God but they wish that there were no God. They are afraid of him, and try to get away from him, or they try to do just enough to please him and to placate him, to buy him off, as it were. But Christianity makes people praise God. These same people in Acts who, a short while earlier, were saying in alarm and terror, 'Men and brethren, what shall we do?' were now praising God. Why?

The first reason I find is this: They praised God because of the great change that had taken place in them, because of this wonderful thing that had happened to them. Here were people who may have been living a desperate kind of life, at any rate, it was a miserable life. They had been trying to get some kick out of the world's pleasures, but had always been fundamentally ill at ease and disturbed and insecure. But then they found themselves day by day in a company in which the Son of God was the centre. They were learning about him and they were amazed at themselves. It is not surprising that they were praising God. They were in a strange, new, wonderful company of people. They had never known anything like it before. Here they had found love: 'All that believed were together, and had all things common; and sold their possessions and goods.' Having come from a background dominated by rivalry and jealousy and spite, they came to a place where people were ready to sell their goods to help somebody who was in need. They were all one and there was an amazing spirit of love. They had never known anything like this. So they thanked God – it was inevitable.

The term that is used here in the Authorized (King James) Version is: 'The Lord added to the church daily such as *should be saved.*' It would be better translated, 'And the Lord added to the church daily such as *were being saved.*' That is why they were praising God – because they were saved. What does that mean? Well, as we have seen, it is important to look at this verb 'saved' in three different tenses.

The people were praising God because they *had been saved.* Peter had said, 'Save yourselves from this untoward generation' (verse 40), and it had happened to them. That means – and I am putting it a the very minimum – that their eyes had been opened, and they had been made aware of their ignorance and darkness. Up to that point, they had not realized the truth about themselves. They had never realized the danger they were in. They had been interested in business and in pleasures and enjoyment but had never thought about their souls. They had never faced the fact of death and of judgment. They had been living on the edge of a volcano and did not know that it might erupt at any moment. That is how men and women always live without God. But they had been awakened by the preaching of the apostle Peter and had been alarmed.

'What shall we do?' they had asked. And they had been given this blessed answer by the apostle Peter: 'Repent.' That is all you have to do. You have simply got to acknowledge and confess your ignorance and your sin against him and believe this message concerning his Son. That is what being baptized into him means. You submit yourself utterly, and believe that your sins are washed away because Christ died for them on the cross on Calvary's hill. So they had done that and they had a sense of peace with God. The burden was gone. Christ had borne the punishment and they were free. Thank God! So they praised him. They had been saved from the judgment of God and from everlasting perdition.

But next let us look at this in the present tense. Something was going on within them: they *were being saved*, a process had started in their hearts. They were having daily instruction, and the more they heard, the more they wondered at it and rejoiced in it. The teaching and the enlightenment made them aware of a new power working in them. They somehow now found that they no longer had a taste for the things that used to entrance them. They could see through them. They saw through the world and its gaudy pleasures. They saw that there was nothing there. They saw that the things that used to excite them made beasts of men and women, and they were amazed that they had once enjoyed them.

This was the new life and the Spirit working within them, delivering them, setting them free from the wiles of the devil and all the enfettering and enslaving influences of the world. They had had an entire change of outlook. They now saw themselves as pilgrims of eternity, as children of God, marching in the direction of their eternal home. What a transformation! So they praised God, and looked to the future.

What, then, was the meaning of this process through which they were passing, this gracious influence of the Holy Spirit, the teaching of these apostles? What was it all for? Why were they being delivered from the world, the flesh and the devil? And the answer is: they saw they were being prepared for the glory. This life is not the only life, and death and the grave are not the end, there is another life, a glorious life, the life into which the Son of God has gone. He had gone to prepare a place for them: 'In my Father's house,' he had said, 'are many mansions . . . I go to prepare a place for you' (*John* 14:2).

And they were getting ready for it. They wanted to be ready to enter into their inheritance. They had been saved, they were being saved, and they would finally be completely saved. These are the things that led them to praise God. And anybody who has ever experienced this change understands exactly how these people felt. Samuel Davies knew all about this:

Praising God

Great God of wonders! All Thy ways
Are matchless, God-like and divine,
But the fair glories of Thy grace
More God-like and unrivalled shine:
Who is a pardoning God like Thee?
Or who has grace so rich and free?

Samuel Davies

Secondly, they praised God still more as they realized increasingly that this wonderful change in them was entirely due to the grace and the mercy of God. This is the crucial test between religion and Christianity, between a pseudo-Christianity and the real Christianity. People who believe that they are Christians because they live good lives do not praise God, they praise themselves. And that is what so many people do. When they attend a place of worship, they take credit to themselves. They have done a good deed. They have put themselves right. It is *their* activity. But here were people who were praising God because they realized that this change in them was the result of God's action, and that it was entirely in spite of what they themselves had been.

In many ways, this is the great theme of the New Testament. Read the Gospels for yourselves and this is what you will find. Read how the angel Gabriel came to Mary and made the announcement to her that she was to bear this extraordinary child, this one who was to occupy the throne of David for ever and for ever. At first Mary did not understand, but when she did she visited her cousin Elizabeth. The moment she did so, the child in Elizabeth's womb was quickened and moved. Then Mary sang, 'My soul doth magnify the Lord, and my spirit hath rejoiced in God my Saviour' (*Luke* 1:46-47). That was her immediate reaction. Why? Because God had done this.

It was the same with Zacharias, the father of John the Baptist. He went into the temple one day to burn incense and, quite suddenly and unexpectedly, he was confronted by an angel who spoke to him and told him that his wife was to bear a child in her old age. Poor Zacharias, he could not believe this, and because of that he was punished by being struck dumb, and he remained dumb until after the child was born. And then, you remember, after the birth of the child, when they came to enquire about his name, Zacharias was still not able to speak, but he wrote down the name – and then suddenly his speech returned. What was the first thing he uttered? Here it is: 'Blessed be the Lord God of Israel; for he hath visited and redeemed his people' (*Luke* 1:68). He praised God for what God had done. It had been entirely of God.

So these early Christians praised God for the same reason that every true Christian praises God. Christians realize the truth about themselves. They are poor in spirit. They hunger and thirst after righteousness. They are sinners with no good in them. Not only that, they realize that they can do nothing about saving themselves. This is basic to the whole Christian position. Those who still think they can put themselves right with God are not Christians. They cannot be because if they can do it, why was there any need for God to send his Son from heaven? Why was there ever need for the death upon the cross and the resurrection? No, no, Christians see the truth of Paul's words:

You hath he quickened, who were dead in trespasses and sins: wherein in time past ye walked according to the course of this world, according to the prince of the power of the air, the spirit that now worketh in the children of disobedience: among whom also we all had our conversation in times past in the lusts of our flesh, fulfilling the desires of the flesh and of the mind; and were by nature the children of wrath, even as others (Eph. 2:1–3).

That is the Christian's confession. This is why Christians praise God. It is all of God from beginning to end. And they find themselves with peace in their hearts, with a knowledge of God, with a new life and a new strength and a new power and a new hope. How have they got this? The answer is: 'By grace are ye saved through faith; and that not of yourselves: it is the gift of God' (*Eph.* 2:8). It is God who, in his everlasting and eternal love, has looked down in pity and compassion upon this world.

Then, thirdly, they praised God because of the amazing way in which he had provided this great salvation for them. They had heard this in the preaching of the apostle Peter and the others whom they had heard speaking in their own languages. The crowd had gathered together to listen to Peter, you remember, because, they said, 'We do hear them speak in our tongues *the wonderful works of God*' (Acts 2:11). That is why Christians praise

God: they have had an insight into the wonderful character of the works of God. That is the great message of the Bible, is it not? God made the world. In the beginning God created the heavens and the earth and the sea and all that is in them. He said, 'Let there be light: and there was light' (*Gen*. 1:3) – wonderful!

Christians know God as the Creator, the Artificer and the Sustainer of everything that is. But that is only the beginning. They know all that great story of the Old Testament. They see God intervening in the life of fallen men and women, coming down to comfort Adam and Eve. They see God making a way of salvation, saving a family at the flood, calling a man named Abraham, turning him into a nation, working through him, revealing himself – the wonderful works of God.

But then they come on to the crucial matters, these very things about which the apostle Peter was preaching on the day of Pentecost. Oh, that I had the voice or the tongue of an angel to put these wonderful things before you! This is why they praised God. They had been told about this Jesus, Son of God, and all that he had done, how God the Father, though he loved his Son with an everlasting love, smote him, and punished him, for us. He died and was buried in a tomb, but God raised him from the dead. Then he ascended into heaven and took his seat at the right hand of God in the glory everlasting. The wonderful works of God!

And they heard that on this day of Pentecost he had sent down the Holy Spirit upon the infant church. That is why they praised God. But they also praised him because of what they knew God was still doing and was yet to do in this same Son of his love. They were beginning to learn about God's plan and purpose of redemption. They were being taught that the church is not just a gathering of those who have been redeemed by the precious blood of Christ. It is the beginning of a new kingdom – the kingdom of God. And it is to continue until all the full number of the elect shall be gathered in and Christ will come again and every eye shall see him. For Christ who has conquered death and the grave and has ascended into heaven will come back into the world and will complete the victory. He will gather his people unto himself and he will destroy the devil and sin and hell and everything that is opposed to God and he will set up his eternal kingdom of glory and of wonder. 'We look for new heavens and a new earth, wherein dwelleth righteousness' (2 *Pet.* 3:13). And God and Christ shall reign over all, and we, these people, these little, despised Christians, we shall be with him in the glory, reigning with him, judging with him.

They began to understand these things, and saw their part and their place in it all. So there was only one thing they could do – they must praise God. These are the wonderful words of God and those who begin to know anything about these things inevitably find themselves praising God.

Then, finally, these people were praising God day by day because, in what had happened and their understanding of how and why it had happened, they began to see something of the glorious being of God. God is worthy to be praised and God alone is worthy to be praised. 'Praise waiteth for thee, O God, in Sion' (*Psa.* 65:1) Read your book of Psalms. The psalmists praised God because of who and what he is. 'O God, who is like unto thee! (*Psa.* 71:19), this great God, glorious in holiness, terrible in power. The moment men and women begin to know something of God, they inevitably praise him and worship him and bow before him in adoration. The tragedy of the world is its ignorance of God. We talk about God. Oh, that we had but a glimpse of him and his everlasting and eternal glory!

These people had seen something of his glorious character and wisdom. Look at his plan of salvation. Who else would have thought of this? Who else would have devised such a plan? Here is the impossible problem: God is holy; man is sinful. How can God forgive and yet remain just and holy – how can it be done? Ask the Greek philosophers. They do not know. They cannot understand.

'But we preach Christ crucified,' said Paul, 'unto the Jews a stumblingblock, and unto the Greeks foolishness; but unto them which are called, both Jews and Greeks, Christ the power of God, and the wisdom of God' (1 *Cor.* 1:23–24). We say with Newman:

> *O loving wisdom of our God!*
> *When all was sin and shame,*
> *A second Adam to the fight*
> *And to the rescue came.*
>
> John Henry Newman

Praising God

Humanity has failed; God sent his Son. What a plan! Have you ever seen it? Have you ever looked into it – Christ, 'the power of God, and the wisdom of God'? It is only as we look at these wonderful works of God that we begin to understand the character and the being of God and, having looked at them, there is only one thing to say and it has been said for us by the apostle Paul: 'O the depth of the riches both of the wisdom and knowledge of God! how unsearchable are his judgments, and his ways past finding out!' (*Rom.* 11:33).

'Come,' says Charles Wesley:

> *Come, Almighty to deliver,*
>   *Let us all Thy grace receive:*
> *Suddenly return, and never,*
>   *Never more Thy temples leave:*
> *Thee we would be always blessing;*
>   *Serve Thee as Thy hosts above;*
> *Pray, and praise Thee without ceasing,*
>   *Glory in Thy perfect love.*
>
> *Finish, then, Thy new creation,*
>   *Pure and spotless let us be;*
> *Let us see Thy great salvation,*
>   *Perfectly restored in Thee;*
> *Changed from glory into glory,*
>   *Till in heaven we take our place,*
> *Till we cast our crowns before Thee,*
>   *Lost in wonder, love and praise!*

Charles Wesley

'Oh that men would praise the LORD for his goodness, and for his wonderful works to the children of men!' 'Let the redeemed of the LORD say so' (*Psa.* 107:8, 2). Have you said it? Are you praising God today, the God from whom all blessings flow? Are you praising him that he loved you so much that he sent his only Son to die for you on the cross, that he rose again to justify you, and that he is now interceding on your behalf? Do you believe it? Do you know it? If you do, you must praise him.

16

Rise Up and Walk

Then Peter said, Silver and gold have I none: but such as I have give I thee: In the name of Jesus Christ of Nazareth rise up and walk (Acts 3:6).

As we have seen, there is considerable confusion in the minds of men and women with respect to the message of the gospel, and that is the tragedy of tragedies. It is, of course, the masterpiece of the devil. As the Bible shows us from start to finish, the devil is the great antagonist of God. He has one ambition, one great idea, and that is to bring ruin into God's perfect creation. He did it at the beginning when God created the world, and he has been most assiduous in his efforts ever since the Son of God came into the world to bring in a new creation. Throughout the centuries, he has been busy doing everything he can to cause confusion with regard to the gospel.

The devil's supreme achievement is to bring this confusion into the church herself. It is not surprising that he confuses the world outside, we do not expect anything better there, but it is terrible that he should succeed with the church herself. And so, let me emphasize this again, perhaps the greatest of all needs in these days, is the need to know exactly what Christianity is and what the Christian church is. What is the message of the Christian gospel? That is what concerns us. Now in the first two chapters of Acts, we are given an account of how the church began, and at the end of chapter 2, we are given a detailed and positive description of the Christian church and her life. Here we see authentic Christianity and nothing else.

This book of Acts is a wonderful book. I have often said that it is the most thrilling, the most exhilarating, book in the world. Anatole France, an infidel French novelist, used to say that when he felt jaded and tired in Paris in the height of the season and at other times, he never went into the country to find refreshment, but into the eighteenth century. I understand that very well. I have often gone into the eighteenth century myself – to the Evangelical Awakening, the blessing of God in revival – but *the* place to go to is the book of the Acts of the Apostles. Here is the tonic, here is the place to get refreshment, where we feel the life of God pulsating in the early Christian church.

Now here in chapter 3, we are also told about the early church but in a different way. There, at the end of chapter 2, we are given a general description of the church; here, in chapter 3, it is put in the form of a picture. There we are given an analysis; here we see the church in operation.

We see what these people were enabled to do because they were the kind of people we have seen described in chapter 2. One of the glories of the book of Acts, as of so much of the Bible, is that it does not confine itself to didactic teaching. It tells stories, it gives examples and illustrations of all that it puts before us theoretically. It gives us the gospel in action, as something living and real. And that is what I am anxious to deal with now.

There is always the danger that we should think of Christianity as something abstract and intellectual. But though we must know the theory, and have the understanding, we must never forget that first and foremost the Christian faith deals with life and living, and is the most revolutionary power that the world has ever known. A dead church is a contradiction in terms. It is a dead something – call it what you like – but not a dead church. The church is life and it is power and it is vigour. All this is perfectly illustrated and exemplified for us in this story in Acts 3. Here is the church in action, the church facing the world. There they are, the first Christians. They have had this tremendous experience. The Holy Spirit has come upon them. They are filled with the Spirit and they are rejoicing, praying and praising God with singleness of heart. But now they face the world as it is – and this is the business of the church. That is why she is here: to help the world. The Lord came from heaven to help men and women. He came 'to seek and to save that which was lost' (*Luke* 19:10) and he has left the church behind him to continue the work. You remember how we made that point at the very beginning. Luke says, 'The former treatise have I made, O Theophilus, of all that Jesus *began* both to do and to teach' (*Acts* 1:1), and he is continuing that work. Now he is no longer here, but he is acting through his chosen servants.

Now here we see a poor man who had been born lame. He was about forty years of age, we are told in chapter 4, and he had never walked in his life. Every day he was carried to the Beautiful Gate of the temple, and there he would sit, asking alms, which means that he was a beggar. He would put his cap on the pavement by his side hoping that people would drop something in as they went into the temple to worship and to say their prayers. We are familiar with this kind of thing. We do not see as much of it as we used to, but throughout the centuries men of this type have always taken up their position outside Christian churches. You are more likely to get help from people who go to church than you are from anybody else and beggars have always known that. So his friends took this man, and put him there by the gate, and we see what happened to him.

Now this is a miracle. What is a miracle? It is necessary to ask that question today in this age that boasts of its scientific knowledge and refuses to believe in miracles. In a miracle, the laws of nature are not broken, but God acts above them. It is the same God acting in a miracle and in the ordinary natural way. God has so made the universe that normally things happen according to what we call 'the laws of nature', though it would be more accurate to say, 'the laws of God in nature'. So if you are ill, you are given treatment, and in time you gradually get better. That is all right, but it is always God who heals. If it is not God's will that you should be healed, you can have the best treatment in the world and you will not get well. God normally heals indirectly, by means of doctors and medicine, but he sometimes heals without them. He heals directly. God is not confined by his own laws. He has made them and if he chooses at times to act independently of them, why should he not? If you make an instrument, you can use it, but you are not bound to use it. Sometimes you can do the same thing without it.

When a miracle takes place, I repeat, it does not mean that the laws of nature are broken, so the scientist need not get anxious or be afraid. No, in a miracle, God in his almighty power is acting in a different way - not laying his laws aside but temporarily acting without them. Now that is what is meant by a miracle.

It is vital to understand that a miracle, by definition, cannot be explained in natural terms because believing people often talk of miracles in a very loose way. They turn everything into a miracle. I remember reading a book called *Ten Thousand Miles of Miracles in Great Britain*. The title was already wrong and it showed that the contents of the book were going to be wrong. You do not get as many miracles as that. This writer tried to say that everything that had happened to him was a miracle. I am therefore tempted to say that nothing that happened to him was a miracle. He may have experienced extraordinary happenings, but they were not miracles.

Why do miracles ever take place? Why did they take place in the time when our Lord was on earth, and also here in the book of Acts? And why have they taken place since then? The answer is that they are meant to be signs. The Gospel according to St John always refers to miracles as signs. They are meant to be demonstrations, proof of this almighty power. And so we find as we read the four Gospels that when our Lord worked a miracle, the people praised God or they were filled with fear because they sensed the power of God. I have always felt that the trouble with people who do not believe in miracles is that they really do not believe in God. They do not know the all-powerful God of the Bible. Their God is someone who is smaller than creation and confined to it, so do not ever argue with such people about miracles; argue with them about God.

So, then, we are confronted here by a miracle. But a miracle also serves another function. It is generally a kind of parable. It has a dual function. It actually is a fact of history, something that has taken place. Yes, but because it is also a sign, it is meant to teach us, to preach to us. It is meant to convey truth to us. And that is exactly what this particular miracle does. So, while we look at this extraordinary thing that was done here by Peter and John and know that it is a fact of history – indeed, the subsequent record proves that abundantly – we are interested in it primarily now as it shows us something of the nature of the Christian church, her business, what she should do in this world and what she can do.

Let us be clear. I accept the miracle exactly as it is, this literally happened, but, further, we must look at its teaching. Indeed, Peter himself, in his sermon that follows this, does explain it. But I am anxious now to take it as a picture of what the Christian church is here to do. So let us first of all look at this man laid there by the Beautiful Gate of the temple as a picture of humanity in a state of sin. The Bible itself does this. It often uses leprosy in both the Old Testament and the New as a very good illustration of what sin is. We are all helped by illustrations. People complain against theology and doctrine, and say they do not like too much reason in sermons, but prefer illustrations and stories. So I am doing that very thing! We have looked at the great doctrine and now let us just look at a picture.

Look at humanity as it is pictured here in the beggar outside the Beautiful Gate of the temple. What are we told? What is the truth about humanity in sin? It is essentially this: this man was born like that. He had never been any different. I do not stay with that, but the first great message of the Christian gospel is that every one of us is born in sin. We are not born innocent. We are not born free from sin. 'Behold, I was shapen in iniquity,' says David, 'and in sin did my mother conceive me' (*Psa.* 51:5). And it is astounding that anybody should dispute that.

Look at the world. Look at the way people behave. Look at how we ourselves have all behaved. What is the matter with that little child? What is it in him that makes him do the very thing you tell him not to do? Why is it that when a child first uses his own will, he is almost invariably disobedient? There is only one answer: we do not start with a clean slate, but we are inheritors of something from our forebears.

This is the first great postulate of the Bible: man and woman created perfect, rebelled and sinned, and all their progeny is born in sin. We see it in the pages of the Old Testament and equally clearly in secular history. It is the whole explanation of wars and troubles and jealousy and envy and malice and spite and all the teeming problems that have always crippled humanity in this world. Sin's effect upon us is to paralyse us. The Bible writers frequently say that sin is paralysis; it leads to helplessness. This beggar could not walk. He could do many other things – he could talk, he could argue about politics and about current affairs, he could hold out his hand – but he could not walk. That was the tragedy of his life. That was what rendered him useless.

And that beggar is a picture of the state of the whole of humanity. That is the presupposition of the gospel. The Son of God left heaven and came to earth precisely because men and women are lost, paralysed and helpless. As we have already seen, they are paralysed in the matter of knowing God. 'Canst thou by searching find out God?' (*Job* 11:7). People can find many things by searching, they can now take photographs on the surface of the moon, but they cannot find God.

They are equally paralysed in the matter of true living. What is life? Can men and women by nature live life in its fulness? Can they live life with enjoyment, with vigour, feeling that nothing is lacking? That is what life was meant to be. Adam and Eve were created perfect. In Paradise they lived a full life with nothing detracting from it. Can we by our own efforts find such a life? Are we really living or do we just exist?

Then another form in which we see the paralysis is this: man's total inability to conquer the devil and temptation and sin. Is there anybody who has never sinned? Can you meet temptation and always defeat it? Do you never do the same thing again, though you know it is wrong? Do you never repeat an action that always leads to misery? These questions are sufficient to bring out the truth, are they not? We are in the grip of some dread paralysis that holds us down and that cripples us. What we want to do we cannot do. This is the whole trouble, epitomized once and for ever in the seventh chapter of Paul's epistle to the Romans.

Then, beyond it all, we see our inability in our inability to die well. Every one has got to die but there is a way of dying that is glorious, that is magnificent, that is wonderful; and we cannot achieve that. Death is an awful spectre. Death to most people – to all people outside Christ – is hateful and ugly, something that they do not like to think about and they object to being reminded of it. And when they meet death, they do not know what to do. They are left, helpless, paralysed, unable to say with the apostle Paul, 'To me to live is Christ, and to die is gain' (*Phil.* 1:21).

The second thing that I find in the picture of the beggar is that the world is unable to help us. All it can do is give us alms. All the world could do for the beggar was to give him alms, and no more. Now this is the way to look at the message of the gospel. The world is full of activity. Look at it in every respect: political, social, educational, entertainment. It is full of people exerting themselves and using their abilities in every conceivable direction. But from the standpoint of humanity's real and ultimate need, that is nothing but the giving of alms. It really does not touch our vital problem. It does not help us at all.

Now the apostle Paul used to make this point. On one occasion we see him in Athens, the great mecca of the philosophers, the place of wisdom above every other place in the world. Athens – the home of philosophy, the home of brilliance, the home of man's flowering understanding. And here was this little apostle, a very able man himself, a man who could have met the philosophers on their own ground, but he did not do so. Why not? Well, in Acts 17 we can read the sermon in which he explained it to them, and he put the same thing in a single phrase in his epistle to the Corinthians where he says, 'The world by wisdom knew not God' (*1 Cor.* 1:21). Complete failure! All that Greece had to offer could not help anybody in the knowledge of God and of life and of living. Indeed, significantly, at the time of the New Testament, suicide was becoming increasingly common among these wise philosophers.

Now all this had already been explained in the Old Testament. Have you ever read the book of Ecclesiastes? It ought to be compulsory reading at a time like this when men and women boast so much of their knowledge and understanding. Here is the wise man, probably King Solomon, and he gives us a bit of autobiography. He says, 'I tried to find the answers to the meaning of life. I tried in every possible way. I tried in the form of wisdom, philosophy and learning. Then I tried in the form of pleasure. I tried by building great buildings and wonderful gardens and parks, and by providing entertainment and music, but I could not find it.' Again, that is another great presupposition underlying the gospel: the world at its best and highest can do nothing but give alms.

Rise Up and Walk

Let me explain what I mean. What the world can do, of course, is give us temporary relief. The world could not cure the man's lameness but it could give him a little money to buy food and to get a certain amount of pleasure. That is all the world does. With all its intellect, it cannot solve our problems. You can ransack the libraries of the world and, apart from this book and its message and books based upon it, you will get no help for your ultimate problem. You will get a lot of entertainment. We have all had entertainment from books, have we not? In a sense, a novel can help you because it so grips you that you forget your problems. Or you go to see a film, or you look at your television, and for a while you feel happy. Then you wake up to the fact that you still have your problem and you are exactly where you were.

Drink can have the same effect, as can many other pleasures. Thank God for great music, and the joy that we get from it. But the greatest music cannot solve the problem of life and of living. Even the men who wrote it still had their problems. Oh yes, these things give us alms. They assuage the anguish for a little while. They give temporary happiness. They enable me to forget my problem. I have something that I can get on with. But each time the activity finishes, I need more. I have not been satisfied. I am still paralysed. I cannot walk. And here it is all put before us in this picture at the beginning of Acts 3. When the world has given us everything it has to give us, the great fundamental problems are still left completely untouched.

The third thing I see about this man is that he expects the wrong things from the church. Peter and John were about to go into the temple when the man asked for alms. Then we read, 'And Peter, fastening his eyes upon him with John, said, 'Look on us. And he gave heed unto them, expecting to receive something of them.' That is where he was wrong, and that is the tragedy of this hour. The world is looking for something the church cannot give. This is the whole reason why I am preaching this entire series of sermons. There is such a false notion about the church and her message and her function that the world is paralysed, and the church, too, in a sense, is paralysed because it encourages this wrong notion – 'expecting to receive something of them'.

The world is expecting all sorts of things from the church. There are some who simply expect the church to give moral teaching, 'moral uplift', as it is called. In the nineteenth century, Dr Thomas Arnold, headmaster of Rugby, a well-known boys' school, proclaimed that the business of Christianity is to make good little gentlemen of us – 'morality tinged with emotion', was his definition. But that is not Christianity.

Then there are people who often go into great cathedrals, but what for? To hear good music. As if it is the business of the Christian church to provide good music! Others go to see the sculpture and the architecture, as if that, too, is the business of the church. You see how sadly astray we have gone.

Others go to church for philosophical teaching and learned disquisitions, as if the church's task were simply to entertain people's minds, to put up rival theories in a dispassionate manner. You must not be passionate, you must always be detached and wise and learned and controlled, and you put the ideas forward and evaluate them just a little! Is that the business of the Christian church? But that is what some people expect from her.

Then others, in increasing numbers, it seems to me, are looking to the Christian church for psychological treatment. I am not surprised. The world is in trouble and people are unhappy. Neuroses are on the increase and psychotherapy has not fulfilled its promises. I remember the beginning of the Freudian era when we were told that all our problems would be solved. But that has not happened, and we are having to resort to physical means and new drugs. The position is almost chaotic and people, including the medical profession, are saying, 'Can the church help us?' The government encourages co-operation between clergy and medical men – psychological treatment to make people better in their minds. There are many who think of the church as simply a place where you go to forget your troubles for a while. You sing hymns and choruses and the church applies psychological remedies, and so-called 'positive thinking'. It tells you to cheer up and assures you that things are never quite as bad as they appear to be because there is always a silver lining to the cloud if you can only see it, and then there are various cults that masquerade in the name of Christianity, as though it were the business of the church just to make people better for a while. I say that is 'giving alms'.

Others expect political pronouncements, and an agenda for political action and reform. The church must always be delivering opinions on the activities of statesmen, and laying down what should be done and protesting against this and that. Others think the church's task is purely a matter of social work and relief work. But that is what the world itself can do. That is what the world is doing. That is not the business of the church. I am not saying that these things do not come in, but I am saying they are not primary. And that is what Peter put so clearly, once and for ever, in this resounding, memorable phrase: 'Silver and gold have I none.' Do not look to me for that. That is not what we are here to provide.

Are you looking to the church for the right thing? What do you expect from the Christian church in this troubled state of the world? Is it any one of the things I have been mentioning? I say she is not here to do that. She is not competent to do it. Who am I to give an opinion and tell the statesmen of the world what to do? I do not even know all the facts. Like you, I have my opinion, but I would not insult you by putting my opinions before you. No, no, that is not my calling. That is not what I am here for. 'Silver and gold have I none.'

So what can the church do? Again, Peter tells us: 'Silver and gold have I none; but' – thank God for this blessed *but* – 'such as I have give I thee.' There is a story of one of the popes of Rome in the twelfth century showing, I think it was Thomas Aquinas, round St Peter's and the Vatican. As they walked around, the Pope pointed to the gold, the silver, the ornate buildings and the magnificence of it all, and said, 'You see, Thomas, the church can no longer say, "Silver and gold have I none."'

'I do see,' said Thomas, 'but I see something further. She also cannot say, "Rise up and walk."'

But that is the church's commission. 'Such as I have give I thee: In the name of Jesus Christ of Nazareth rise up and walk.'

The church is not here to talk politics, to play music, to give philosophical disquisitions, to produce art, or to provide social amelioration or psychological treatment. God forbid that anybody should be depending on my little ministry. Do you simply go to church to get temporary relief, to forget your troubles and feel happier for a moment? God have mercy upon you if you do! No, the business of the church is to deal with the *real* problem of men and women: not to give alms, but to offer a cure for the paralysis. This is the unique message of the church and this is what differentiates it from every other institution under the sun. The church is an expert on the soul. It is not a cultural centre or a psychological clinic or a social agency. No, her call, her commission, is to deal with the souls of men and women, with what causes their paralysis. Their trouble is not in the mind, nor in the heart nor anywhere else, primarily, but in the soul – that is, in the essence of their being, the centre of their life.

The trouble of men and women is their sinfulness. It is not lack of knowledge, there is plenty of that. They know theoretically that war is madness but that does not prevent their fighting. They know perfectly well that to drink too much alcohol is sheer lunacy, but they do it. Their trouble is this paralysis of the soul, that twist, that fatal thing that holds them down, that sends them astray. It is their estrangement from God. It is the violation of the law of their own being – that is the trouble.

The problem of the world today is the direct, immediate, central problem that men and women do not know God, and do not know how to live and do not know how to die. And this central problem leads to all the misery, the unhappiness, the failure, the shame, the remorse, the agony, the bitterness, and heartbreak of life. This is the problem. What is the value to you of scientific knowledge, if it does not help you to live? What is the point of being thrilled by great music, if it still leaves you a slave to sin? What is the value of admiring art and showing your great cultural understanding, if you cannot control your temper? The problem of the world is the problem of the souls of men and women, fallen, with the image of God defaced almost out of recognition. Human beings are almost worse than animals because the possibility of greatness is there in them. It is this contradiction, this paradox, that is humanity; greatness and smallness, achievement and failure, here is the essential problem.

And the church is here to tell you what you need to know above everything else, namely, how your soul can be redeemed and be put right with God; how you can be set upon your feet; how the paralysis can be cured. The church does not give you alms, it gives you a cure – a radical, a complete cure.

So how does the church do this? This is what I want to leave in your mind. Peter said, 'Silver and gold have I none; but such as I have give I thee' – then – 'In the name of Jesus Christ of Nazareth rise up and walk.' Here is the message: Jesus Christ of Nazareth. Our message is not culled from the philosophers nor from human wisdom. Peter talked of 'Jesus Christ of Nazareth' (3:16). *Jesus*: the babe born in Bethlehem, the man who lived and worked in Nazareth; *Christ*: the Messiah, the promised Deliverer, indeed God in the flesh, proved by the resurrection, proved by the descent of the Holy Spirit; *Jesus Christ*: God the Son come in the flesh. All the great apostolic teaching is summarized in these two words.

Yes, and *of Nazareth*: 'Can there any good thing come out of Nazareth?' asked Nathanael (*John* 1:46). The world had rejected him because it had despised him. It had said, 'Is it possible that the Saviour of the world can be just a carpenter, especially one who comes out of a place called Nazareth?' Peter rammed this home to them: *Nazareth*. The one despised is the Lord of glory and the Saviour of the world. He is the one, and it is all in him. 'Apart from him, we are nothing and nobody,' said Peter in effect. 'But in him we are tremendous. We are his agents. We are – as it were – almost his limbs. We are the body through which he is now acting.'

'In the name of Jesus Christ of Nazareth' – he is God, the Son, the eternal Son. He came into the world. He lived; he died; he rose again. What for? To bring redemption, to deal with the fundamental problem of the human soul, lost and estranged from God. That was what Peter said to this man. He said: Listen, I am here to put you in touch with him, this Jesus Christ of Nazareth. And, thank God, that is still our message. The Christ of God – Jesus of Nazareth – is alive. He is there in the heavens, seated at the right hand of God, saying to men and women in this world: 'All power is given unto me in heaven and in earth' (*Matt.* 28:18). Whatever your needs are, I am able, I am willing. He can give all that we need and infinitely more. He came into this world to deal with our radical problem, the paralysis of our souls. Like Peter, I cannot save you, but he can. He is filled with pity joined with power, and is looking down upon you. He knows all about your paralysis. That is why he came into this world and he is using me to tell you that he can do this for you.

Furthermore, what he does for us entirely transcends all our expectations. We come and we expect alms. This poor fellow, even when Peter and John had spoken to him, looked at them expecting to receive something. And what a surprise he got! He thought he was going to have some unusual present, perhaps. But what he got was something he had never imagined because he had lost hope. Everybody loses hope. He had been put down at the Beautiful Gate of the temple and the world could do nothing. Who were these two? They did not look anything. But in a few moments, look at him, walking, leaping, praising God, rushing into the temple and causing one of the greatest sensations that had perhaps ever been known in Jerusalem.

What does this mean for us? What we get in Christ is not merely temporary relief but a cure. Well, a cure for what? Here is my problem – we have already seen it – my guilt, my past sins rising before me, especially on my death bed. How can I meet God? I cannot. I am helpless. I am paralysed. But by dying on the cross Christ has dealt with it. God gives absolute forgiveness. If you believe on God's Son and his object in coming into this world, God assures you that he will never look at your sins again. He has punished them in him. He has borne them away once and for ever.

But he does not stop at forgiveness. We need life and he gives us life which is life indeed, life and life more abundantly. This is a gospel that offers regeneration, a new birth, a new start, a new beginning. It is a gospel that tells you that the Holy Spirit will take up his residence in you and give you power and strength and might. As Peter took hold of that man's hand and lifted him up, Christ was lifting him through Peter. And so we are told, 'Immediately his feet and ankle bones received strength. And he leaping up stood, and walked, and entered with them into the temple, walking, and leaping, and praising God.' Now that is exactly what Christianity does. It is not merely a hard task and a painful duty performed in the hope that God will forgive us. No, no, it is the knowledge of sins forgiven: walking, leaping, praising God. For the first time in his life this beggar was able to walk. The paralysis was gone. He was able to live a full life. That is the promise and the offer of the gospel.

Notice also the word 'immediately' – 'and immediately his feet and ankle bones received strength'. That is a vital part of the message. The message of the gospel does not tell you: Start doing this and that. Read your Bible and pray. Stop doing this and stop doing that. Come to church. Then after a while you will gradually make yourself a Christian. No, no – *immediately*, now, at once, without a second's delay. It is not something you have to do, it is Christ who does it: 'In the name of Jesus Christ of Nazareth rise up and walk.' That is a picture of justification by faith only.

> *If you tarry till you're better,*
> *You will never come at all.*
> Joseph Hart

> *Just as I am, without one plea.*
> Charlotte Elliott

That is the invitation. It is all of grace. It is the gift of God, the action of the risen Christ, and he has all power. He is a miracle-worker. He will give you his own life and he will do it now. He postulates nothing in you except that you see your need. He does not ask you to produce any works. He does not ask you to produce anything that can in any way recommend you to him. He says, 'They that are whole have no need of the physician, but they that are sick: I came not to call the righteous, but sinners to repentance' (*Mark* 2:17). Are you paralysed? Are you hopeless? Listen. He is life. He is power. He has everything to give you that you need and he will give it to you at once.

There is only one condition. We read, 'Peter, fastening his eyes upon him with John, said, Look on us.' This is, again, most important. This poor man had become so hopeless that he did not even look at the people who gave alms to him. Perhaps he had become a little bit cynical, so he put the cap there, and though these kind people dropped something in, he did not even trouble to look at them and to thank them. It had just become a habit to receive alms in that way. So Peter said to him, 'Look on us,' and he looked at them. In effect, Peter was saying to that man, 'My dear man, look at us. We are not ordinary men. We are not like most people who pass by you into the temple and have dropped something into your cap. Look at us. We are the apostles of Christ. We are new men in Christ Jesus, we are filled with the Holy Spirit. We are not just men, we are agents of the divine and the eternal. Concentrate on what I am saying.'

And I repeat that to you. If you would know the benefits of Christian salvation, you must pay attention. If you listen to this gospel with your own ideas in your mind, half listening and half not, half arguing against it, you will remain paralysed. You must give yourself utterly and absolutely to this. As long as you think you can do anything, you will remain paralysed. 'Look on us,' said Peter. And you must give undivided attention to the message of the Christian church. Forget everything else – this is all.

We need to become desperate. We must abandon everything and listen to this blessed knowledge, as the beggar did. 'He gave heed unto them.' This might be translated, 'He directed and held his mind towards them.' He was wrong and muddled still, but at any rate he did pay undivided attention to these extraordinary men.

And then came the liberating word. It is always like this. It happened to the great St Augustine himself. For all his great knowledge of philosophy, and his brilliant intellect, there was a moral sore, a failure, an unhappiness, and he was at the end of his tether. But the voice came, 'Rise and read!' And he did. He gave undivided attention and the liberating word came to him. Spiritually, Augustine rose up, and walked and continued to go on walking and leaping and praising God.

Now I am a very unworthy man. I have only one reason for being a preacher – it is that he has called me and put me here. I am the purveyor of his message. I have nothing else. It is his power, his command, and through me he is saying to you in your utter helplessness and your misery and hopelessness, perhaps your cynicism, perhaps your final despair, 'In the name of Jesus Christ of Nazareth rise up and walk.'

'Believe on the Lord Jesus Christ, and thou shalt be saved' (*Acts* 16:31). Amen.

17

The God of Abraham, Isaac and Jacob

And when Peter saw it, he answered unto the people, Ye men of Israel, why marvel ye at this? or why look ye so earnestly on us, as though by our own power or holiness we had made this man to walk? The God of Abraham, and of Isaac, and of Jacob, the God of our fathers, hath glorified his Son Jesus; whom ye delivered up, and denied him in the presence of Pilate, when he was determined to let him go. But ye denied the Holy One and the Just, and desired a murderer to be granted unto you; and killed the Prince of life, whom God hath raised from the dead; whereof we are witnesses. And his name through faith in his name hath made this man strong, whom ye see and know: yea, the faith which is by him hath given him this perfect soundness in the presence of you all, and now, brethren, I wot that through ignorance ye did it, as did also your rulers. But those things, which God before had shewed by the mouth of all his prophets,that Christ should suffer, he hath so fulfilled (Acts 3:12–18).

In our last study, we left the once-lame man going into the temple, healed, walking and leaping and praising God. Now this, of course, led to great excitement. The people knew who the man was and were amazed at what had happened. As the man held on to Peter and John, all the people ran towards them to Solomon's Porch in the outer court of the temple. When Peter saw this he began to preach to them, and then we are given the account of the sermon which goes on to the end of chapter 3.

We have considered the sermon preached by Peter on the day of Pentecost in Acts chapter 2, and now we are looking at his next sermon. These sermons are important for us because here we are face to face with the authentic Christian message and above everything else, as we have seen, this is what the world needs to-day.

The crowd had gathered and they wanted to know what had happened to the lame man. So Peter took advantage of the oppor-tunity, and told them about this new phenomenon that had come into being – the Christian church – and he explained its message. This is what is so wonderful about the Scriptures. We have the picture, the dramatic incident, and then we are given the explan-ation, a sermon, teaching. We need that, too.

First, I want to deal with the sermon in general. It is such a rich sermon, an amazing sermon. Of course, what we have here is the essence of the message. Undoubtedly, the total sermon was much longer. Here in Acts we are given synopses of the great sermons preached by the apostles at the beginning. So what is the teaching?

The first great principle, one that stands out on the very surface, is that Christianity is a phenomenon. It is not primarily, nor essen-tially, a teaching only. There is teaching here, that is what the sermon is, but Christianity is essentially something that happens, something that has happened, something that is happening, something that is going to happen. Again, I take you back to the first chapter of Acts: 'The former treatise have I made, O Theophilus, of all that Jesus began both to do and to teach, until the day in which he was taken up, after that he through the Holy Ghost had given commandments unto the apostles whom he had chosen.' I have already told you, says Luke, of all that he began to do. I am now going to tell you what he continued to do, and what he is yet going to do.

We see the crowd staring at the beggar, and they were 'filled with wonder and amazement' (verse 10). This is repeated in verse 11: 'All the people ran together unto them . . . greatly wondering'. We saw exactly the same thing in the second chapter, when the Holy Spirit descended upon the apostles and the others and they began to speak with other tongues. We are told that at the time devout people were gathered together in Jerusalem from different parts of the world and, 'They were all amazed and marvelled, saying to one another . . . And how hear we every man in our own tongue? . . . And they were all amazed, and were in doubt, saying to one another, What meaneth this?' (*Acts* 2:7–8, 12). That is what I mean by a phenomenon, that is how Christianity began, something happened.

Now this is the point which so many miss at the present time. This is one of the most grievous and fatal misunderstandings of the Christian message and the whole purpose of the Christian gospel. People are for ever reducing it to ethical or political teaching, or, perhaps still more serious, a kind of religious teaching; one of the great teachings which they put into a series with the so-called great world religions: Confucianism, Buddhism, Islam, and so on. Now those religions are nothing but teachings. They do not claim to be anything else. They are teachings with regard to how people should live, philosophies which take a religious form. And the danger is that people put the Christian faith into that category. They reduce it to a point of view, an attitude with regard to life. But here, at the very beginning, we are reminded that this is not true. Christianity is unique. It is historical. It is phenomenal. It is primarily something that is done, and then it is followed by the teaching which explains what it is that has happened. This is not only true of the New Testament, it is equally true of the Old Testament.

The Old Testament is primarily a book of history. It tells us of things that have happened. Look, for example, at the story of Moses in Exodus chapter 3. Moses had had to escape from Egypt and he had been in the land of Midian for forty years, earning his living as a shepherd. So there he was, guiding his sheep to fresh pasture over the mountains, and no doubt he was feeling quite hopeless. He had perhaps stopped thinking about his people in the land of Egypt, from whom he had had to flee. He had forgotten all about his great days when he had been brought up as the son of Pharaoh's daughter and all the glittering prizes that had dangled before him; all that was past history. Now he was just a shepherd tending his sheep like every other shepherd.

So on that day he took the sheep to 'the backside of the desert' (*Exod.* 3:1), near Mount Horeb, and suddenly he was arrested by God. He did not sit down, as it were, and read a book. It was not that he began to meditate and to ruminate about life, to try to see if he could draw up a plan of living and a philosophy of existence. Not at all! In the midst of a most ordinary vocation he was suddenly confronted by something. By what? A phenomenon, a burning bush, a bush burning and yet not being consumed, and he said, 'I will now turn aside, and see this great sight' (*Exod.* 3:3). He was about to investigate when the voice came. It was a meeting with God – a phenomenon.

We must get rid of this old notion that Christianity is a kind of theoretical teaching. This can never be said too frequently to an age like the present one that boasts of its intelligence and learning. Christianity is not a philosophy. Indeed, its greatest enemy is philosophy, whatever form it may chance to take, whether the formal philosophy of the university and the academy, or the pseudo-philosophy of the newspapers and the journals. Christianity is something that happens, something that confronts us, that is there facing us. That is why the people in Acts 3 came together. It was because of the event of the miracle, the man healed, as before, on the day of Pentecost, it had been because of the event of the baptism with the Holy Spirit and the strange results produced in the apostles and in others.

Has Christianity ever come to you as a phenomenon? If it has not, you know nothing about it. You can have a theoretical interest in Christianity, many people have. God forgive me, so had I for many years. I had a mere intellectual interest in it, and that can be very fascinating, but it is not the real thing. One becomes a true Christian when one is confronted by something which is a phenomenon, something arresting, something shaking, something inexplicable. So this is the first thing that strikes us at once, and of course this is the very essence of the message. The Christian church herself is a phenomenon that has baffled the ages and the centuries. She is baffling this present age. Why does she still exist at all? Why does she still continue when so many other institutions have come and gone?

The Christian faith is something that changes the lives of men and women. It produces saints. It is a series of phenomena. Read this book of Acts, read the history as far as it is known in the early centuries, and that is what you will find. There was something about these Christian people. Not only could nobody understand it, they could not put a stop to it either. The Jews tried to do so and so did the Romans. There were grievous persecutions so that the church was repeatedly driven underground, and yet she still went on. They murdered the Christians, they tried to murder all the leaders, but, as we are reminded, 'The blood of the martyrs was the seed of the church.'

In the early eighteenth century, conditions in Britain were, if anything, even worse than they are today, morally and religiously. You can read an account of this in a book called *England Before and After Wesley*. There was degradation and vice and sin. The book describes the gin shops in London where you could get drunk – if I remember rightly – for a ha'penny or a penny, and if you paid just a little extra you were given the straw as well on which to lie in your drunkenness and recover. Moreover, in that Hanoverian period devil worship was rampant. But then something happened, a phenomenon took place, a mighty revival, and the face of England was changed, as men and women were taken up out of the degradation of the gutters of life and were washed and cleansed and changed to become new men and women. You cannot explain the history either of the nineteenth or the twentieth centuries except in the light of that event. And it all happened through the Christian church.

That leads me to ask you a question: Have you ever been arrested by the Christian message as those people were in Jerusalem, or do you feel – to use the modern language – that you have got it taped, that you understand the whole thing? Have you been confronted by something that pulls you up? That is always the first step in becoming a Christian.

But now let us listen to what Peter said to all this. What was his reaction? He was the spokesman of God on this occasion. First of all, it is really interesting to notice what he did *not* say. I am sorry that there is such a grievous misunderstanding of Christianity that we have to start with a negative again. Some people might say that this would have been a wonderful opportunity for Peter to preach about miracles, to offer to heal others. One man has just been healed: 'Anybody else want to be healed? Come along.' He did not do that, though today that often passes as Christianity. People are offered physical healing, friendship, guidance, experiences of different kinds. But that is not Christianity. Christianity does do things like that, but it does not preach them, that is what the cults do. Indeed, that is precisely the very method of the cults. They come to you and say, 'What is your problem? How are you feeling? Come along, we can put you right.' Christianity has so often been turned into one of the cults. The church in her folly, because she wants to attract people, has presented herself in that guise. But that is not what Peter did and we must not do it.

No, Peter gave the explanation of the miracle. He dealt with what had happened and showed its significance. He did not, to use the modern language again, cash in on what had happened. He did the exact opposite. In effect, he said, 'You are marvelling and looking at us and I want to explain to you what has happened.' And my business now is just to expound the apostle's sermons. I am not preaching as someone on my own, I am preaching Peter's sermon.

This is how Peter began: 'Ye men of Israel, why marvel ye at this? or why look ye so earnestly on us, as though by our own power or holiness we had made this man to walk?' Now there, you see, Peter started with the wrong explanation of this phenomenon. He said in effect, 'I am amazed at the fact that you are surprised at this. Why do you marvel at it? You should not. If you understood things as you ought to, you would not be marvelling, still less would you be looking at my friend John and myself as if we, by our own power or holiness, had enabled this man to walk.'

In other words, Peter understood the congregation to which he was preaching and he knew that their greatest danger was to regard him and John as miracle-men. There were people like that in the ancient world. We read about the magicians in Egypt and Luke refers to other magicians, such as Bar-Jesus (chapter 13). There were clever men who were regarded as seers and as strange and extraordinary people. They had some curious powers whereby they were able to treat people and heal their diseases or charm away a curse that had been put upon them. That kind of thing has been very common, not only in the East but in this country also. I even remember the relics of this. I remember a man in Wales whom everybody called 'the wise man', and people used to go to him for help. In those days a farmer might suddenly find that his cream or his milk kept turning sour and then he believed that somebody had put a curse on him. So he would go to the wise man, this man with understanding who had books and signs, and after paying a fee, he would be given a message. Sometimes the wise man would make people write their message on a piece of paper, fold it up and sew it inside a shirt or other garment. If they did not look at it for a given number of days, it would act as a charm, the curse would be dispelled and all would be well.

Now that kind of thing was rampant in the ancient world and Peter recognized this at once. He said: We are not miracle-workers. We have not got some strange power such as these other people claim to have. You must not explain it like that. Neither must you attribute the healing to some extraordinary piety on our part, our own power or holiness or godliness. Indeed, in a sense it has nothing to do with us at all.

Peter was anxious to make that clear and it is equally necessary that it should be clear at the present time. When people become Christians, it cannot be explained in any human terms. No one can make another person a Christian. People foolishly talk about being 'so and so's convert'. What a ridiculous thing that is! People can persuade one another, of course. They have persuaded others to join churches, but that does not mean conversion.

No human being can change a soul, or regenerate a soul, or give life to somebody who is dead spiritually, which is what makes a man or woman a Christian. Men and women can be used as instruments, as Peter and John were, as Paul was, as the great preachers of the centuries have been, but they have been nothing but instruments, and they do not want personal followers. They are not interested in that and they do nothing to advertise themselves. They keep out of sight. Oh, it is not us: 'Do not look at us.'

In the same way, it is made equally clear that there is no formula which can be taught and which we must apply. You know the sort of thing I mean – the cults again, or psychology. Here is a man who is finding trouble in walking. There is nothing really wrong with him, it is imaginary, functional. And what do you do with him? Well, you say, 'If you do what I tell you, you will soon get rid of this difficulty in walking. Say to yourself, "Every day and in every way I am getting better and better." Repeat the formula, go on repeating it, suggest it to yourself.' And the man suddenly finds he is all right. It is nothing like that here! That is not

Christianity. Psychology, I suggest to you, like philosophy, is one of the greatest of the enemies of Christianity.

So what made the beggar walk? It was, said Peter, something that happened to him. It happened quickly, immediately. It was not a course of treatment, it was an action: 'His name [Jesus] through faith in his name hath made this man strong' (verse 16) has given him this perfect soundness in the presence of you all This was in an entirely different category.

So Peter told the people not to believe the wrong explanation of the beggar's healing. But as you read Peter's account of the true explanation, does his sermon come as a bit of a surpise to you? Here was the man who had been healed, walking, leaping and praising God, holding on to the apostles and embracing them, and the crowd gathered. Have you been rather surprised at Peter's words? 'Ye men of Israel, why marvel ye at this? or why look ye so earnestly on us, as though by our own power or holiness we had made this man to walk?' Then notice, 'The God of Abraham, and of Isaac, and of Jacob, the God of our fathers, hath glorified his Son Jesus.' Here is the very essence of the whole matter and to the natural person it is one of the most astonishing things.

It is surprising for these reasons: First, what Peter was saying to them is, You are concentrating on the wrong thing. It is not the miracle, as a miracle, that is important. The vital thing is that to which it points. Humanity in its cleverness is always interested in the phenomena, and these people came rushing together crying out, 'This is wonderful!' You can always get a crowd if you produce some kind of a phenomenon. They want to understand and investigate. That was the very thing that Moses was tempted to do when he saw the burning bush, and, indeed, he was beginning to do it. There he was, leading his sheep, when suddenly he saw the phenomenon. He was a very able man, and he had been trained in Egypt. He knew something about the magicians and the lore and learning of the ancient Egyptians, which was considerable. Egypt was a great civilization. And Moses, with the science of those days, said: Ah, I shall turn aside. I'm going to investigate this phenomenon.

But out of the bush came the voice: Stand back. 'Put off thy shoes from off thy feet, for the place whereon thou standest is holy ground' (*Exod.* 3:5). The phenomenon is a phenomenon, yes, but not for our detached, academic, scientific investigation. 'Ah yes, I'll get a book out of the library on Christianity. I've read the others. I want to evaluate it all.' But if you continue like that you will never become a Christian. 'Take off your shoes. The ground on which you are standing is holy ground.' The phenomenon in itself is not important, it is that to which it points.

I repeat, this is not mere theory. If you have not felt something of awe and amazement and wonder, you have not even started yet. Peter did not give a disquisition on miracles. That is what modern men and women like: 'Is a miracle possible?' 'Is it any longer possible for the modern, educated, scientific person to believe in the supernatural and the miraculous?' These are the great debates, and we are tremendously intrigued. But Peter did not preach on miracles – of course not. The Bible does not defend miracles; it is a record of them. It just tells us that they have happened. It confronts us with them. And as long as you think that with your intellect you can understand them, you have not started, you are right outside. You must take your shoes off your feet. You must be humble. You must become as a little child.

So Peter did not preach on miracles, nor did he attempt to give explanations. He said: Look at this, yes, but what does it point to?

But I must go even further and to me this is in many ways the most astonishing thing of all. Peter's sermon did not even start with the Lord Jesus Christ. Have you ever been struck by that? Peter had healed the man in the name of Jesus Christ of Nazareth, yet when the people said, 'What is this?' Peter's answer was: 'The God of Abraham, and of Isaac, and of Jacob.'

I speak carefully because I know that I am liable to be misunderstood at this point, but this to me is a very vital part of Christian teaching and of the Christian message. You do not start even with the Lord Jesus Christ. I am not at all sure but that most of our troubles in the Christian church today are not just due to that. We must start with God. We start with the whole message of the Bible.

There is a modern conception of evangelism which regards it as simply saying to people, 'Come to Jesus.' This view says that you need not talk to people about repentance, but if they are in trouble, or are unhappy, you just tell them to come to him. You start with him and end with him. But that is not Christian preaching. Here we see Christian preaching. A miracle had just taken place and the great apostle was preaching. And he started with God – the God of Abraham and of Isaac and of Jacob. This is how all these apostles preached. The apostle Paul did exactly the same thing.

In Acts 14 we are given an account of Paul in a place called Lystra. Paul, too, had healed a lame man and the people were so carried away by this that they began to worship Paul and Barnabas, calling them Mercury and Jupiter. We read:

Then the priest of Jupiter, which was before their city, brought oxen and garlands unto the gates, and would have done sacrifice with the people. Which when the apostles, Barnabas and Paul, heard of, they rent their clothes, and ran in among the people, crying out, and saying, Sirs, why do ye these things? We also are men of like passions with you, and preach unto you . . .

What?

. . . that ye should turn from these vanities unto the living God, which made heaven and earth, and the sea, and all things that are therein (Acts 14:13–15).

That is Christian preaching. You do not even start with the Lord Jesus Christ. There is even a danger of people turning him into nothing more than some kind of miracle-worker. No, you start, as Peter started here, with the whole message of the Bible.

The first step in Christian preaching is to tell men and women that they and all their problems must always be considered in connection with God. That is the whole message of the Bible. You do not start with particular problems, but with men and women as they are in this world. How are they to be understood? It is in their relationship to God. So when people come together because of a miracle or anything else, you do not talk about the miracle, you do not even talk about the Son of God, you talk about God and man.

Yes, but notice that Peter did that in a special way: the God of Abraham, and of Isaac, and of Jacob. Why do you think he said that? This is the very essence of the matter. I have already referred to that great experience that came into the life of the brilliant mathematician, Blaise Pascal. Some think that he is probably the greatest mathematician of all time. He was a brilliant philosopher, a genius in every sense, who lived in France in the seventeenth century. But he was not only a great scientist, he was also a godly man, a man who was seeking God, and one evening he had an overwhelming experience of God. This is what he wrote: 'I have met the God of Abraham and of Isaac and of Jacob, not the God of the philosophers.' That is it.

I sometimes think that this is the greatest lesson needed by this world of ours. Our trouble is that we do not know God. That is our first need – not the God of the philosophers, not the God of speculation. There are clever people writing books about God at the present time – *Honest to God, Down to Earth, New Reformation* – all those clever books, and what are they? They are nothing but speculation. What is God? Well, we are told that he is ultimate reality. He is the ground of being. He is the uncaused cause. But that is not the God the apostle Peter preached. No, no: the God of Abraham, the God of Isaac, the God of Jacob, the God of our fathers. Peter's God is a living God, and he is a personal God. That is what these philosophers are writing against today. They laugh at us. They say, 'You think of God as some old man up in the heavens. You describe God as "up there" or "out there". But that's primitive, that's childish. God is not personal. Where there is love, that's God. Where there is kindness, that's God – the ground of being, ultimate reality.'

Out upon the suggestion! Thank God that that is a lie. God is personal. He is living. He is not an abstraction. He is not a number of theories or categories or concepts. God is eternally different from all that, and entirely unlike the false gods of the pagans. They made their gods out of wood or stone or silver or gold. They carved them in the likeness of a man or a beast and they erected a temple round them. Then they worshipped them and they took their oblations to them. But there is nothing there. There is no life, no reality, no power. They are vanities, and emptiness. But God is the God of Abraham, Isaac and Jacob. He is the God who says, 'I am that I am' (*Exod.* 3:14). He is a living God. He is a personal God, who speaks as a person. But it does not stop at that. The God of the Bible is the God who has created the universe. 'In the beginning God created the heaven and the earth' (*Gen.* 1:1). He is a God who acts, a God who does things, a God who plans, who thinks and who orders.

But, thank God, by using this term, Peter tells us something much more precious for us, something much more wonderful. He is the God who reveals himself. He is the God who appeared to Abraham when he dwelt in paganism in Ur of the Chaldees. He spoke to Abraham and called him out. The philosophers have been trying to find God from the beginning but, said Paul, 'The world by wisdom knew not God' (*1 Cor.* 1:21). The philosophers cannot arrive at God. The more intelligent may come to a point at which they say that there must be a God. But they cannot get further. They cannot arrive at him because, by definition, he is inscrutable. He is eternal. He is everlasting. He is infinite in every way.

> *Immortal, invisible, God only wise,*
> *In light inaccessible hid from our eyes,*
> *Most blessed, most glorious, the Ancient of Days,*
> *Pavilioned in splendour and girded with praise.*
> William Chalmers Smith

What human being can arrive at him or any knowledge of him? They cannot. But the whole message of the Bible is to say that God is a God who reveals himself. There would not be a Bible but for that. There would be no history of the Jews, there would be no Christian history, but for that, nor would this beggar have been healed at the Beautiful Gate of the temple. God makes himself known, and all we know about him is what he has revealed. 'The God of Abraham' – he appeared to Abraham, and to Isaac. In Genesis we read the story of Jacob running for his life from his brother Esau. Tired at the end of a day, he felt he could not go on another step. There was no bed there. He had to gather stones together to make a pillow. But when he fell asleep he had an amazing dream and vision with a ladder from earth to heaven and angels coming up and down. He woke up and said, 'This is none other but the house of God, and this is the gate of heaven' (*Gen.* 28:17). God had spoken to him. That is the God of the Bible. In his infinite grace and kindness he draws back the veil and gives us a revelation of himself.

Let me go further. He is a God who can be spoken to. Read the story of Abraham, Isaac and Jacob. Look at them when they were in trouble and did not know what to do and everybody was against them. What did they do? Thank God, they could turn to him and speak to him. He is a God to whom you can pray.

> When all things seem against me
> To drive me to despair,
> I know one gate is open,
> One ear will hear my prayer.
>
> Oswald Allen

You can have fellowship and communion with him. You can address him. You can listen to him: the God of Abraham, of Isaac and of Jacob.

Then, still more wonderful, though he is so high and great and lofty and eternal, he is a God who is concerned about the state of this world. That is something that he keeps on making plain and clear to us. Men and women in their folly have rebelled against him and brought chaos down upon themselves, but Christianity brings the message that God is concerned and determined to do something about it. So we do not start even with Jesus Christ, but with God who thought out a plan of redemption before the foundation of the world. It is the most comforting and consoling fact that though statesmen fail, having done their best, though the clever men propound their theories, but do not help us, and though civilization advances but immorality increases, in spite of that, all is not lost and all is not hopeless, because the everlasting God is concerned.

Notice those wonderful words in that third chapter of Exodus. God told Moses to take off his shoes and not to come near for, he said, 'I am the God of thy father, the God of Abraham, the God of Isaac, and the God of Jacob' (verse 6). So Moses hid his face because he was afraid to look upon God. (Have you ever known the fear of God? You will never know his salvation until you have.) Then we read, 'The LORD said, I have surely seen the affliction of my people which are in Egypt, and have heard their cry by reason of their taskmasters' – and this blessed phrase – *'for I know their sorrows'* (verse 7). And it is my privilege to tell you that God knows your sorrows. That is why he gave his only-begotten Son. He put it like this to Moses: 'I am come down to deliver them out of the hand of the Egyptians, and to bring them up out of that land unto a good land and a large, unto a land flowing with milk and honey' (verse 8). Oh, yes, he is concerned. He erupts into the world and its affairs. He intervenes. He comes down.

But also Peter said to these Jews, 'Ye are the children of the prophets, and of the covenant which God made with our fathers, saying unto Abraham, And in thy seed shall all the kindreds of the earth be blessed' (*Acts* 3:25). He is a God who has a great plan and purpose, the God who has determined to do something about this world, to restore it to the condition in which he made it. He will not let the devil triumph. God has a plan and he has made an agreement – that is, a covenant – with men and women. He made it especially with Abraham. He visited Abraham and said, 'In thee shall all families of the earth be blessed' (*Gen.* 12:3). He repeated the promise of that covenant to Isaac, and then to Jacob. That is why Peter talks about the God of Abraham and of Isaac and of Jacob. I am the covenant God, he says. I am the God who has determined before the foundation of the world to redeem men and women and to restore this world to its original perfection.

And then I leave you with this thought: the God of Abraham, of Isaac, of Jacob – three generations but only one God. He did not merely reveal himself to Abraham. He did not only act for Abraham, for Isaac and for Jacob, he also appeared to Moses. 'I am come down,' he said (*Exod.* 3:8). He took the people of Israel from the hopeless captivity and bondage of Egypt. He reminded Moses that he was the same God. He always was, he always would be, from eternity to eternity.

In Sinai he gave the law. He revealed himself. He gave the plan. Later, he spoke through the prophets. The same God who starts, continues and will finish. Then, 'When the fulness of the time was come, God sent forth his Son, made of a woman, made under the law, to redeem them that were under the law' (*Gal.* 4:4–5). If you just stand there and look at the baby in the manger in Bethlehem, and try to understand, you never will, any more than Moses could understand the burning bush.

What is the message? Well, it is this: the same God is just continuing the carrying out of his plan and purpose. Here it is in its supreme form, in his Son Jesus. Peter said: 'Unto you first God, having raised up his Son Jesus, sent him to bless you' (*Acts* 3:26). God sent his Son into the world. It was a part of the ancient plan, the promise to Abraham repeated to Isaac and repeated to Jacob, that in Abraham's seed he would bless all the nations of the world. Ah yes, but that Son was killed. Well, said Peter, 'This Jesus hath God raised up' (*Acts* 2:32).

Then the Son ascended into heaven. Had God finished? No, no, on the day of Pentecost, the Holy Spirit was sent down. God is still active. He has gone on throughout the running centuries. What is a revival? God acting – the God of Abraham, Isaac and Jacob, the same eternal, changeless God, the God who is 'the Father of lights, with whom is no variableness, neither shadow of turning' (*James* 1:17). What has the miserable science of the mid-twentieth century to do with this God? He is everlasting. He is absolute – the same covenant God – and he will go on until the times of revival shall come, the times of refreshing, yes, and until the restitution of all things has taken place, and God is all and in all.

That is the message, though this is but a specimen of the activity of that God. Do not stop at the phenomenon of the beggar who was healed. Do not exercise your cleverness in trying to dissect miracles. 'Do not look at us.' This is God, the eternal God, at work. His plan is certain and sure. Nothing can stop it, nothing can deflect it from its course. 'Why do the heathen rage,' says the psalmist, 'and the people imagine a vain thing . . . Yet have I set my king upon my holy hill of Zion' (*Psa.* 2:1, 6). The God who can defy and conquer death in the resurrection will bring his purpose to pass. That is the message.

Did you know that you are in the hands of this God, that he made you and that the world is his and not yours? Did you know that 'It is a fearful thing to fall into the hands of the living God' (*Heb.* 10:31)? He is the God who at the beginning said, 'Let there be light: and there was light' (*Gen.* 1:3). Do you know God? What is your relationship to him? You have to give an account of your life to him. This covenant-keeping God calls upon you to repent and to turn unto him, to believe that Jesus of Nazareth was his only-begotten Son who came into the world to die for you and your sins and to reconcile you to God according to God's plan and purpose and covenant. At this moment he will receive you to himself if you but turn to him. Blessed be the name of the God of Abraham, the God of Isaac, the God of Jacob!

18

What Do You Think About Jesus?

And when Peter saw it, he answered unto the people, Ye men of Israel, why marvel ye at this? or why look ye so earnestly on us, as though by our own power or holiness we had made this man to walk? The God of Abraham, and of Isaac, and of Jacob, the God of our fathers, hath glorified his Son Jesus; whom ye delivered up, and denied him in the presence of Pilate, when he was determined to let him go. But ye denied the Holy One and the Just, and desired a murderer to be granted unto you; and killed the Prince of life, whom God hath raised from the dead; whereof we are witnesses. And his name through faith in his name hath made this man strong, whom ye see and know: yea, the faith which is by him hath given him this perfect soundness in the presence of you all. And now, brethren, I wot that through ignorance ye did it, as did also your rulers. But those things, which God before had shewed by the mouth of all his prophets, that Christ should suffer, he hath so fulfilled (Acts 3:12–18).

We have seen how in his sermon to the Jews in the temple court, Peter did not start with the Lord Jesus Christ, but took them back to the foundation of the world and beyond, to the everlasting God who made a covenant with his people to redeem them through his dear Son. In other words, Peter preached the great message of the whole Bible.

Throughout his sermon, Peter's basic point was that we are to be concerned primarily and fundamentally about our relationship to God. That is the one thing that really matters, and the way in which that is crystallized for us once and for ever is in our relationship to the Lord Jesus Christ.

Peter would not allow an idle curiosity, an intellectual approach to the problem of Christianity. He brought his hearers immediately to a consideration of themselves and their own condition. Now the popular technical term for all this is that the problem is an *existential* one. This means that you do not sit back in an armchair and theoretically consider the problem of God and of Jesus of Nazareth. You are not a spectator, not a theoretician. No, you consider it as if under judgment, with a sense of personal judgment, with a sense of personal relationship, realizing that it vitally affects your soul and your eternal destiny.

It is always the task of the church to hold us, as Peter did here, face to face with this historic person. What you think about miracles is utterly irrelevant. That is not your problem, though, as we have seen, that is what people want to be arguing about. Can twentieth-century people believe in miracles? Can they believe in the supernatural, even? We are told this is impossible, so we have to cut out bits of the Bible. But the real issue is that this Jesus, this person who appears before us in the pages of the New Testament, is a person who belongs to history. We are not interested primarily in Christian teaching, but in him, the Teacher.

So you see how people go astray today with their tremendous interest in his teaching. In all the annual assemblies of the great denominations, resolutions are passed and sent to the governments of Britain and of the United States and of other countries. That is regarded as Christianity – what we think about various international problems. These are the things that are occupying people's minds. They think that your view on these subjects determines whether or not you are a Christian. But it does not. Here is the question: What do you think of this person, this historical person?

What is our relationship to Christ? That is what Peter preached about and he would not allow his listeners to have an interest in anything else. Do not look at us, he said, look at him. Peter's manner here is most dramatic. Looked at merely from the standpoint of language, this is an extraordinary passage. Are you interested in paradoxes? Well, here you have them.

The God of Abraham, and of Isaac, and of Jacob, the God of our fathers, hath glorified his Son Jesus; whom ye delivered up, and denied him in the presence of Pilate, when he was determined to let him go. But ye denied the Holy One and the Just, and desired a murderer to be granted unto you; and killed the Prince of life, whom God hath raised from the dead; whereof we are witnesses (Acts 3:13–15).

Peter put it in this dramatic form because he was preaching to them, bringing the message home to them, and pressing upon them the relevance of this person - Jesus of Nazareth.

Peter said, 'I wot [know] that through ignorance ye did it, as did also your rulers' (verse 17). He was kind to them, sorry for them. He said in effect, 'When you shouted, "Away with him! Crucify him!" I know you were ignorant and your rulers were equally ignorant.' These people thought that they had finished with Jesus of Nazareth once and for ever, but they had not. Peter put it like this: You are interested in this miracle. You are interested in us. You think we have some special power or holiness. But you are quite wrong. Do you know what this is? Do you know what we are? It is he – the one you thought you had finished with. This was the essence of Peter's message and it is the message of the Christian church to the whole world today.

The one whom those Jews in Jerusalem thought they had got rid of was confronting them in the very miracle that they were inter-ested in. They could not see him, but he was there. Jesus whom they had rejected was the explanation of the phenomenon which they had observed, and so Peter proceeded to preach the Lord Jesus Christ to them. And, I repeat, this is the message of the Christian church in all ages. The world rejects him. In its clever-ness it denies him and thinks it has disposed of him. People explain him in their various categories. They have 'got him taped', as they think, and they put him where they think he belongs, but they cannot. He keeps on coming back. He still confronts us. We cannot get away from him. Today he dominates the universe and the whole of history, just as he has always done.

Now these people in Jerusalem, like all succeeding generations, were baffled by Jesus of Nazareth: Jesus the person, but especially

Jesus in his death upon the cross. Listen to Peter putting it all before them. Jesus – Peter calls him that because he had been known by these people as Jesus of Nazareth. You are confronted by a man who belongs to history, who has divided all history into BC and AD. You are confronted by this person as he is portrayed in the pages of the four Gospels. And as you look at them, you see that he is truly a man who was born in a stable, brought up in Nazareth, and worked as a carpenter. Then, at the age of thirty, you suddenly see him setting out in an extraordinary public ministry which lasted for some three years. Go through his teaching, and you feel like the officers who were sent to arrest him and came back saying, 'Never man spake like this man' (*John* 7:46). There was something strange and extraordinary about his teaching.

And then you read the accounts of his miracles. These were always arresting attention. How anybody can deny the miracles and believe anything about Jesus Christ, I do not know. They are part and parcel of the whole story. If you take them out, how do you know what you have left? What can you believe? The moment you begin to pick and choose, you have no authority except your own subjective feeling. And that is not only to be disloyal to the Scriptures, it is to be foolish, because you are setting yourself up as the one who can decide. But how can you? No, no, you must take the picture as it is. Why did he ever make this impact? Why did a carpenter from Nazareth create this disturbance? Why has he, as I say, dominated human history?

But the most amazing thing of all about him is the claim which he constantly made. He claimed a unique authority. He would say without any hesitation, though he was a carpenter and had never been trained in any of the schools, 'Ye have heard that it was said by them of old time . . . but I say unto you' (*Matt.* 5:21–22). He kept on saying this. He said that he was to be believed and followed. He did not hesitate to turn to a man – Matthew – sitting at the receipt of custom and say to him, 'Follow me,' expecting the man to leave everything and to follow him, which he did. He did the same with the sons of Zebedee, and the fishermen left everything and followed him. He claimed a unique authority, he demanded an absolute allegiance, but above all, he claimed that he was in a unique relationship to God. He did not hesitate to say, 'I and my

Father are one' (*John* 10:30). He did not hesitate to say that he was the light of the world (*John* 8:12). He did not hesitate to say that he had come to give his life a ransom for many (*Mark* 10:45). He is the Saviour of the world (*John* 4:42).

Those were his astounding claims and they were well-known to those people. As we read the Gospels, we find that at first he made quite an impression upon people, but gradually they, their leaders especially, turned against him. So we are confronted by an apparent contradiction. Here is one with such extraordinary knowledge yet never having learned. Here is one with such amazing power. Here is one who made these exalted and exceptional claims. Yet he ended his life on a cross. This one who could even raise the dead was arrested in apparent weakness, and charged as a felon. He seemed almost incapable of defending himself.

And then came the great climax. Pilate, the Roman governor, was an intelligent man who could see that there was no case against Jesus, and wanted to set him free. Pilate's wife had had an extraordinary dream and she sent a message to her husband telling him about her dream and warning Pilate to have nothing to do with Jesus because he was innocent (*Matt.* 27:19). Pilate agreed with her – this was what he felt himself. His own intelligence had brought him to the conclusion that the Jews had no case at all against Jesus but were motivated by some personal spite and jealousy.

So Pilate was anxious, as Peter reminded the people in the temple, to let him go; indeed, he was determined to do so. But the Jews would not have it, even when, according to the custom, Pilate offered to release a prisoner. Pilate gave them the choice but they chose a murderer, Barabbas, to be set free, and said that this Jesus should be put to death, that he should be crucified. So he was taken and we see him in utter weakness, staggering, faltering and falling under the weight of the cross, as he carried it through the streets of Jerusalem to Golgotha.

Then we look at the Roman soldiers nailing him to the cross. And the extraordinary thing is that he appeared to be so utterly helpless. The people at the cross hurled this at him. They said: 'He saved others; let him save himself, if he be Christ, the chosen of God' (*Luke* 23:35). You say you are the Son of God, if you are, prove it. Come down. Save yourself. Even one of the two men who was being crucified with him threw his weakness in his teeth and said, 'If thou be Christ, save thyself and us' (*Luke* 23:39). But he did not, and he died, and he died before the other two. The soldiers who came to examine the executions were amazed that he was already dead. His friends took down the body and laid it in a tomb. They rolled the stone in front of the entrance, and put a seal upon it, and soldiers were ordered to guard the tomb. And the crowd and the rulers came to the conclusion that that was the end of the story, that all his claims were nonsense and he was an impostor.

Everyone had different reasons for their action. The Pharisees saw in him one who endangered their jobs. The Sadducees, clever politicians, saw there was a danger that he might upset the Roman authorities. He was a political threat, and they said it was better to get rid of him and save the nation. That is how Caiaphas, the High Priest, figured it out. But they were unanimous in this: he was only a man, and now, having disposed of him, they would have no more trouble with him. He had made these great claims and foolish people who were following him, ignoramuses, mere workmen, artisans, had believed him. But, of course, that is what you would expect of such people. However, it had all been proved to be wrong. He had died in weakness, so what could he have been but a man? He was a failure and that was the end of the story.

Peter was preaching to people who had believed that verdict on Jesus. And before I go any further, I must ask you a question: What do you make of all this? What do you make of Jesus of Nazareth? What have you made of this figure who appears here in the four Gospels? What is your reaction to him? Have you considered his message to you? Have you considered what all this means? Is he only a man to you? Perhaps you are not like these Jews of old; perhaps you say, 'I regard him as the greatest man who ever lived, the most moral individual, the greatest teacher the world has ever known.' Indeed, perhaps you go further. Perhaps you would say that if only the whole world, especially the leaders of the nations, would put into practice his teaching, the Sermon on the Mount in particular, then we would get rid of war and there would be no more bombs. If we would only implement his teaching in a political sense we would make the world a better place to live in. Is that what you think – just a man, a teacher, a political agitator, a great seer, one with unusual understanding – but only a man?

Some people today go further and say that of course he was a failure, he died of a broken heart and when he said, 'It is finished,' what he really meant was, 'It's all up. I've failed. They won't listen to me.' But these people add, 'That's all right. The world has never understood its greatest men. "Truth for ever on the scaffold, wrong for ever on the throne." He was a great man but the world wasn't ready for him. It didn't understand him. So, though he died with a broken heart, his memory and his teaching have continued and still have their influence upon humanity. Furthermore, it's our business to see that they have an even greater influence.' Is that your attitude? Here is the question of all questions: Is that all? How do you understand him? How, especially, do you understand his death? That is what Peter expounded to the temple crowd.

Notice, too, the way Peter gave his message. All I shall do is take Peter's headings, not mine. Preaching is a great thing if you let others preach for you! I do not understand the sort of preacher who is in great difficulty every Saturday looking for a text for Sunday and trying to get a sermon. It is all here. I am not preaching – it is Peter preaching. I am simply holding his words before you. 'Now,' said Peter in effect, 'how do you approach this question? You shouted, "Away with him! Crucify him!" Why did you do that? Well,' said Peter, 'you did it because your whole approach was wrong.'

And Peter says exactly the same to the modern man and woman. The way to look at Christ and to consider him is to take him in his setting, in his background. In other words, as we have seen, you start with prophecy. Notice how Peter kept on saying this. 'Those things, which God before had shewed by the mouth of all his prophets, that Christ should suffer, he hath so fulfilled' (verse 18). Listen to him again:

Whom the heaven must receive until the times of restitution of all things, which God hath spoken by the mouth of all his holy prophets since the world began. For Moses truly said unto the fathers, A prophet shall the Lord your God raise up unto you of your brethren, like unto me; him shall ye hear in all things whatsoever he shall say unto you . . . Yea, and

*all the prophets from Samuel and those that follow after, as many as have
spoken, have likewise foretold of these days* (Acts 3:21–22, 24).

This is preaching! 'Look here,' said Peter in effect, 'you're looking at this, you're looking at us. You say: "What's this?" But the
way to understand it all is to go back to the prophets.'

Here, to me, is the most profound insight into this whole matter.
Modern men and women start with a picture of Jesus which they
find from books rather than the Bible. But if you want to understand Jesus of Nazareth, you must know your Bible, the whole of
it. You must listen to what this book has to say about him. Listen
again to the language of Peter: 'God before had shewed by the
mouth of all his prophets' (verse 18). In other words, when you
read the prophecies of the Old Testament, you are reading what
God has said. It is God who has shown it. These prophets were not
just ordinary men; they were men who were given a message by
God. He was speaking through them. Indeed, in verse 21, Peter
goes back even further and says: 'God hath spoken by the mouth
of all his holy prophets since the world began.' And then he
mentions Moses who was one of the first of the prophets. Moses
lived fourteen hundred years before the birth of Christ. He was
the man whom these Jews revered, their national leader, their
great lawgiver and teacher. Moses, Peter told them, spoke of these
days. Then he said: Samuel, your great prophet, did exactly the
same thing. These men have all spoken of these days, and it was
not they who were speaking. It was God who was speaking
through them.

Our Lord himself did the very thing that Peter was doing on this
occasion. Peter was now filled with the Spirit and in preaching to
this crowd, he was repeating what Christ had said to him and the
others in the upper room at Jerusalem. All the disciples had been
utterly cast down when Christ had died. They did not understand
and had felt it was the end. Two of them on the road to Emmaus
had been joined by our Lord who had said to them, 'Oh fools, and
slow of heart to believe all that the prophets have spoken: ought
not Christ to have suffered these things?' (*Luke* 24:25-26).And we
are told that he expounded unto them in all the scriptures the
things concerning himself. Then later that evening, when our Lord
appeared in the upper room, he said, 'All things must be fulfilled,

which were written in the law of Moses, and in the prophets, and in the psalms, concerning me' (verse 44). 'What is the matter with you?' he said in effect. 'You are looking at me – can you not see who I am? Read your prophets. See that I am the fulfilment of their words.'

This is God's Word, why do you pay so much attention to modern books? Who are the writers? What do they know? They know no more than you do. But here is God speaking centuries before the events, through the mouth of his holy prophets. And in the prophets we find an account of this person. Because men and women, in listening to the devil, had put themselves under his dominion, they could now never set themselves free. But God had promised away back then that he would send a Deliverer, a Messiah. He described him, he even told them that the Messiah would be born of a virgin in Bethlehem. He gave them all sorts of details, including the fact that he would ride on the foal of an ass into Jerusalem and would be led as a lamb to the slaughter, and would rise again afterwards. In his holy prophets, God gave a description of this person, a description of his word: 'A bruised reed shall he not break, and the smoking flax shall he not quench' (*Isa.* 42:3).

Have you not often been struck, as you read your four Gospels, by the multiplicity of Old Testament quotations, and the constant refrain, 'That it might be fulfilled which was spoken of the Lord by the prophets'? All that is true of him had been prophesied. It is all there – he himself, his life, his teaching, and above all, as Peter reminded them, his death. 'Those things, which God before had shewed by the mouth of all his prophets, that Christ should suffer, he hath so fulfilled' (verse 18). That is the way in which you begin to approach the question of Jesus. Go back to Genesis and read right through. Keep your eye on him and you will see him everywhere. You will see this person fulfilling it all. That is how you begin. That is how Peter began.

Then Peter came to the fact of the resurrection, and this is a vital part of the preaching. Why was this lame man hanging on to Peter and John? Why was he embracing them? Why was he able to do it at all? Why was he not still sitting on the pavement?

You are looking at us, said Peter, but you cannot understand us except in terms of Jesus. '[You] killed the Prince of life, whom God hath raised from the dead; whereof we are witnesses' (verse 15). Would there ever have been a Christian church at all if it had not been for the fact of the resurrection? And remember that 'resurrection' means that he literally rose in the body, not that his influence went on, nor that he is now in the spiritual realm and you can make contact with him, as you can with the spirits of the departed, through some spiritualistic medium, which is what many today preach as resurrection. But that is not what the New Testament talks about. Peter said, 'We are witnesses.' And they were witnesses in this sense: he had said to his disciples in the upper room that he was not a ghost; he was not a spirit. They were frightened because he had suddenly appeared in their midst, though the doors were bolted. They had thought: This is a ghost, an apparition. But he said, 'A spirit hath not flesh and bones, as ye see me have' (*Luke* 24:39). And he asked, 'Have you anything to eat?'

'Yes,' they said, 'we have a bit of broiled fish and a honeycomb.'

'Let us have it,' he replied. And he sat and ate in their presence.

Peter said in his sermon, 'We are witnesses of these things.' And you and I would not be considering these things now if this had not literally happened. There would never have been a church but for this. Those men were shattered when he died. What gave them new life, what gave them this message? It was he. He is risen. 'We are witnesses of these things.'

This is how you understand Jesus Christ. You do not just take the Sermon on the Mount and his teaching and say, 'That is what they need to know in the trouble spots of the world,' or, 'That is what they need to understand in our government.' No, no, you look at this blessed person. And you do not only look at the prophecy and the resurrection, but also at Pentecost. Here were Peter and John working this miracle: What enabled them to do it? It was not their power, nor their holiness, said Peter. What was it, then? Well, the power came from God. 'His name through faith in his name hath made this man strong . . . the faith which is by him hath given him this perfect soundness in the presence of you all.'

There is nothing in us, said Peter. We were like you. I was a craven coward. I myself denied him to save my own skin. What has happened to me? I have been baptized with the Holy Spirit. He has sent down the Spirit, as he said he would. Pentecost power, the risen Christ enduing his servants with authority and might and power. And, said Peter, he is still exerting that power. Do not look at the miracle. Look at the one who worked it. Do not try to understand this marvel. Can you not see there is only one who can produce it? He has made us what we are. He has made him what he is. It is this risen Christ who sent down his Spirit. This is the result.

How do you explain the persistence of the Christian church? Men and women would have ruined her long ago. Look at the heresies that have come in. Look at the false teaching that has had to be cleared out. Look how people put organizations in the place of the living Christ. See how the church has become an institution, dead and filled with pomp and power, having silver and gold but no spiritual authority. See how she has become political. Ah, people would have destroyed her long since. There is only one reason why she still persists: it is this living Christ. And throughout the centuries, he has taken hold of men and women – lame, hopeless, impotent, helpless, in sin and iniquity and shame – and lifted them up and sent revival and authority and power, and on goes the church.

What does all this mean? Peter now gave the answer. 'There are the facts,' he said in effect, 'why don't you face them?' Let me tell you what you have done, said Peter: 'Ye denied the Holy One and the Just . . . And killed the Prince [the Author] of life.' There is only one explanation of these things: he is not only a man. As Peter said at the beginning of his sermon: 'The God of Abraham, and of Isaac, and of Jacob, the God of our fathers, hath glorified his Son [his servant] Jesus.' Yes, he is a man, but he is not only a man, he is the Son of God. You remember how Peter, preaching on the day of Pentecost, had made this point. He had quoted David's words in Psalm 16, 'Thou wilt not leave my soul in hell, neither wilt thou suffer thine Holy One to see corruption' (*Acts* 2:27). Peter had said:

Let me freely speak unto you of the patriarch David, that he is both dead and buried, and his sepulchre is with us unto this day. Therefore being a prophet, and knowing that God had sworn with an oath to him, that of the fruit of his loins, according to the flesh, he would raise up Christ to sit on his throne; he seeing this before spake of the resurrection of Christ, that his soul was not left in hell, neither his flesh did see corruption (Acts 2:29-31).

What Do You Think About Jesus?

Who is Jesus of Nazareth? He is 'the Holy One and the Just'. Before his birth, before his conception even, the angel Gabriel had said to his mother Mary, 'That holy thing which shall be born of thee . . .' (*Luke* 1:35). He was not born of natural generation. He had no human father. 'The Holy Ghost shall come upon thee, and the power of the Highest shall overshadow thee: therefore also that holy thing which shall be born of thee shall be called the Son of God.'

That is the only explanation of the healing of the lame man, and the resurrection proves it. Here is the only one who has ever risen from the dead. There had been holy men before, but they were all imperfect, they were not 'the holy one', but here he is, the Son of God. This is the message of the incarnation. He is man, yes, but he is God. He is the eternal Son of God. He is that Holy One. He is as holy as God the Father, and he is just.

You preferred a murderer, said Peter. You preferred one who is utterly unjust. But Jesus is just. He is without sin: 'In all points tempted like as we are, yet without sin' (*Heb.* 4:15). He had no blemish, no imperfection. There was nothing wrong in mind or thought or action.

And above all, Peter said, he is 'the Prince of life'. That means the author of life, and this is what the whole of the New Testament claims for him. The apostle John says, 'In the beginning was the Word, and the Word was with God, and the Word was God. The same was in the beginning with God. All things were made by him; and without him was not any thing made that was made. In him was life; and the life was the light of men' (*John* 1:1-4). He is the author of life. He is the one through whom God has created the whole cosmos, and he sustains it all by the word of his power. That is who he is. The resurrection proves it.

Paul puts this point to the Christians in Rome. 'Jesus Christ our Lord,' he says, 'which was made of the seed of David according to the flesh; and declared to be the Son of God with power, according to the spirit of holiness, by the resurrection from the dead' (*Rom.* 1:3–4). Who is this? Yes, man, teacher, miracle-worker, but not only that. He was killed, he was buried, but then he burst asunder the bands of death: 'Thou wilt not leave my soul in hell, neither wilt thou suffer thine Holy One to see corruption.' It was impossible that he should be held by death, and he rose, proving that he is the eternal Son of God – God and man – the man Christ Jesus; Jesus the Son of God.

'Well,' you may say, 'that sounds very plausible to me, but you leave me with a problem. Why did he ever die if he is the Son of God? If he is the Son of God, why did he not escape to heaven? He could have done it. According to you, he could work miracles. He could raise the dead. Why, then, did he die? Why did he suffer?'

You are asking a good question. It is the most important question anyone can ever ask. There is only one answer and Peter gives it here: 'Those things, which God before had shewed by the mouth of all his prophets, that Christ should suffer [which can be translated, 'which his Christ *must* suffer'] he hath so fulfilled' (verse 18). Here again is the message of the whole of the Bible. Here is the explanation of the Old Testament. All the prophets, Peter said, from Moses onwards, indeed, from the foundation of the world, have all been saying and writing about these days.

What have the prophets all been saying? They have been saying, 'By faith Abel offered unto God a more excellent sacrifice than Cain' (*Heb.* 11:4). Why? Because it was a blood offering and not merely an agricultural offering. They have been telling us that God commanded Moses to build a tabernacle and to introduce some great ceremonial. Among other things, the priests had to take a beast and then put their hands upon its head, metaphorically transferring their sins to it. Then they had to kill it, take the blood and offer it to God at the altar. A lamb was always to be slain morning and evening, with no intermission. The sacrifices described in the Old Testament were all types and shadows of Christ.

He was the lamb provided by God as an offering for sin. God had taught his people and prepared them for the coming of his Son by means of types and shadows, by analogies and illustrations. They all pointed to the one who was coming – the Lamb of God. At last he appeared, and John the Baptist, the forerunner, said to the people, 'Behold the Lamb of God, which taketh away the sin of the world' (*John* 1:29). Here is God's lamb, the lamb that will really do that. The blood of bulls and of goats and the ashes of an heifer, used in the old temple worship, could never cleanse the soul and the conscience from sin, but God could and he alone. Christ offered his own blood. The prophets had prophesied it, and he had done it. All that God had said by the mouth of his prophets that the Messiah should suffer, had been fulfilled by Jesus Christ.

Why did this have to happen? Peter told the people in Jerusalem: 'Repent ye therefore, and be converted, that your sins may be blotted out' (verse 19). That is why our Lord died on that cross. The great problem confronting us is how our sins can be blotted out. All of us are as we are because of our sins. They stand between us and God, and the great problem confronting each of us is: 'How should man be just with God?' (*Job* 9:2). What can I do with my sin? Have you faced that problem?

You thought the problem was whether, with your great intellect, you could accept miracles. But your problem is your sinfulness, the uncleanness of your mind and heart, the evil actions you have performed, your wrong relationship to God, your blasphemy against him, your arrogance in questioning him and in querying him. That is your problem – your moral failure, your blindness, your darkness. You have sinned against him. You have taken his name in vain. You have broken his commandments. Your sins are heavy upon you, and if you die like that, you go to perdition. So how can you get rid of your sins? How can you blot them out? You cannot. That can only be accomplished in one way – and it is the very thing that happened on the cross on Calvary's hill.

At Calvary God was laying your iniquity on his Son. God was taking your sins and punishing them in him. His blood was shed that your sins might be blotted out. That is the only answer and the only explanation for Christ's death. Our Lord's own disciples warned him about going to Jerusalem and they did their utmost to dissuade him, but, as we have seen, he set his face steadfastly to go to Jerusalem. He said: I must. I have come into the world in order to do this, cost what it may. This is the hour for which I have come. 'As Moses lifted up the serpent in the wilderness, even so *must* the Son of man be lifted up' – on a cross – 'that whosoever believeth in him should not perish, but have eternal life' (*John* 3:14–15).

That is what Peter preached; that is what I preach. Peter was saying: Do not be interested in the miracle. Do not be interested in us. The question for you is: Do you realize that you killed the Prince of life, the Son of God, the Saviour of the world? Do you realize that you denied and rejected the only one who can save you? Repent, change your minds, believe in him, and the moment you do, your sins will be blotted out. God will justify you and regard you as if you had never sinned at all.

And you, too, are thinking of the wrong problems, the wrong questions. The problem is – you. You must die -- you do not know when – and stand before God in the judgment. Then the Christ who has been in this world will confront you. What did you believe about him? What did you make of him? What conclusion did you come to with regard to him?

In the ultimate analysis, there are only two views of the Lord Jesus Christ. You either take the world's view of him or else you take God's view. Look at the contrast. The world's view is that he is only Jesus, a man like Barabbas. God's view of him is that he is his dearly beloved, only begotten Son. The world cries, 'He is only a man.' God speaks from heaven at the baptism and on the Mount of Transfiguration and again just before the end that this is his beloved Son in whom he is well pleased (see *Mark* 1:11; 9:7; *John* 12:28).

There is another contrast. Peter said, '. . . whom ye delivered up, and *denied* him in the presence of Pilate, when he was determined to let him go. But ye *denied* the Holy One and the Just, and desired a murderer to be granted unto you' (verses 13–14). The world denies him – denies him as the Son of God, denies him as the Lamb of God, denies him as the Saviour who shed his blood that the world might be forgiven. But what did God do? 'The God of Abraham, and of Isaac, and of Jacob, the God of our fathers, hath glorified his Son Jesus' (verse 13). The world denies him and rejects him; God has glorified him. He glorified him in his life. He spoke from heaven authenticating him. He gave him power to work miracles, to teach. He glorified him in his death. He said: Here is one who is big enough and great enough and holy enough to bear the punishment of sin. He is my lamb. But above all, God glorified his Son in the glorious resurrection. Have you denied him or have you glorified him?

But listen to another contrast. 'Ye . . . *killed* the Prince of life . . .' The world is always killing him, killing him metaphorically. 'Away with him!' it says. But, said Peter, '. . . whom God hath raised from the dead' (verse 15). Are you still killing the Son of

God or are you looking unto him in the glory and in the exaltation, bowing your knee before him and saying to him, like the apostle Paul: 'Lord, what wilt thou have me to do?' (*Acts* 9:6).

Finally, there is one extraordinary thing in this sermon of Peter. So far I have shown you the utter contrast between the way men handled the Son of God, and the way in which God himself handles him. But there is one thing that both man and God have done to the Lord Jesus Christ, the Son of God. Here it is: 'The God of Abraham, and of Isaac, and of Jacob, the God of our fathers, hath glorified his Son Jesus; whom ye delivered up, and denied him in the presence of Pilate, when he was determined to let him go.' They delivered him up to death. And God did exactly the same thing. The apostle Paul says in Romans 8:32, 'He that spared not his own Son, but delivered him up for us all.' It is the same word exactly. Men delivered him up to death, but the message of the gospel is that God delivered him up to death, for us all.

So you are confronted now by this Jesus of Nazareth, the Son of God, and you always will be. He will be confronting you on your deathbed, but, much more important he will be confronting you beyond death in the judgment. He came to give his life a ransom for you. God delivered him up for you, whatever you may have been, whatever you may have thought of him until this moment. Do you see now that you have done it all in ignorance? So repent and believe on the Lord Jesus Christ and you shall be saved.

19

The Return of Christ

Repent ye therefore, and be converted, that your sins may be blotted out, when the times of refreshing shall come from the presence of the Lord; and he shall send Jesus Christ, which before was preached unto you: whom the heaven must receive until the times of restitution of all things, which God hath spoken by the mouth of all his holy prophets since the world began (Acts 3:19–21).

In this one sermon here in Acts 3, we have a very wonderful summary of what constitutes the essence of Christian preaching. Why should we be interested in that? As we have seen, it is because of the state of the world in which we live and because of our own state and condition by nature. None of us would be considering this were it not that we had found life hard, full of problems and trials. We have tried everything else and have found it to fail. We know that what the world has to offer is no solution and we want to know what the Christian church has to say to us and to the whole world in which we live. In a world that in so many respects is collapsing round and about us, it is urgently important that we should know exactly what the Christian message is and what it has to offer us. And in this sermon the apostle gives us the answer.

We saw in our last study how Peter expounded the meaning of the death of Jesus Christ, this Son of God, 'the Holy One and the Just'. We have seen how he told the people in the temple court that Christ's death was God's way of giving them forgiveness, giving them an opportunity to have their sins blotted out. But Peter had more to say, he did not leave it there, and it is very important that you and I should realize that the gospel does not end at that. It starts like that. The first need of every human being is to be reconciled to God. But then the apostle went on to say that what Jesus had done so far was only a part of what he was going to do. What had already happened was not the end of God's plan and purpose. There was more to follow, indeed, the bulk was to follow.

It is very interesting to me to notice the way in which the apostle preached to the people. You see, he made use of the miracle. He said: 'This man ... whom ye see and know' (verse 16). Peter kept on reminding them of that and, of course, they all did know him. This poor fellow had been placed at the gate every day and of necessity everybody knew him. As they went into the temple through the Beautiful Gate, they had to pass him. Peter made use of it like this: he said in effect, 'You are amazed to see this man now walking and leaping and praising God. Yes, but the questions you must concentrate on are these: What made him as he was, and what is the meaning of his healing? I want to try to show you,' said Peter, 'that what happened to that man is but a foretaste of what will happen to the whole universe.' And that is the theme to which I now want to call your attention.

The healing of the lame man is but an illustration of what God, in Christ, will do to the whole cosmos. In other words, we must realize that a part of the preaching of the gospel message is that salvation is not merely a personal matter, but concerns the entire universe. The personal is a vital part, but it does not stop at that, it is included in a greater whole. Peter put it like this: Jesus is the Christ, which means that he is the Messiah, he is the one appointed by God, foreordained by God before the foundation of the world, to lead a great move of deliverance. He is a leader. He is a Saviour. And Peter went on in a very interesting manner. He said:

Moses truly said unto the fathers, A prophet shall the Lord your God raise up unto you of your brethren, like unto me; him shall ye hear in all things whatsoever he shall say unto you. And it shall come to pass, that every soul, which will not hear that prophet, shall be destroyed from among the people. Yea, and all the prophets from Samuel and those that follow after, as many as have spoken, have likewise foretold of these days (Acts 3:22–24).

Peter was saying that the Lord Jesus Christ was not only foretold by Moses, but was prefigured by him. Moses was the great leader who led the children of Israel out of the bondage of Egypt to the Promised Land of Canaan. He did not have the privilege of actually taking them in, but he took them to the river Jordan and all they had to do was cross it. He was the appointed leader, God's man to lead this people from captivity to liberty, to a land flowing with milk and honey. But as Moses himself had said: 'The Lord thy God will raise up unto thee a Prophet from the midst of thee, of thy brethren, like unto me' (*Deut.* 18:15). The work of the Messiah was to lead the whole universe from bondage to paradise. Now that is how the apostle works out this great statement and it is a vital part of the preaching of the gospel.

Here, then, is the message: God has a plan for this world, this whole universe, in which we live. In Christ it will be delivered and restored. But here come the great questions: When will this happen and how will it happen? And the answer given by the apostle comes as a direct challenge to the modern world. This is what men and women not only do not accept but dislike, and reject with scorn and contumely. The answer is that this deliverance lies in the future. It is apocalyptic. It is a great event to which the whole of creation is moving.

Let me put this in its modern context. People heartily dislike this 'other worldly' view, as they call it. They ridicule it and call it 'pie in the sky'. 'Ah,' they say, 'people in the past used to talk about the next world, this wonderful future world, and they sang about golden harps and golden streets and so on. But, of course, we've grown up, and we no longer believe in that kind of thing. What we want is a message that will help us in the here and now. We want something *this* worldly. It's no use telling us that something marvellous and wonderful will happen some time. What we want is a message that will put this world in order while we are in it and give us some sort of security and happiness. And,' they say, 'surely that is the real gospel. The gospel teaches us how to reform this world, how to put things right by legislation, by sociological movements, and education, and things of that kind.'

This has been the popular theme of the twentieth century. It used to be known as the social gospel, but it goes under many names. It is the belief that Christianity is just a view of life, a view of the social order, and a set of principles. So all we have to do is persuade the statesmen and employers and trade unions to put these things into practice. 'In this way,' people say, 'we'll get rid of our problems. We'll reform the world. We'll have a happy society. We'll get them to destroy the bombs and banish war. We'll have a great league of all the nations of the world, and will all live happily ever after.' They may not be so sure about the 'happy', but they say, 'At any rate, we'll not be bothered by wars. We'll have plenty of time to go on drinking and dancing and gambling and doing the things that really make life worth living.'

That is about it, is it not? But I want to show you that it is a complete denial of the gospel. That is my first objection to a social gospel. It is the exact opposite of what was taught here by the apostle Peter. Notice what he did: having reminded his listeners of the tragedy of their denial of 'the Holy One and the Just', he said, 'Repent ye therefore, and be converted, that your sins may be blotted out, when the times of refreshing shall come from the presence of the Lord.' And then immediately Peter took them to this: 'And he shall send Jesus Christ, which before was preached unto you: whom the heaven must receive until the times of restitution of all things, which God hath spoken by the mouth of all his holy prophets since the world began.'

There is not a word in Peter's sermon about reform. There is not a word about going out to preach the gospel in order to make people live better lives, and to influence the imperial government of Rome in order to get these things put into practice. No, no, that is not how Peter preached. Remember, here is the first preacher in the Christian church, here is the authentic summary of this great message, and what a wonderful opportunity! The crowd had gathered, they wanted to hear, and Peter told them something that is in the distant future. Now this was not only true of the preaching of the apostle Peter, but was equally true of the preaching of our blessed Lord and Saviour. Our Lord never claimed to have come into the world to reform it. He never said the world was going to get better and better, indeed, he said the exact opposite:

As it was in the days of Noe, so shall it be also in the days of the Son of man . . . Likewise also, as it was in the days of Lot; they did eat, they drank, they bought, they sold . . . But the same day that Lot went out of Sodom it rained fire and brimstone from heaven (Luke 17:26, 28–29).

Our Lord said that evil men would get worse and worse. And he said, 'And when ye shall hear of wars and rumours of wars, be ye not troubled: for such things must needs be' (*Mark* 13:7). So the apostle Peter was but repeating what he had heard from the lips of his Lord and Master. Our Lord held out, as the only hope, something that he was yet going to do.

We find exactly the same thing in the preaching of the apostle Paul and in all his epistles, as Peter himself said in his second letter. Talking about the coming day of the Lord, Peter wrote, '. . . even as our beloved brother Paul . . . in all his epistles, speaking in them of these things; in which are some things hard to be understood, which they that are unlearned and unstable wrest, as they do also the other scriptures, unto their own destruction (2 *Pet.* 3:15–16).

And if you read in Acts 17 the little summary of Paul's sermon in the city of Athens, you will find that Paul preached precisely what Peter preached here. We find this throughout the New Testament, and, as Peter reminds us, it is the great message of the Old Testament. The prophets, too, spoke of a great future age when the lion shall lie down with the lamb and when the wolf and the ox shall eat straw together. It is the universal message of the whole of the Bible.

So the modern idea that Christianity is just a movement for world reform and that it is mainly political and social, is a complete denial of the teaching of the Scriptures. That is what makes it so tragic. Not only that, but, secondly, this teaching is entirely disproved by history. Christianity has been in this world for nearly two thousand years and it has not reformed it. History is against this modern idea. History has been a matter of ups and downs, advances and retrogressions.

To me, this is the most important point of all. I imagine that there is no one single consideration that stumbles so many people with regard to the Christian faith as this very thing that we are considering together. If Christianity is a movement for world reform, if the business of Christianity is to get rid of war and to teach people how to live together and to solve labour and industrial problems, if it is just a social, political programme, then the man of the world makes this point, and he is perfectly entitled to do so: 'All right, that's why I'm not a Christian. That's why I don't believe your message. Christianity has been going for nearly two thousand years. It claims that it will put the world in order and that it will get rid of all our problems. But after two thousand years of preaching – and the church has been in control in many centuries and could do anything she liked – look at the state of the world! I'm not interested,' says the modern person. 'Your Christianity has proved to be a failure. There's nothing in it. It doesn't work. It's all right as idealistic talk, but in the actual world of practicalities it has nothing to give us. If Christianity is true, then why, in this one century, have we already had two world wars, and why are the nations behaving as they are? It's impossible. It's ridiculous.' And, of course, that is a perfectly valid argument and the people who misrepresent Christianity as a social, political programme have no answer to give.

But Christianity has never promised to be a vehicle for world reform. There is no statement anywhere in the Bible to that effect. The tragedy of this false view of the Christian message is that it cannot explain the past centuries; it cannot explain the state of the world today; it has nothing to tell us with respect to the future. It is utterly bankrupt. The proponents of a social gospel can only go on repeating that people must be persuaded to accept this ethic. They must enter politics. They must organize this and that. Yes, and though nothing has come of it, there is nothing to do but to go on doing it. It is hopeless.

Of course, it sounded very plausible and very likely in the nineteenth century, but then the world really seemed to be advancing towards perfection. There had not been a very serious war since the Napoleonic Wars. There had been the odd incident, like the Crimean War, but that was something local. The whole world seemed to be settling down to a great advance and in 1859 Darwin came along with his theory which was going to prove it. He said: I found this law in biology and it works out everywhere.

Then came Thomas Huxley who said: This is not only biologically true, it is true all along the line. Herbert Spencer, the philosopher, added that this was a principle of the whole of life. Everything is advancing, moving steadily in the direction of perfection. The poets caught the fire and Tennyson sang about the parliament of man and the federation of the world – the glorious age that is coming. I admit that it seemed very plausible then, but how anybody can believe anything like that now passes my comprehension. No, this twentieth century has shattered it; it has ridiculed it and made nonsense of it. Nothing is so discredited as this whole notion that man and the universe are moving in the direction of perfection by a process of evolution. This century has smashed that idea once and for ever. There is no explanation of history along that line. Is it not time that the world began to listen to the apostle Peter? Is it not time that the world began to listen to the authentic Christian message? Peter said: You want to know what this is all about? You look at this man and see him walking, leaping and praising God. He was paralysed, so you ask: What is this? It is a picture, a parable. This will happen to the whole universe.

How?

Well, said Peter, this same person, the one you thought you had got rid of, is the key to it all. 'He [God] shall send Jesus Christ, which before was preached unto you: whom the heaven must receive [retain, contain] until the times of restitution of all things, which God hath spoken by the mouth of all his holy prophets since the world began.'

What does all that mean? Well, let me expound the phrases to you. Again, my task is very simple. I just have to underline the headings used by the apostle Peter himself. Here is the first phrase: 'Whom the heaven must receive'. Peter had just told the people that this Christ did die on the cross on Calvary's hill, and he told them why Christ died. Then, as we saw, he reminded them that Christ did not remain in the tomb. 'Ye . . . killed the Prince of life, whom God hath raised from the dead; whereof we are witnesses.'

But Peter took it a step further. Not only did the resurrection take place, but something else followed after forty days – the ascension: 'Whom the heaven must receive'. Go back to the first chapter of Acts and you will find our Lord talking to the disciples and telling them to stay at Jerusalem where they would receive power 'after that the Holy Ghost is come upon you'. Then we are told, 'And when he had spoken these things, while they beheld, he was taken up; and a cloud received him out of their sight' (*Acts* 1:9). Therefore the ascension, too, is a part of the preaching of the gospel.

When Peter said, 'whom the heaven must receive', in effect, he was telling the people, 'We are not only witnesses of his resurrection, we are witnesses of his ascension.' Many sections of the church observe Ascension Day.[1] It happened ten days before the Feast of Pentecost which we call Whit Sunday. It is a part of the preaching of the gospel to say that Christ was taken up into heaven. And the New Testament Scriptures tell us that after he ascended, he passed through the heavens into heaven itself and took his seat at the right hand of God, in the glory everlasting and is seated there still.

We know a good deal about what our Lord is doing in heaven. We know he is reigning. Before he ascended into heaven, he told his disciples, 'All power is given unto me in heaven and in earth. Go ye therefore, and teach [disciple] all nations . . . teaching them to observe all things whatsoever I have commanded you: and, lo, I am with you alway, even unto the end of the world' (*Matt.* 28: 18–20). Now here is the Christian philosophy of history. Do you want to understand the modern world? Do you want to understand the last two thousand years? Do you want to know the future of this world and of the human race? I can tell you, and not because I have had a vision or because I claim to have had some unusual understanding, but because it is all here. The Christian message gives the only explanation of history. It is that this same Jesus is seated there at the right hand of God's glory in the heavens and he is ruling.

What else is he doing? He is calling out a people to himself. He sent these disciples and said, in effect, 'I leave my message with you. You are going to be witnesses to me. I am going to give you power to enable you to speak and testify to what you see and what you know and what you have experienced. I am sending you to Jerusalem, to Samaria, to the uttermost parts of the earth. I am sending you to tell the universe that I am the Son of God and the only Saviour.' And our Lord has been doing that ever since. From that moment until now, he has been calling out a people and he has been forming a new kingdom, the kingdom of God, the kingdom of heaven.

That is the story that begins in this New Testament and is continued in the long history of the Christian church. Throughout the

[1] This sermon was preached on the Sunday before Ascension Day, 1965.

running centuries, this gospel has been preached, and men and women individually, sometimes in small companies, have had their eyes opened. They have seen it. They have believed it. They have been separated from the world and become members of the church, members of the body of Christ. They have started living a new life with a new hope. They have lost the fear of death and the grave. They are enabled to conquer sins that used to get them down. And this is still going on. He is still sending out his messengers. Men and women are still being converted and renewed.

But the apostle went on to say that there would be an end to that process: 'whom the heaven must receive until the times of restitution of all things'. When will that be? Well, he tells us: 'He shall send Jesus Christ, which before was preached unto you.' Have you ever realized this? Jesus of Nazareth, the Son of God, will come back into this world. I have already told you how he ascended up into heaven in the sight of these men on Mount Olivet. You remember the sequel? 'And while they looked stedfastly toward heaven as he went up, behold, two men stood by them in white apparel; which also said, Ye men of Galilee, why stand ye gazing up into heaven? this same Jesus, which is taken up from you into heaven, shall so come in like manner as ye have seen him go into heaven' (*Acts* 1:10-11). That is exactly what Peter was saying. The heavens would retain him until God sent him again. Where to? Back into this world! This is the very heart and centre of the cosmic message of the Christian gospel, the Christian evangel.

How will our Lord come back? This is what the angels said to the disciples: 'In like manner as ye have seen him go into heaven.' He will come visibly. He will come bodily. Ah yes, but it will be very different from his first coming. He will not come as a helpless babe, but as the King of kings, as the Lord of lords. He will come riding the clouds of heaven surrounded by an innumerable host of holy angels. It is a part of God's plan, and it is an essential part of the Christian message.

I am simply expounding Peter's sermon to you. This is not my theory; it certainly is not the theory of modern man. Not only do people today not speak like this, they laugh at it and ridicule it. Of course they do! They laughed at him when he was in the world. They would not believe that he was the Son of God, the Holy One and the Just. Who is this fellow?' they said. 'Who is this impostor?' But he made this lame man walk. He was there. As they ridiculed the first coming, they ridicule the idea of the second coming. Peter has already said it for us in his second epistle where he refers to 'scoffers' who say, 'Where is the promise of his coming?' (*2 Pet.* 3:4). You Christian people, with your talk about the second coming, for nearly two thousand years now you've been saying that the Son of God is going to come back into this world, but where is this promised coming? The whole world looks as it's always looked. Everything is the same as it's always been. What's the use of talking about this? When is he going to come?'

And you remember Peter's answer? You think you are clever, says Peter, because you think that God is like you. You count your days and weeks and months and years. 'But, beloved, be not ignorant of this one thing, that one day is with the Lord as a thousand years, and a thousand years as one day' (*2 Pet.* 3:8). I do not know when he is coming, says Peter; there is only one who knows and that is God himself. All I know is that he will come. He will send him. God has not finished.

Why will God send his Son back into this world? The answer is: for the restitution of all things. If you prefer, you can translate restitution by the word restoration. God is going to send his Son back into the world to restore, reconstitute, all things. He has promised to do this, says Peter, from the foundation of the world. He has said so through all his holy apostles and prophets. He will send his Son back again in order that everything may be restored.

'What do you mean?' asks someone.

Well, if you really want to understand history, if you want to know why the world is as it is today, if you want to know whether there is any hope for the world, listen, as you have never listened in your life. Here is the only explanation. God will send his Son back into this world so that everything shall be restored. This is prefigured, as Peter says, by Moses and the children of Israel of old. The children of Israel were God's people. He had called Abraham and led him to the land of Canaan. But owing to a famine, they had had to go down to Egypt, and there, after the days of Jacob and Joseph, they had been maltreated and had had a very hard time. They had lost their freedom and their greatness and were slaves groaning in a foreign land. But God sent a deliverer called Moses, and he, the prophet of God, led them out, in spite of all difficulties, to the Promised Land. And, said Peter, when God sends the one who was prefigured by Moses back into his world again, he will send him into it in order that all things shall be reconstituted, regenerated, restored.

Now the apostle Paul put that in a great and striking phrase in the first chapter of his epistle to the Ephesians, 'Having made known unto us the mystery of his will, according to his good pleasure which he hath purposed in himself: that in the dispensation of the fulness of times he' – God – 'might gather together in one all things in Christ, both which are in heaven, and which are on earth; even in him' (*Eph.* 1:9-10). That is the principle.

Christ will come back to reconstitute the universe, but why does it need to be reconstituted? Ah, here is the question, and here is the relevance of all this to you and to me. This world in which we are living is not the world as God created it. He made it perfect. There were no thorns in it, no briers, no illness, no paralysis, no disease, no death. It was perfect, paradise, and man and woman were perfect in it, made in the image and likeness of God. So why is the world as it is? Why is a man born lame? Why have we had two world wars? Why is the world in its madness heading for a third? Why are they making these bombs? Why is there jealousy and envy and malice and spite? Why is there tension among the nations? What is the cause of it all? And there is but one answer. It was all caused by the fall of man. The devil tempted Adam and Eve. They listened and fell and brought chaos upon themselves and upon the whole universe. When Adam and Eve fell, humanity suffered in every respect. From thereon men and women suffered spiritually; they lost the face of God; they lost his original righteousness; they lost God's peace; they lost his happiness; they lost his joy; they became afraid. Internal conflicts began and they could trust no one. Not only that, the whole cosmos suffered.

The apostle Paul has put this in a memorable statement once and for ever, in the eighth chapter of the epistle to the Romans. This is what the modern world does not know but needs to know: 'I reckon that the sufferings of this present time are not worthy to be compared with the glory which shall be revealed in us. For the earnest expectation of the creature waiteth for the manifestation of the sons of God.' Then, 'For the creature [the creation] was made subject to vanity, not willingly, but by reason of him who hath subjected the same in hope' (*Rom.* 8:18–20). This means that the creature, the creation itself, 'also shall be delivered from the bondage of corruption into the glorious liberty of the children of God' (verse 21). Adam and Eve were the lords of creation, and God put them in the universe to manage it for him. When they fell, the universe fell, and God cursed the ground. That is when diseases came in. That is when paralysis came in. That is when thorns and briers came in. That is when wars and murder came in. That is when all that makes life a hell came in.

The world has been upset; it is turned into chaos. It is a place of disorder, a place of trouble. It is cursed. But when God sends his Christ, his Son, again into the world, he will send him back into it to put it right again – this is the restitution of all things. The world at the moment is being partly governed by the devil. He is 'the god of this world'. He is 'the prince of the power of the air, the spirit that now worketh in the children of disobedience' (*Eph.* 2:2). That, and not lack of education, is the explanation of the world. The most educated men and women in this country are as bad as the most illiterate. Oxford and Cambridge are not free from sin – why, the problem is acute there. An enquiry is having to be made because those students, the best brains in the country, are living on drugs, 'getting kicks', they say, committing suicide. Our hearts should break and bleed as we think of them. This is not a problem of knowledge and of education. Can you not see, this is a world that is being governed by Satan. There is disorder, licence, lust, passion. The world is upside down. But God will not allow the devil to have the final victory – of course he will not!

So what will happen? Oh, you say, preach Christianity and you will gradually educate people. But will you? It has been tried for two thousand years, but that is the very thing that does not work. It never will succeed because man is so rotten that he must be born again. No, no, there is only one hope – it is the coming back of this Christ. He will come back and will judge the world in righteousness and not only will he condemn all who have died in evil and sin and who have rejected him and what he offers them, but also Satan will finally be destroyed. Christ, while he was in this world, already defeated the devil – he is already in chains – but he will be destroyed with an everlasting destruction. The devil and hell and evil and sin and all that is against God will be burned with a holy fire until there is nothing of it left, and there shall be 'new heavens and a new earth, wherein dwelleth righteousness' (2 *Pet.* 3:13).

And, blessed be his name, he will restore not only the whole universe. Paul says: 'We know that the whole creation groaneth and travaileth in pain together until now' (*Rom.* 8:22). The day is coming when 'the creature itself also shall be delivered from the bondage of corruption into the glorious liberty of the children of God' (*Rom.* 8:21). What does this mean? Paul tells us: 'The earnest expectation of the creature waiteth for the manifestation of the sons of God' (*Rom.* 8:19). They are the men and women who have believed this gospel throughout the centuries. They are the people who have listened to this message and have accepted it while the world has ridiculed it. They have become fools and have been made wise. They have been the laughingstock of the world, but they are children of God, and when he comes and reconstitutes the whole cosmos – not only this earth but Mars and Jupiter and the sun and the moon and all the universe – it will all be restored to its original, absolute perfection. And you and I who believe in Christ, whose sins have been blotted out, we shall be reconstituted, our spirits shall be perfect, we shall know him even as we are already known.

And, wonder of wonders, this transformation will apply even to our physical bodies. We long and look for the Saviour, says Paul to the Philippians, 'Who shall change our vile body, that it may be fashioned like unto his glorious body, according to the working whereby he is able even to subdue all things unto himself' (*Phil.* 3:21). Look, said Peter in his sermon, you are interested in this miracle. Here is a man born lame, standing, walking, leaping, praising God. But the whole universe will be the same and the children of God will walk and leap and praise God in this renovated universe. Death is caused by evil and sin and rebellion against God, but he will come and destroy it all and the world will be restored to its glorious, original perfection, and all who believe in him shall be like this man. Here is a specimen. Here is a sample, an illustration. There shall be no more sighing, no more sorrow, no more sickness and disease. God shall wipe away all tears from their eyes. There shall be no more death. It will be glory and everlasting glory. There will be nothing wrong, nothing reducing the glory. It will be absolute and eternal and entire.

That is future history. That is Christian preaching. This world is not going to get better and better, it is much more likely to get worse and worse. But let this world do whatsoever it wills, it cannot make any difference to the plan and the purpose of God. In his own appointed time, in the fulness of time, as he sent his Son the first time into the world, he will send him again. He will destroy every enemy of man and of God and:

> *Jesus shall reign where'er the sun*
> *Doth its successive journeys run,*
> *His kingdom stretch from shore to shore*
> *'Til moons shall wax and wane no more.*
> Isaac Watts

As certain as we are alive today, these things will happen.

So I say to you what Peter said to these people in Jerusalem of old. The problem for you is not to try to understand miracles, it is not to be bothered about your intellectual difficulties, the problem for you is this: Are you ready for this great event when the Son of God will come in his righteousness to judge the whole world and send to everlasting destruction those who have not believed in him? That is your problem. For he is coming. The only hope for this world is that the Son will deliver it from the bondage of corruption into the glorious liberty of the children of God. Nothing matters but this.

So in the light of this, what is this world, what is even death itself? It is nothing. The one thing that matters is that we should know him, that we should be reconciled to him. Listen to Peter: 'Repent ye therefore, and be converted, that your sins may be blotted out' (verse 19). Then you will become the children of God and you will begin to wait for that great day. That is what the apostle Paul also and all the others exhorted those early believers to believe and to do. Paul writes to Titus:

The grace of God that bringeth salvation hath appeared to all men, teaching us that, denying ungodliness and worldly lusts, we should live soberly, righteously, and godly, in this present world; looking for that blessed hope, and the glorious appearing of the great God and our

Saviour Jesus Christ; who gave himself for us, that he might redeem us from all iniquity, and purify unto himself a peculiar people, zealous of good works (Titus 2:11–14).

If you believe these things, says Peter in his letter, 'What manner of persons ought ye to be in all holy conversation and godliness . . . Wherefore, beloved, seeing that ye look for such things, be diligent that ye may be found of him in peace, without spot, and blameless. And account that the longsuffering of our Lord is salvation' (*2 Pet.* 3:11, 14).

But let us end with a word from the apostle John, the companion of Peter on this famous occasion when the miracle was worked. This is how John puts it: 'Beloved, now are we the sons of God, and it doth not yet appear what we shall be: but we know that, when he shall appear, we shall be like him; for we shall see him as he is. And every man that hath this hope in him purifieth himself, even as he is pure' (*1 John* 3:2–3). Forget your great intellect, and all your supposed intellectual problems. Face your relationship to God and your eternal future, and believe on this Son of God who was crucified and died that you might be forgiven and who, blessed be his name, said this just before he left this world:

Let not your heart be troubled: ye believe in God, believe also in me. In my Father's house are many mansions: if it were not so, I would have told you. I go to prepare a place for you. And if I go and prepare a place for you, I will come again, and receive you unto myself; that where I am, there ye may be also (John 14:1–3).

Repent, if you have never done so until this moment, and believe on this crucified, risen, ascended, glorified Son of God with whom you shall spend your eternity in the glory, in the new heavens and the new earth wherein dwelleth righteousness. God will triumph over the devil and hell and all his enemies. Christ will reconstitute all unto the glory of God. Make certain that you will be in it and enjoying it for ever and for ever.

20

Ignorance

And now, brethren, I wot that through ignorance ye did it, as did also your rulers (Acts 3:17).

We have been looking into the essence of Peter's sermon to the crowds in the temple, and have seen how he pointed the people to the God of the covenant, to the centrality of Jesus Christ and to his death, resurrection, ascension, and coming again. But now, in the light of that amazing, extraordinary power that can heal a man born lame and send him into the temple walking and leaping and praising God, the question arises: Why, then, does the whole world not believe this? Why are men and women not walking and leaping and praising God like the lame man? Why is the whole world not at the feet of Jesus Christ, worshipping and adoring him and following him? Why is it that the whole world is not Christian? Why does it not believe this message and submit itself to it? Why does it not rejoice in this great hope that is set before it? Why is it that so many in the world, yes, the majority, are not at all interested in Jesus Christ, and dismiss him and especially dismiss his death upon the cross, and his shed blood, and do not believe in the resurrection, and certainly do not believe in his second coming? Surely this is a most urgent problem for us to face.

The answer is given here in verse 17 and it is given in one word: *ignorance* – 'And now, brethren, I wot [I know, I am aware] that through ignorance ye did it, as did also your rulers.' Ignorance is the central problem of men and women. So let us look at this as the apostle Peter puts it here, and let us see how, in a sense, this is the great theme of the New Testament message.

Let me first of all note what an astounding statement this is, and if it was astounding in the first century, it is still more so today. Twentieth-century men and women are amazed to hear that their greatest trouble is ignorance. They have come of age. They are knowledgeable and educated. Their attitude is that it was all right for their ignorant forebears to believe this gospel, as it is perhaps still all right for the superstitious to believe it, but to ask modern, scientific men and women to believe this gospel, why it is insulting!

Yet this old gospel still comes to us and tells us that the main trouble in the world is ignorance, and, indeed, it is very simple for me to prove that this is still the right diagnosis. Does the state of the world not prove it? If people know as much as they claim to know, then in the name of God, why is our world as it is? If we are so clever with our scientific research and psychology and social studies and multiplicity of educational facilities, why are we as we are?

I am not here to oppose any of these things. Thank God, I have received a little education myself and I am grateful for it, it is all of help and value. All I am trying to show you is that clearly that is not enough. I am in this pulpit to testify that it was not enough in my own personal life, and it is not enough in the life of any individual.

If this knowledge that we have, of which we boast so much, is adequate, then I ask again, why is our world as it is? Why have we had these wars in this century? Why are nations piling up these terrible instruments of death and torture? Why the tension between nations? Why all the difficulties in our own society – capital, labour, master, servant? Why are there disputes in families? Why rivalries and jealousies among people who have been brought up together? Oh, why all the things that make life so tragic? Why does any individual fail? Why does any one repeatedly go down to the same sin?

Ignorance

Can anybody dispute the diagnosis that the main problem in the world is ignorance? Not ignorance about how to conquer the force of gravity, we have that knowledge, we have done it. Not ignorance about how to invent gadgets. You press buttons and everything is done for you. You sit down and enjoy yourself looking at the television while the washing is done and the cooking is done.

Oh yes, we have all that knowledge. But that is not the knowledge I am talking about. I am referring to the knowledge of how to live; the knowledge of what humanity is and what it is meant to be; the knowledge of how to resist temptation; the knowledge of how to go straight and to be clean and pure and wholesome; the knowledge of how to die without a fear; the knowledge of what lies beyond – this is the knowledge we need. The problems of living and of life today are exactly as they have always been, in spite of all this vast knowledge that we have accumulated. All the knowledge that we have, and of which we are so proud, does not help us with the fundamental problems of the individual and of society, for society is nothing, after all, but a collection of individuals, and the state of the world today proves that the main trouble is still individual ignorance: 'And now, brethren, I wot that through ignorance ye did it.'

What are the causes of this ignorance that stands between us and the salvation of God? Fortunately for us, that is dealt with, not only here by the apostle in a very brief way, but elaborated in the further teaching of the New Testament. What is it in men and women that makes them reject the gospel, as did those who crucified Christ? What is the cause?

Let me give you a negative first. This ignorance has nothing to do with intellect or brain power, or a person's capacity for reason or understanding. Modern people say they are not Christians because of their great intellects, that only fools are Christians. As for people of intellect and understanding, of reason and ability, of course, it is almost an insult to ask them to believe such a thing. That is the central fallacy and Peter deals with it in a very interesting way. He says, 'Now, brethren' – he is speaking to the crowd – 'I wot that through ignorance ye did it, as did also your rulers.' If it had been only the rabble that had cried, 'Away with him! Crucify him!' then you could say, 'Of course, the rabble never does understand, the majority are always ignorant, but the discerning people, the rulers, with brains and understanding, they never do such a thing.' But, of course, we happen to know from the accounts in the Gospels that the common people shouted, 'Away with him! Crucify him!' at the instigation of their rulers. It was the Pharisees and scribes, the doctors of the law, the Sadducees and the priests who provoked this rejection of the Christ of God – 'ye did it, as did also your rulers'. And this is a point that the New Testament makes so frequently.

The apostle Paul writes to the Corinthians, 'Ye see your calling, brethren, how that not many wise men after the flesh, not many mighty, not many noble, are called' (*1 Cor.* 1:26). He says again, in the second chapter, 'Which none of the princes of this world knew: for had they known it, they would not have crucified the Lord of glory' (verse 8). This gospel has always been 'Unto the Jews a stumblingblock, and unto the Greeks foolishness' (*1 Cor.* 1:23). 'The natural man receiveth not the things of the Spirit of God: for they are foolishness unto him: neither can he know them, because they are spiritually discerned' (*1 Cor.* 2:14). But the point I want to emphasize is that Peter, here in this pregnant phrase, disposes of this whole argument.

And modern men and women need to be told that. Someone says, 'I'm a person who reads. I don't go to a place of worship and sing hymns and have a little bit of sob stuff on a Sunday night. I'm a thinker and I watch the experts on the television. I see the philosophers and scientists. None of them are Christians and I'm not a Christian for the same reason. They are people with brains – so am I.' But what such person forgets is that for every great intellect that rejects the gospel, there are probably a least a thousand people who are not intellectual who also reject it. 'Ye did it,' said Peter, 'as did also your rulers.'

If it were a matter of intellect, all the people who do not have great brains would believe the gospel; but they do not. Indeed, one of the greatest tragedies and problems in this country is just this – and every Christian should be tremendously concerned about it – that Christianity is rapidly becoming something that only applies to the middle classes, and the majority of people are right outside and uninterested. The ordinary people and the rulers unite in rejecting him. It has nothing at all to do with learning.

What, then, is the cause of the ignorance? The answer is quite simple, unfortunately. It is not the state of the head, it is the state of the heart and, ultimately, it comes back to pride. Oh, how plainly these people showed it, and so did their rulers. If you want to know why people reject the Son of God and cry, 'Away with him! Crucify him!' make a study of the Pharisees and the scribes, those doctors of the law, and the Sadducees, and then you begin to get at the answer.

If you read about those people in the Gospels, what do you find? Well, you find malice, bitterness, spite, malign cleverness. What had he done to them? He had come to do good. He had never hurt any of them. We read of him: 'A bruised reed shall he not break, and smoking flax shall he not quench' (*Matt.* 12:20). But look at all this antipathy, all this vituperation. Indeed, Peter brought this out in a very striking way here. He said, 'The God of Abraham, and of Isaac, and of Jacob, the God of our fathers, hath glorified his Son Jesus; whom ye delivered up, and denied him in the presence of Pilate, when he was determined to let him go.' There was the Roman governor, far from being a godly man, but at any rate an intelligent man, and, as we have seen, he felt he must have some sort of reason for condemning a prisoner and as there was no reason at all, he was determined to let Christ go. Pilate did everything he could to set him free.

Now is this a matter of calm, dispassionate reason? People say that Christians are just sentimentalists and emotionalists, who do not know how to think, whereas non-Christians look at things objectively, dispassionately and calmly, and as a result of their assessment of the facts, they reject him. Well, all I would ask is this: Why did the Jewish leaders press the common people to shout, 'Away with him!'? Why did they fight against Pilate when he was determined to let him go? How do you explain this hatred, this antagonism? When we have explained this, we will have an explanation of the ignorance.

There is evidently an element of perversity in all this. These people preferred to have a robber delivered to them: 'But ye denied the Holy One and the Just, and desired a murderer to be granted unto you.' My friends, I ask you as intelligent people, have you ever considered this question? Here was a generation that preferred a robber and a murderer to God's holy, only-begotten, just Son. That is the problem. What made people do that? What made them do it with such malice, hatred and spite that they mocked him and jeered at him and taunted him as he died in agony on the cross?

Again, the explanation is quite simple. They felt like this about him because he condemned them. He did not come to condemn them, as he constantly told them. He said, 'God sent not his Son into the world to condemn the world; but that the world through him might be saved' (*John* 3:17). What was the matter, then? Oh, I will tell you. These authorities, these experts, suddenly saw this carpenter who had never been to the schools, an apparent ignoramus, and yet he was able to teach in a manner that they could not. They could just quote their authorities. They looked up their text books: 'So and so said this; that one said that.' But here was one who spoke 'as one that had authority, and not as the scribes' (*Mark* 1:22), and they hated him for that.

And though our Lord did not directly condemn them at first, they understood his teaching, and they saw that it condemned them. He made their righteousness, of which they were so proud, to appear as filthy rags, and they hated him. He eclipsed them as a teacher, he eclipsed them as a person, he eclipsed them in all his pronouncements, and they hated him with a terrible hatred, especially when he said, 'Ye must be born again' (*John* 3:7), and when he said, 'The Son of man is come to seek and to save that which was lost' (*Luke* 19:10), and, 'The Son of man came not to be ministered unto, but to minister, and to give his life a ransom for many' (*Mark* 10:45).They hated him and killed him because of it.

But that is not the only explanation of this ignorance. Let me take you to the second factor. The apostle, here in verse 19, says, 'Repent ye therefore, and be converted, that your sins may be blotted out.' *Sins.* In verse 26, I read this: 'Unto you first God, having raised up his Son Jesus, sent him to bless you, in turning away every one of you from his iniquities.' Oh, this is the cause of the trouble – sins and iniquities. What are these? They are transgressions against God's holy law. They are our violations of the law of our being and the law of life. They are our deliberate refusal to live as God intended us to live – missing the mark, falling short of righteousness, deliberately doing that which is evil, delighting in it and glorying in it. What is the result? This is one of the great themes of the Bible. Sins and iniquities always blunt every single human faculty. The case of the Bible is that ever since man and woman fell, they have never been able to think straight. They are muddled. You cannot go on sinning and preserve your faculties. That is a theme in itself, I know. I am only just glancing at it now in terms of what the apostle says here.

That was the whole trouble with the Jews at the time of our Lord. The apostle Paul says to the Corinthians: The trouble with my fellow countrymen, the Jews, who reject Christ and the gospel, is that their minds were blinded. 'For until this day remaineth the same vail untaken away in the reading of the old testament; which vail is done away in Christ. But even unto this day, when Moses is read, the vail is upon their heart' (2 *Cor.* 4:14–15). That was the tragedy of the Jews. They were proud of their Scriptures. They said: We alone have the oracles of God. The Gentiles are ignorant.

'But,' says Paul in effect, 'they don't understand their Scriptures. A veil is upon their hearts. They cannot think straight. They've been like that for centuries and they're still like that now.'

When man fell, all his faculties fell with him, and man has never been free since he fell. There is no such thing as 'free thinking'. Everyone is a creature of prejudice. Is that not the cause of all our troubles? Look at the outcries against certain acts of this government, but then remember the outcry against the acts of the previous government. Each person looks at a subject entirely from his own standpoint – prejudice. The other person is always wrong. Nobody can look on dispassionately and with a free mind.

In writing to the Ephesians, Paul gives a great psychological analysis of sinful humanity: 'This I say therefore, and testify in the Lord, that ye henceforth walk not as other Gentiles walk' – then – 'in the vanity of their mind, having the understanding darkened, being alienated from the life of God through the ignorance that is in them, because of the blindness of their heart: who being past feeling have given themselves over unto lasciviousness, to work all uncleanness with greediness' (*Eph.* 4:17-19).

There is nothing to add to that. Paul is saying that because people are sinners all their powers are blunted and vitiated, and the more they sin, the more twisted their thinking becomes. The heart governs the mind, and prejudice arises. They are out to defend themselves at all costs. They are perverts and creatures of prejudice. So that is an additional reason why men and women reject the Lord Jesus Christ.

The third and the last explanation is terrifying. The apostle Paul was a great preacher and evangelist, and sometimes he seems to have been disappointed at the meagre results of his preaching, so he takes up the question in 2 Corinthians 4:3-4 where he says, 'If our gospel be hid' – if men and women are not seeing it, are rejecting it, if there is still ignorance – 'it is hid to them that are lost: in whom the God of this world hath blinded the minds of them which believe not, lest the light of the glorious gospel of Christ, who is the image of God, should shine unto them.' This is why men and women do not believe in Christ, in this century as in the first. It is not because of their great brains, but because the devil – the god of this world – has bludgeoned their minds, has held them as captives, and they are not free. The devil has blinded them so that they cannot see the light of the glorious gospel of Christ.

There, then, is the explanation of the ignorance of which Peter spoke: 'I wot that through ignorance ye did it, as did also your rulers.' I have been arguing out of a holy indignation and righteous anger at the way in which the devil confuses the minds of people, and I want you to see his work for what it is. But I speak with compassion, also. Oh, the tragic ignorance of the world, the needless unhappiness, the needless pain and sorrow! The world is as it is and it is in an agony because it is ignorant.

But, in the third and last place, what is it ignorant of? Just let me give you some of the answers and you can then work them out for yourselves. First, the world is ignorant of God. That is the central trouble always. Our Lord in his last prayer that is recorded for us, his great high priestly prayer, put it like this: 'O righteous Father, the world hath not known thee: but I have known thee, and these' – the disciples – 'have known that thou hast sent me' (*John* 17:25). If only men and women knew God, the God of glory, the God whose name is love, the God who is righteous, the God who is holy, the God who is light and in whom is no darkness at all. If the world but knew God! That is the tragedy. Men and women think God is against them. People who have never thought of God, who never go to a place of worship, say, when something goes wrong, 'Why does God allow this – if there is a God?' The trouble is that they do not know the only true and living God.

If the world had but some glimmering of an understanding of all God's divine and holy and eternal attributes, it would fall down before him. But the world has listened to the lie of the devil. He came to our original parents and he said, 'Hath God said?' Can't you see he is trying to keep you down? If only you ate of that fruit you would be like gods, your eyes would be opened.

'Ah,' they said, 'he's right. God is against us.'

And that is the greatest folly of all, the tragedy of tragedies, and the world is still like that today.

But they are not only ignorant of God, men and women do not know themselves, either. They do not know their own state and condition. They do not really understand their essential problem. They do not realize that they are as they are, and this world is as it is, because they are sinners. It is the only explanation. Of course, in international affairs, the people on one side say wars are all due to the people on the other side, but those on that other side are saying exactly the same thing! And it is the same with every quarrel and dispute, is it not? People do not know that they are sinners. They do not know that they have sinful natures. They do not know about the blindness that I am speaking of. They think that they are all right really. 'Of course,' someone says, 'I don't claim that I'm a one-hundred-percent saint, you know, but I really am a good fellow, and my troubles are due to the fact that I'm not being given an opportunity to show what a good fellow I am!' If this is put right, and that is put right, and all these other things are put right, all will be well.

No, no, men and women are too big for that. I have said it before, and I say it again, thank God you do not make people new by giving them new houses. Every one is entitled to a decent house, but the fact that you put people in new houses does not mean that they are new people. They will turn their houses into pigsties if their natures are those of a pig. Men and women are content to think of themselves as reasoning animals and they think that all they need is food and drink and sex and clothing and cars. God have mercy upon us! They do not realize that human nature has gone wrong and that they are twisted, perverted, vicious and vile.

In Romans 7 you will read the apostle Paul telling us the truth about himself. 'In me,' he says, '(that is, in my flesh,) dwelleth no good thing' (*Rom.* 7:18). 'The law is spiritual: but I am carnal, sold under sin' (verse 14). What is the matter with me? With my mind I recognize the holiness and the righteousness of God's law. 'But I see another law in my members, warring against the law of my mind, and bringing me into captivity to the law of sin which is in my members' (verse 23). I do not know what I am. I am a fool. I am right; I am wrong. There is excellency in me; there is that which is ignoble and vile and foul. 'O wretched man that I am! who shall deliver me?' (verse 24). But modern men and women think that they need more money, better conditions, a better environment, better circumstances. They have not yet come to the knowledge that even Shakespeare possessed, and he was not a Christian: 'The fault, dear Brutus, is not in our stars but in ourselves, that we are underlings.'

People are also ignorant of the fact that there is a final judgment and that they are moving in that direction. Of course, we are all interested in life and it is right that we should be, but it is equally right that we should be interested in death: every one of us has to die. You do not expect governments to address you on that, do you? I agree that it is not their prerogative; but it is mine. They are very interested in how you will be able to pay for your funeral, but I am much more interested in how you are going to die. The disposal of your body is not the great question; the great question is the destiny of your soul. According to the Bible, 'It is appointed unto men once to die, but after this the judgment' (*Heb.* 9:27).

Men and women are beings responsible to God. God observes them and God will judge them. Every one of us will have to give an account of the deeds done in the body, whether good or bad. But people are ignorant of that; they are living for the hour. They say, 'Let us eat, drink and be merry, for tomorrow we die.' And they say, 'Death is the end.'

But that is sheer ignorance. 'I wot that through ignorance ye did it, as did also your rulers.' The rulers do not know it any more than the common people. The rulers desecrate the Sabbath as much as the common people. It is all the result of an ignorance of their souls and their ultimate destiny. They stand before God in judgment and if they die in sin they go on to eternal misery and unhappiness. The world would not be able to go on as it does if it realized this. And this is what Peter preached. 'Repent,' he said,

'. . . that your sins may be blotted out, when the times of refreshing shall come from the presence of the Lord.'

Then that leads to the next thing: the world does not know that it needs a Saviour. That is why the world rejected Christ when he came in the flesh and that is why it has gone on rejecting him. He said, 'Come unto me, all ye that labour and are heavy laden, and I will give you rest' (*Matt.* 11:28). He said, 'The Son of man is come to seek and to save that which was lost' (*Luke* 19:10); 'I am come that they might have life, and that they might have it more abundantly' (*John* 10:10). And they said to him, in effect, 'What are you talking about? We have life.'

On one occasion when he was preaching, he said, 'If ye continue in my word, then are ye my disciples indeed; and ye shall know the truth, and the truth shall make you free.'

The Jews answered, 'We be Abraham's seed, and were never in bondage to any man: how sayest thou, Ye shall be made free?' (*John* 8:31-33). They said: You're insulting us. We're free and we've always been free.

The world never realized its need of a Saviour and it still does not realize it today. People think they can reform themselves and that they can reform their world. But they do not realize their weakness, their utter hopelessness and the uselessness of all their works. 'But I'm a good man,' says somebody, 'I'm a moral man. If I were a drunkard or an adulterer or a wife beater I could understand your argument, but I'm not. I'm always there to help my fellow man. My aim is to do good.'

Oh, my dear friend, you do not know what you are talking about. You are ignorant. Look at the apostle Paul, once Saul of Tarsus, a righteous Pharisee, a man living to please God and to carry out the moral law as he understood it. He says: I excelled above everybody in my obedience to the law of God (see Philippians 3:4–6). But it was all ignorance, because when Paul met the Lord of glory on the road to Damascus, he suddenly saw the value of his supposed righteousness. He says, 'What things were gain to me, those I counted loss for Christ . . . and do count them but dung [refuse]' (*Phil.* 3:7-8). It is no good at all, it has no value, said Paul, echoing the sentiments of the old prophet: 'All our righteousnesses are as filthy rags' (*Isa.* 64:6). Men and women in their ignorance compare themselves with some obviously evil person lying in the gutter. But what they need to do is compare their goodness with the goodness of Jesus Christ. He said, 'Except your righteousness shall exceed the righteousness of the scribes and Pharisees, ye shall in no case enter into the kingdom of heaven' (*Matt.* 5:20). Men and women do not have righteousness and will never produce it. There is nothing they can do. They are vile and lost and helpless and hopeless. But they do not know that, so they do not see their need of a Saviour.

Further, as Peter went on to show, people are in this appalling ignorance because they really do not understand the Scriptures. Peter said, 'All the prophets from Samuel and those that follow after, as many as have spoken, have likewise foretold of these days' (verse 24). These people were without excuse. They were Jews. They had their Old Testament and they read it and they listened to the preaching of it every Sabbath in the synagogues and they thought they were experts on the Scriptures; but they did not know them. The Scriptures spoke of these very things, or, as Paul again puts it, to the Corinthians, when Moses was read every Sabbath they were blind; the veil was over their eyes.

Our blessed Lord said the same thing on that famous occasion when he addressed the two men who were going down from Jerusalem to Emmaus after the resurrection. The women had come back from the tomb saying that it was empty and that Christ had risen. But the two did not believe them. They thought the women were mad and that their words were 'idle tales' (*Luke* 24:11). So they were walking down the road in utter dejection. Then this stranger drew near and began to talk to them. He said: What is the matter with you? They said: Have you not heard about Jesus of Nazareth? 'We trusted that it had been he which should have redeemed Israel' (*Luke* 24:21), and brought in the kingdom. But he is dead. He is buried. It has all come to nothing.

Then our Lord began to speak, and this is what he said: 'O fools, and slow of heart to believe all that the prophets have spoken: Ought not Christ to have suffered these things?' (*Luke* 24:25–26). And then he began to expound the Scriptures to them. You see, the world is as it is and these people were like that, because of their ignorance of God's revelation. We are left without any excuse at all. It is all here. It is all open before us and yet people are ignorant.

Ignorance

But the height of the tragedy is that the world is ignorant of the Lord Jesus Christ. 'Oh, brethren,' says Peter, in effect. 'I know that it was because of ignorance that you crucified him, spat upon him, and cried out with the crowd, "Away with him! Crucify him!"' And this is just what Paul said. In his sermon at Antioch in Pisidia, he said, 'For they that dwell at Jerusalem, and their rulers, because they knew him not, nor yet the voices of the prophets . . . they have fulfilled them in condemning him' (*Acts* 13:27).

This world does not know him, and what a tragedy this is. The great leaders of the world, the princes of this world, the great philosophers, the scientists, they all reject him. Why? They do not know him, 'for had they known it, they would not have crucified the Lord of glory' (*1 Cor*. 2:8). It is almost inconceivable, is it not, but there was the Son of God standing in the flesh. Oh, what must his face have been like! They had the privilege of looking at him and looking into those eyes of love, that holiness and that purity. They saw his miracles. They listened to his teaching. They did not recognize him. They missed the splendour of his presence, the accents of his voice, the purity of his teaching, they could not get it. But, oh, above all, how they missed the glory and the wonder of the cross, and all because of ignorance.

According to Peter and all the New Testament, 'Those things, which God before had shewed by the mouth of all his prophets, that Christ should suffer, he hath so fulfilled' (verse 18). They mocked him and jeered at him. They did not know that God's plan, worked out in eternity before the very creation of the world, was being put into practice. What was that? It was God, taking your sins and mine and putting them on his own dearly beloved Son.

Oh, what love! He took our guilt and put it on to his Son and punished him in our stead – the most glorious thing that has ever happened. But they did not see it, they were completely ignorant of what was happening, that holiday crowd in Jerusalem, mocking and jeering and laughing. Yet there God was doing – I say it with reverence – the greatest thing that even God could do. He was giving up his only begotten Son to death and to the tomb. He was slighting him for us, and was making this glorious way of salvation. They did not know that and the world still does not know it. If they did, they would join Isaac Watts in saying:

When I survey the wondrous cross
On which the Prince of glory died,
My richest gain I count but loss
And pour contempt on all my pride.
                                        Isaac Watts

They do not know that and they are ignorant of the glory of the resurrection.

And the world is ignorant, too, of the blessings of salvation, the very blessings that it stands in need of. What are your greatest needs? Here they are: forgiveness of sins. When you are in a tight corner, when the world has failed completely, what can you do? You say, 'There's only one thing left: I must pray.'

During the war we used to read of those poor fellows whose ship had been torpedoed. They got out into their little boat or dinghy, and there they were, thirteen or fourteen days on the ocean, with no sight of help, with food finishing, water finishing – everything gone. What should they do? And then somebody would say, 'Let's pray.'

But how can a sinful man, who has not thought of prayer for years, suddenly go into the presence of this holy God? Your sins are between you, something has got to be done about them. The greatest need of men and women is forgiveness of sins, reconciliation with God. And here it is offered, that is the blessing of this gospel. Christ died that you might be forgiven, that your sins might be blotted out. And the world is ignorant of it.

And it is ignorant of the new birth, the new life. Look at that poor man who is a slave to the sin which is ruining his life, ruining his reputation, ruining his family, ruining everything. He has tried, he has exerted his will, he has made his vows, his resolves, he has done everything. But he cannot do anything about it. And the world cannot help him. What does he need? Does he need education? Some of the most educated people in the country are the greatest sinners. There is only one thing that poor fellow needs. He needs a new nature, a new heart. He needs a nature that will love the light and hate the darkness, instead of loving the darkness and hating the light. He needs to be made anew. He needs to be born again. It is offered him in the Gospels, but he does not know it. He is ignorant.

Ignorance

Are you still ignorant? As you look at the world, as you look at your own life, as you look at history, as you read this word, are you still ignorant – of God, of your immortal soul and, in between, of God's own Son, Jesus of Nazareth, the Saviour of the world. God forbid that anybody should still be in ignorance.

Let me plead with you in the words of Peter: Repent, think again, ere it be too late. Turn to him quietly and say quite simply:

> *Lord, I was blind! I could not see*
> *In Thy marred visage any grace;*
> *But now the beauty of Thy face*
> *In radiant vision dawns on me.*
> William Tidd Matson

Tell him that, and he will receive you and you will be with him in the glory everlasting.

21

The Heavenly Breeze

Repent ye therefore, and be converted, that your sins may be blotted out,
when the times of refreshing shall come from the presence of the Lord
(Acts 3:19).

Peter, you remember, had been preaching to the people on the
person of the Lord Jesus Christ and his place in connection
with God's great purpose of redemption. Peter had preached our
Lord's death and burial, his mighty resurrection and then his
ascension, and had showed how our Lord would come again to
establish new heavens and a new earth, and to reign for evermore
in glory everlasting. Peter applied this by saying that the lame
man had been healed through faith in the name of Jesus (verse 16).
Peter and John had not healed this man by their own power or
holiness (verse 12). The power of the Holy Spirit whom the risen
Jesus had sent down upon them was the sole explanation of this
miracle. 'But above everything, what I want you to know,' said
Peter in effect, 'is that you can share this, you can become partici-
pants in it. You need not look on in astonishment. This can happen
to you as it has happened to him and as it has happened to us.'

Peter put it like this: 'All the prophets from Samuel and those
that follow after, as many as have spoken, have likewise foretold
of these days' (verse 24). Peter said: These are the days of the
Messiah. This is a new age. There is a new liberty. God's plan of
salvation is working in a new power, as all the prophets have

prophesied. And there is a yet more glorious age to come, but here and now you can begin to participate in the blessings of that coming age. I know you are ignorant of all this, and it is because of that that you crucified the Son of God. But I want you to see that, in spite of that, you can participate in the blessings. All you have to do, said Peter, is to repent and turn from your sins: 'Repent ye, therefore, and be converted' (verse 19).

What interests me is the way in which Peter put all this. He said, 'Repent ye therefore, and be converted, that your sins may be blotted out, when [that so] the times of refreshing shall come from the presence of the Lord.' Now there are some who think that that is a reference to the second coming of our Lord. I disagree entirely, as do many authorities, because Peter went on after that to talk in a separate way about the second coming – 'And he shall send Jesus Christ' (verse 20) – that is God's act. But here it is the people's repentance that leads to the times of refreshing. So this is not a reference to the second coming, but is, rather, a really wonderful way of giving expression to the blessings of salvation.

What, then, are these blessings? Salvation, Peter said, is exactly comparable to a man recovering from the effects of heat, or to a man who, on the point of suffocation, is revived by fresh air – 'times of refreshing'. It is not surprising that the apostle should put it like that. Peter said in effect, 'If you only repent, if you only believe this message, you will experience a most glorious refreshing. You will be like those who are almost dead under some oppressive heat when suddenly the fresh air is let in.'

Why did Peter use this illustration? Well, you see, he had just passed through Pentecost. You remember the story in Acts 2. The disciples and others were all together in an upper room with the doors locked because they were afraid of the Jews when suddenly there was a sound of a mighty rushing wind. The Holy Spirit came as a breeze, as a gale. So what was more natural than for Peter to use this particular illustration? Here he was, filled with vigour and power, a man who but a few weeks back had been denying his Lord, and saying he did not know him, because he was so afraid of being put to death. He was now filled with boldness, with confidence and assurance. He was ready to preach to the rulers and to the people. He did not hesitate to condemn them all and to say that they were ignorant. What had happened to this man?

He was like a giant refreshed. He had been refreshed by the coming upon him of the Holy Spirit. He had been baptized with the Holy Spirit. He was a man upon whom the gale of the Holy Spirit had blown. And, therefore, it was but natural that, when he came to commend the gospel to these people who had gathered to listen and to look at the healed man, he should have used this illustration. He said: Repent and you will be refreshed – 'Times of refreshing shall come from the presence of the Lord.'

This comparison is used in other places in the Scripture. Our Lord used the same illustration in dealing with Nicodemus. Nicodemus did not understand this being 'born again'. 'How can a man be born when he is old?' he asked. 'Can he enter the second time into his mother's womb, and be born?' (*John* 3:4). This all sounds ridiculous. How can these things be?

But our Lord said, 'Marvel not that I said unto thee, Ye must be born again. The wind bloweth where it listeth, and thou hearest the sound thereof, but canst not tell whence it cometh, and whither it goeth: so is every one that is born of the Spirit' (verses 7–8). The word translated 'spirit' is the same word as the word translated 'wind' – this breeze, this gale, this fresh air that comes. So Peter here was not only thinking of his own experience on the day of Pentecost, but was also remembering the words of his blessed Lord and Master.

That is how salvation comes. It comes like a breeze in a heavy, oppressive and heated atmosphere, and let me commend this gospel to you in those very terms. Look at it like this: look at humanity as it is by nature, look at the world, look at the whole history of the human race apart from Jesus Christ, apart from Christianity – what is it like?

Well, the Scriptures use many pictures and illustrations in order to convey some impression of this condition of the human race in sin. In the last study, we were seeing it as ignorance, and it is often depicted as slavery, but here is an entirely different picture. All these illustrations are true; they just convey different aspects of the same thing.

Now here the picture is of the human race like a body of men and women shut up in some confined space. There are no windows, there is no opening, and the heat is tremendous. The sun is shining upon the building and here they are in this sultry room without ventilation. The more they exert themselves, the greater the sense of oppression.

That is the picture which is used here to convey the whole notion of the condition of humanity in sin, as the result of the fall of Adam, as the result of man's original rebellion against God. And how perfectly true this is. Take, for instance, the element of oppressiveness. What is your view of life? What has been the view of men and women who have really thought deeply about these things? Have they taken a light, optimistic view? Is that the report that has been given of life in this world by the greatest and profoundest thinkers, irrespective of whether or not they have been Christian? No, that is not their picture at all. It is rather, to quote Wordsworth, that:

> *Shades of the prison-house begin to close*
> *Upon the growing boy.*

Up to a certain age we do not understand life. We live in a realm of fantasy, a realm of romance, and there is a kind of freedom. But the moment we begin to think, we realize that we are in a prison house.

I do not know if Wordsworth was a Christian, but he was a profound observer and that is how he saw life in this world, and, of course, he was simply repeating the old Platonic philosophy. The Greek philosophers had studied life, they had pondered this whole business and they had all come to that conclusion. Wordsworth also wrote about the 'still, sad music of humanity'. The great literature of the ages and of all countries, as someone has put it, all tends to be tragedy. Shakespeare's greatest plays are his tragedies, and look at the Greek tragedies. Why tragedies? The answer is that that is how these men found life. They found it to be a place of tragedy. There is an oppressiveness about life in this world.

Take, for example, the well-known expression, 'the burden and heat of the day'. Is there anything that is more characteristic of life today, as at all other times, than fatigue? Men and women are tired, tired of the problems and the trials and the troubles of life. We seem to be surrounded by them. Life is full of them. And we soon get over the stage when we see life through rose-coloured spectacles. We know that life is real, life is earnest, and life is a battle. It is full of difficulties, and we feel at times that they are closing in upon us. We are like people shut up in that room without windows, and we are breathing one another's breath and air. It is polluted, and it is so hot and oppressive.

But not only is it life in general, with its attendant circumstances – illness, accident, disappointment, the treatment we receive at the hands of other people, the competition, what they call the rat race – that is an oppression upon the soul, but in addition, there is the terrible moral conflict in which we find ourselves. There is a fight within, there is a fight without, the world and the flesh and the devil – is this not a part of life? Are you perfectly happy? No, the world seems to be against us. Then, above all, there is the law of God. We have a conscience, and a sense of condemnation. There is a feeling of guilt, a feeling of disease. We have a sense of unworthiness which we try to get rid of.

And then, ruling over it all, there is the thought of death, that thing which is ever coming nearer and nearer and nearer, and about which we can do nothing. Now all this leads to a tremendous sense of oppressiveness, the very thing that is referred to in the comparison used by the apostle Peter. We feel that we are fighting a losing battle.

That is one aspect and, of course, that inevitably leads to weariness. Our Lord gave out his gracious invitation: 'Come unto me, all ye that labour and are heavy laden, and I will give you rest' (*Matt.* 11:28). He knew human nature. He knew that our greatest need is our need of rest. We labour and are heavy laden, struggling, fighting against all the discouragement of life, so that we become utterly weary. We are exhausted and wonder whether we can last much longer. If you talk to the doctors, they will tell you all about it. Newspaper and magazine articles deal more and more frequently with the strain of life. This is the modern disease and problem – psychosomatic illness, neurosis, stress.

It all means that men and women find the strain too much. It is all shutting in upon them. The heat is upon them and there is not enough air. They say, 'I just cannot go on. I must have a stimulus, a tonic, some pep pills.' They need something to keep them going, and at the same time something to make them sleep because they are so badly overtired that they cannot sleep. This is life, this is the need that Peter was talking about – 'times of refreshing'.

The Heavenly Breeze

Oh, the battle of life does not get easier as you get older. Experience does not solve the problems. It helps you to avoid certain obvious pitfalls, but the older you get and the more you know, the more you realize the nature of the problem and you no longer have that foolish optimism which so many of us start out with in our youth. When we are young, we say, 'It doesn't matter what happened to people before us; we're different! These older people, these middle-aged people, don't understand. People over thirty, perhaps, don't understand any longer. It's only the young who really understand. We're going to make a new world, a new life.' But, my dear young friends, we have all said the same thing at your age, and as you go on you find that in fact life seems to get worse and worse.

Life gets worse as you get older because your powers begin to fail. The problems remain the same, but your ability to withstand becomes less and less. You find your faculties failing. You are amazed at yourself and the things that happen to you. You thought you would have outgrown certain things, but you have not. They are still there and you find the pressure increasing upon you. Every day you get older and death gets nearer.

And away beyond it all is the great question: What lies beyond death? Every one of us has a sense of mortality, every one of us has a sense of judgment. That is why the thought of death has always been a tyranny. It is shutting in upon us. It is coming and we cannot do anything. The air becomes more fetid, more humid, more impossible. We are trying and struggling and failing. So we feel there is only one thing to do and that is to let go, to give in, to get out of it, anything to get out of this stress and strain and struggle and fight and the hopelessness of it all.

Is that not a true picture of life? This has often been pointed out. Many learned writers have shown that the time when our blessed Lord came into this world was characterized above everything by this very kind of lassitude, lethargy and weariness. Just before he came, there had been the great flowering period of the Greek philosophers, that age of hope. They began to talk about Utopia. They planned for a perfect world. There were great ideas, great hopes and everything was alive and alert. But it had gone, and all the teaching had led to nothing. Then the Roman Empire had come with its brilliance in law and administration and local government and there was a new hope. But it, too, had come to nothing. The world was tired and oppressed, weary and exhausted; cynicism was spreading. That was the condition of the world when the Son of God came into it, and it has been repeated many, many times. Brighter periods are followed by oppression again, that end-of-the-century feeling that was often referred to at the end of the nineteenth century. So there, according to the Bible, is the condition of humanity as it is by nature, as it is as the result of the fall.

What, then, is the gospel message? 'Repent ye therefore,' said Peter, 'and be converted, that your sins may be blotted out, when the times of refreshing shall come from the presence of the Lord.' This is Christianity. It is not a kind of conference to decide whether we have enough energy left to make a hole in the wall so that we can let in some air. No, no, it is not that. It is a message that comes from the outside – from the presence of the Lord, the one Peter had been preaching about. It is the coming of the Son of God into this world that changes everything. This is the message of salvation. He can do it, and he alone can do it.

Do you know what civilization is? Have you ever been in the conditions that I am describing to you? Have you ever been in some of those cities in America where there is terrible humidity? In America they not only measure the heat, they measure the humidity, and they are quite right. Have you ever been in the city of Boston, say, on a hot August Sunday afternoon when it is not only very hot, but very humid as well? No sun to be seen, but it is there above the clouds.

The whole universe seems to be pressing down upon you, hot and humid. And you are tired, and you sit in a room and what can be done? Before they had air conditioning, people used to put on electric fans. The electric fan causes the air to circulate and while you are sitting somewhere near this fan you feel a little cooler. You are quite convinced that the fan is cooling the atmosphere. But you are wrong. It is actually increasing the temperature because the energy of the electricity is adding to the temperature. You have the impression that it is cooling the air, because there is a movement, but the fan does not bring in any fresh air at all. It makes the same air go round and round. You merely get the illusion that the position is being dealt with.

That is all civilization does. It does not touch the problem. It does not make any difference to the real condition of men and women. We change this and improve that, and there is a sort of movement, but nothing new is brought in. Let me use a medical illustration. You cure one disease and you say, 'Now we shall be all right.' Then you suddenly hear that another disease has come. Penicillin cures some of the most terrible diseases, yes, but that, in turn, produces certain germs that are resistant to penicillin and they are the real killers.

A few years back there was a great outcry because hospitals had become dangerous places. The talk was of a penicillin-resistant staphylococcus which was unknown until penicillin came in. You see what happens? You circulate the same fetid, oppressive atmosphere. The same heat remains, it is even increased, but you are under the illusion that things are better. They are not. You are simply moving round and round in exactly the same condition.

Here is the message of the New Testament. Humanity has shut itself in. It has shut the windows to heaven and it cannot open them. It has been trying to desperately, but it cannot do it and the more it tries, the more exhausted it becomes. But here is one who can bring us seasons of refreshing – this is the whole message of the gospel of salvation. All the Old Testament prophets had been looking forward to him. They had said, 'Comfort ye, comfort ye my people, saith your God' (*Isa.* 40:1). There is one coming who will set us free. Christ came into the world to open a window into heaven.

This is a great theme in the Bible from beginning to end. Something like that happened even at the original creation. We read, 'The earth was without form, and void; and darkness was upon the face of the deep' (*Gen.* 1:2). How did order and creation come? Here is the answer: 'The Spirit of God moved upon the face of the waters' (verse 2); the wind of God, the breath of the Almighty, originally formed creation and, when man was made out of the dust of the earth, it was only when God breathed into him the breath of life that he became a living soul. That was the first creation, and the new creation is similar. The window is opened so that the heavenly breezes may enter in:

> *O loving wisdom of our God!*
> *When all was sin and shame,*

A second Adam to the fight
And to the rescue came.
John Henry Newman

And what is the result? It is 'times of refreshing' – *the breath of hope*. Think of the Black Hole of Calcutta. There those people were, shut in, and the longer they were there, the more poisoned the atmosphere became, and the weaker they got. No effort was of any value at all. They were simply shut in, in this fetid, putrid, polluted atmosphere. They were dying, and there was no hope. The coming of the Lord Jesus Christ into this world has brought a breath of hope. That is why the introductions to the Gospels are so lyrical. 'The people which sat in darkness saw great light . . .' (*Matt.* 4:16). The people who were shut in the confined space in that awful room suddenly felt a slight breeze. It is like a traveller going through a trackless desert, seeing nothing but sand and sand and sand. The sun is shining upon him, he is oppressed by the heat, and suddenly he sees an oasis; the mirage has become a pool. These are the expressions which are used in the Bible to convey to us some impression of the blessings of this great Christian salvation. When everything else has failed, when all is sin and shame, when humanity is defeated and hopeless, he comes and at once there is a hope.

Handel caught this to perfection in his great music in *The Messiah*. Have you noticed that amazing turning point when suddenly, from the oppression and the darkness and the failure – 'All we like sheep have gone astray' – Handel moves into, 'For unto us a Child is born', and the whole atmosphere is changed. This is the blessed hope. It means that God is concerned about this world of ours. We have put ourselves in the prison house. We have shut and blocked the windows of heaven, but 'God sent forth his Son, made of a woman, made under the law' (*Gal.* 4:4), to make an opening to let in the air. It is, I repeat, the breath of hope. In other words, this is the great message, surely, of Whit Sunday.[1] There the disciples were in the upper room, and, 'Suddenly there came a sound from heaven as of a rushing mighty wind' (*Acts* 2:2). It was not generated in the room. It was not produced by man's

[1] This sermon was preached on Whit Sunday, 1965

machinery. No, no, it came from the outside and it always does. It comes from heaven, from eternity. This is a supernatural gospel, this is a miraculous message. Because God is concerned, there is an eternal hope for us, the breath of hope.

But then, think of *the breath of relief*: seasons of refreshing. Just imagine what people feel like under the conditions I have been describing. They have lost all their energy. There is no oxygen and the humidity and the heat are terrible. But suddenly they are conscious of something new – a freshness, a coolness, a balm, something that makes them feel that they will be able to breathe after all, that they are not irretrievably doomed to death. What is it? Peter gives us the answer: 'Repent ye therefore, and be converted, that your sins may be blotted out.'

It works like this: when men and women really understand life, when they are enlightened and delivered from this terrible ignorance, they realize that they have only one real problem and that is their relationship to God. There is a sense of guilt, a sense of condemnation, a sense of being a rebel against a holy God and a consciousness that they can do nothing about it. But just when they feel that finally it is hopeless, just when they say with Augustus Toplady –

> *Not the labours of my hands,*
> *Can fulfil Thy law's demands,*
> *Could my zeal no respite know,*
> *Could my tears for ever flow,*
> *All for sin could not atone.*
>
> Augustus Toplady

– just when they feel they are finished and done for, just at that point, the breeze begins to blow. The fresh air comes in through the new window opened by the Son of God, and they realize that they can be forgiven, their sins can be blotted out.

Is there anything in life comparable to that knowledge? You remember the picture painted by John Bunyan? He puts it in terms of a man carrying a terrible load, a pack upon his shoulders that is crushing him. But suddenly, at the cross, it falls off and goes tumbling down, and he can stand erect. The Son of God came into the world to remove your guilt. He died that we might be forgiven. He bore our sins in his own body on the tree. He has taken away the thing that is crushing us. The guilt has gone and with it goes the fear of judgment and the sense of condemnation. At one moment we are cringing in utter hopelessness and the next moment we cry out with Paul, 'There is therefore now no condemnation to them which are in Christ Jesus' (*Rom.* 8:1).

No condemnation! Christ has taken it away. 'For what the law could not do, in that it was weak through the flesh, God sending his own Son in the likeness of sinful flesh, and for sin, condemned sin in the flesh: that the righteousness of the law might be fulfilled in us, who walk not after the flesh, but after the Spirit' (*Rom* 8:3–4).

And as you are feeling that the struggle is utterly useless, and all is futile, and just when you are on the point of giving up, and you say, 'I cannot do it, nobody can,' you hear his gracious words: 'Come unto me, all ye that labour and are heavy laden, and I will give you rest' (*Matt.* 11:28). We cannot stagger on any more. 'Come,' he says, '. . . Take my yoke upon you, and learn of me; for I am meek and lowly in heart . . . my yoke is easy, and my burden is light' (verses 29–30). You are not left alone. He says: I am with you. I have come in. I have brought the heavenly atmosphere and I will be with you. Yoke yourselves to me. I will take you on.

So the oppression begins to vanish; the fresh air has come in: the breath of relief as well as the breath of hope.

But then it is also *the breath of life* – the reviving breath of God that gives us new energy, new power. Listen to him as he says to you, 'I am come that they might have life, and that they might have it more abundantly' (*John* 10:10). Listen, said Peter to these people at Jerusalem, what you need is new life. Think of this man, forty years old, unable to move. Then look at him walking, leaping, praising God. What has done it? Oh, this risen Jesus has put life and power into him. You are amazed at us, but we are nothing. I am nothing but a fisherman. I have no strength, no power. It is not my godliness that enabled me to say to this man, 'In the name of Jesus Christ of Nazareth, rise up and walk.' I was staggering. I was dying in that putrid, fetid atmosphere. But he opened the window. He sent in the breath of life. I am born of the Spirit and I am a new man. That is the message.

This breath of God, this Holy Spirit, gives us new life. Our Lord said to Nicodemus:

Verily, verily, I say unto thee, Except a man be born of water and of the Spirit, he cannot enter into the kingdom of God. That which is born of the flesh is flesh; and that which is born of the Spirit is spirit. Marvel not that I said unto thee, Ye must be born again.

This is it.

The wind bloweth where it listeth, and thou hearest the sound thereof, but canst not tell whence it cometh, and whither it goeth: so is every one that is born of the Spirit (John 3:5–8).

This wind of God will create in you a new principle of life. You will start a new existence. You will be a new person, a new creation. You will scarcely be able to believe that you were that exhausted person who was dying of poisoning in that fetid atmosphere. You will be so strong, you will have such confidence, you will have such a blessed hope, that you will scarcely know yourself. You will have new power in your life because the Holy Spirit will be dwelling within you, and, above all, you will know a spirit of gladness, a spirit of rejoicing that you never knew before.

'The fruit of the Spirit is love, joy, peace, longsuffering, gentleness, goodness, faith, meekness, temperance' (*Gal.* 5:22) – that is it. The apostle Paul asked: What is the kingdom of God? He tells you, 'The kingdom of God is not meat and drink; but righteousness, and peace, and joy in the Holy Ghost' (*Rom.* 14:17). To be a Christian does not mean that you are just managing to walk about this room, that you have not yet fallen, that you are fairly moral and decent. No, no, the Christian is like this man walking, leaping and praising God. Christians are not miserable men and women who are just managing to drag themselves round the world. They are people to whom the Spirit of God has come through the Lord Jesus Christ. They have new life and energy welling up within them.

As we have already seen at the end of the second chapter of Acts, that is what happens to all who believe this message. We read of these early Christians, 'And they, continuing daily with one accord in the temple, and breaking bread from house to house, did eat their meat with gladness and singleness of heart, praising God, and having favour with all the people.' That is the message of the Christian church. Peter was saying: Do not look at us. Do not look just at this man who has been healed. Look at the explanation of it all. Where has he found the power? Where has he found the life? Where have *we*? Why can I – Peter, Simon Peter – preach as I preach? Why have I lost my fear of the authorities and powers? Where do I get this divine energy? That is the question. Why am I filled with a spirit of rejoicing and gladness and of praise? There is only one answer: 'His name through faith in his name . . . hath given him this perfect soundness in the presence of you all.'

Listen, said Peter, do you not see that this is what you need? How are you getting on? You may not be physically paralysed but what about your spirit? What about your soul? Is your mind free? Is your heart filled with gladness? Has your will any power left in it at all? Are you living or are you just existing? Are you crushed by the problems of the battle of life? Are you at the point of exhaustion? Are you almost desperate? Do you just keep going by pleasure and entertainment, but then return to the same problem? Oh yes, for a few hours you are out of the home, but you have to go back to the problem. While you are moved by the film, you forget your heartache, but the film ends and back comes the heartache, you have only circulated the fetid air for a while. Is that it?

Do you not see, my dear friend, that what you need is the breath of God in your soul? Can you not see that your need is of that heavenly oxygen – the Holy Spirit? Oh, said Peter, repent. Think again about it. See the truth. See the enormity of what you have done. See that you are proved to be wrong, by this man walking and leaping and praising God. It is the risen Christ, whom you crucified, who has done it. See him, believe in him, and he will send into you, as he has done into us, this breath of life that will put you on your feet, that will make a new person of you, that will give you a joy unspeakable and full of glory. You know, Peter said, He is going to come back one day and then he will destroy all his enemies and he will set up his eternal kingdom. It will be a kingdom of glory. It will all be pure. There will be no clouds, no sorrow, no darkness, no death. It will be glory.

Would you not like a foretaste of that now? Would you not like to be refreshed and prepared for that? All you need to do, said

The Heavenly Breeze

Peter, is to repent. 'Repent ye therefore, and be converted.' Not only will your sins be blotted out, but you will begin to experience a season of refreshing. It will be permanent. It will be complete. It will be absolute.

> Sometimes a light surprises
>   The Christian while he sings;
> It is the Lord who rises,
>   With healing in His wings:
> When comforts are declining,
>   He grants the soul again
> A season of clear shining,
>   To cheer it after rain.
>   William Cowper

You have but to pray and he will give you his coolness and his balm.

22

Thinking Again

Repent ye therefore, and be converted, that your sins may be blotted out, when the times of refreshing shall come from the presence of the Lord (Acts 3:19).

Peter had preached to the crowd in the temple, Jesus Christ crucified, risen, ascended; Jesus Christ coming again; Jesus Christ the great Deliverer; the baptizer with the Holy Spirit; Jesus Christ who alone can refresh us and give us new life and health and vigour and strength. He had expounded all that, but still he had not finished, and we have not finished. God forbid that we should finish without looking at this subject that is left here for us to consider. Far too often we stop at the wrong point, we do not go all the way, but here it is.

In the light of all this, said Peter, 'Repent ye therefore . . .' Here is the focus of the whole sermon and this is the point that pierces. This is an essential and a vital part of the preaching of the gospel and the first thing we must realize is that this message, this gospel, is not something theoretical and academic. It is not just one of a number of views of life that you can take up and read about, or listen to lectures or sermons concerning it, and still remain in the position of a spectator. One can have an intellectual interest in various subjects – 'Very good, very intriguing, very enjoyable.' But this is not like that; this is the most practical thing in the world. This is something that concerns life and living. This is a life and death matter. This is what the apostle said, so it is vital that we should get this note in his sermon.

This emphasis was present, in exactly the same way, in the sermon Peter preached on the day of Pentecost and it characterizes the whole of the New Testament teaching. It is a note of urgency: 'Repent ye therefore . . .' Peter was urgent and insistent. He was not entertaining these people. He was not just out to deliver an address. He was not a kind of orator. Not at all! This man had been a fisherman, but suddenly he had been called and commissioned. He had been sent to do something, and he was alive. He was alert. He was insistent and urgent. Listen, he said, 'Repent.' He pressed his message upon his listeners and thereby he showed them that it was not just of general or theoretical interest. Oh no, he said: This is the most urgent and practical thing in the world. And he pleaded with the people.

The apostle Peter preached like this because he was concerned about those people in Jerusalem and he was anxious to produce a change in them. He had a great feeling of compassion for them. He told them, as we have already seen, that he knew that they, and their rulers, had acted in ignorance. He saw the condition they were in and he was troubled about them. For their own souls' sake he tried to make them see what he had to tell them, and he pleaded with them to listen and to do something about it. That was his whole object and purpose in preaching and that is still the business of the gospel; it is still the primary function and purpose of preaching. It is an evil day in the history of the church when men read essays from pulpits or when they are more interested in the form than in the content, in the externalities rather than in the living principle. Far too much attention is still being paid to things that are comparatively irrelevant. Peter stood up and he preached. He did not spend hours in a study polishing his phrases, thinking of clever illustrations – oh, such a thing is so repugnant to the New Testament gospel. Here was a man, alive, and he wanted other people to be alive. Here was a man who felt the burden of souls and so he brought his whole great statement of the gospel to this focus, to this point of application. And that should be the aim of all preaching.

So now I want to put this point to you, and I want to put it first of all as a question. You have heard this gospel: Has it done anything to you? Has it had any effect at all upon you?

'Ah,' you say, 'but I enjoy listening to preaching.'

I am not asking you that. I am asking you: Has your listening to the preaching affected you? Has it produced any change in you? That is what it is designed to do, and I do not hesitate to say that unless we can say that we are what we are because of this gospel, we are not only not Christians, but we have never really heard the gospel. We have listened, but we have not heard. There is a distinction between seeing and perceiving, and there is exactly the same difference between listening and really hearing. 'He that hath ears to hear, let him hear' (*Matt.* 11:15). That is it. Have we heard like that? Has this come to us in such a way that it has led to a result?

So what is the intended result? What does this gospel call upon us to do? And the answer is put here quite simply: first, repent. Obviously, to the apostle Peter this was a very important matter and in his sermon on the day of Pentecost he said exactly the same thing. There he was, in the midst of his sermon when suddenly we are told that the crowd were pricked in their hearts and said to Peter and the rest of the apostles, 'Men and brethren, what shall we do?' And Peter's answer was this: 'Repent, and be baptized every one of you in the name of Jesus Christ for the remission of sins' (*Acts* 2:37-38). And here again, on the second occasion when he preached, he said, 'Repent ye therefore, and be converted [turn] . . .' And he ended the sermon by making the same point, because it is so important: 'Unto you first God, having raised up his Son Jesus, sent him to bless you, in turning away every one of you from his iniquities.' Repent!

It is absolutely right and essential that we should realize that repentance always comes at the very beginning of the gospel. It is important that we should realize this because there is a popular teaching at the present time which tells people not to worry about repentance. You come to Jesus. You make your decision. You come forward. You sign the card or whatever it is. Repentance? That will come later. But I am here to remind you that it does not come later. It is the first step. And I have a most uncomfortable feeling that it is because this is forgotten, that the Christian church is as she is. We are not to get people interested in religion anyhow, somehow. We must follow the apostolic pattern and here repentance is something that comes at the very beginning. It is amazing to me that anybody should be in any trouble over this. Repentance must come first because our state and condition by nature makes it an absolute necessity.

Notice what the apostle Paul said about himself in the first chapter of 1 Timothy. He said: Here I am. I am an apostle and a preacher. He could not get over the fact that he was in such a position because when he looked back, what did he see? 'Who was before a blasphemer, and a persecutor, and injurious' (*1 Tim.* 1:13). Or, as Paul again puts it in writing his great epistle to the Romans: 'The carnal mind is enmity against God: for it is not subject to the law of God, neither indeed can be' (*Rom.* 8:7). And that is true of every one of us by nature. So is it not obvious that the first thing that must happen to us is that we must repent? And when people say that repentance can look after itself and come later, they are telling us that they know nothing about the doctrine of man as the result of the fall, that they are ignorant of the whole doctrine of sin. God have mercy upon us! But this is not only something that is obvious from the whole theological teaching of the New Testament, it is actually something that invariably did come first in the history of the formation of the Christian church.

Take your New Testament. Start at the beginning – who was the first preacher? John the Baptist. What was his message? Here it is: he preached 'the baptism of repentance for the remission of sins' (*Mark* 1:4). The first preacher preached a doctrine of repentance. He was called by God: 'The word of God came unto John the son of Zacharias in the wilderness' (*Luke* 3:2), and that was the message.

The second preacher was the Lord Jesus Christ himself and he preached exactly the same thing: 'The time is fulfilled, and the kingdom of God is at hand: repent ye, and believe the gospel' (*Mark* 1:15). Repentance is always the first note, and when, towards the end of the Gospels, our Lord rounded upon the Pharisees and pressed his message upon them, this is the way he put it: The final condemnation you have to face is that the Word of God came to you as it did to everybody else, but, 'The publicans and the harlots go into the kingdom of God before you. For John came unto you in the way of righteousness, and ye believed him not: but the publicans and the harlots believed him: and ye, when ye had heard it, repented not afterward, that ye might believe him (*Matt.* 21:31–32). So repentance invariably comes first in all the Gospels.

And here it is again. Here was the beginning of the Christian church, and the moment the apostle Peter began to preach in the name of the church and somebody said, 'What shall we do?' the answer was: 'Repent.' And here, without their asking, he said, 'Repent ye therefore . . .' In other words, the logical and the inevitable result of true listening to this gospel is repentance.

Then when we go on to the account of the ministry of the great apostle Paul in the second half of the book of Acts, we find the same thing. Take, for instance, that most lyrical passage in the twentieth chapter, where the apostle Paul, hurrying up to Jerusalem, had no time to go up to Ephesus, and so sent a message to the elders to come down to meet him at the seashore. When they came down, Paul said to them: I warn you that all sorts of things are going to happen after I have gone (see verses 29–30). He said, '[I] have taught you publicly, and from house to house . . . I ceased not to warn every one night and day with tears' (*Acts* 20:20, 31). And what did he teach? 'Repentance toward God, and faith toward our Lord Jesus Christ' (verse 21). These are the twin poles of the gospel.

What, then, does repentance mean? It is a very interesting word. Our word 'to repent' comes from a Latin word which means 'to think again'. But the corresponding Greek word for 'repentance' means 'a change of mind'. Let us work it out. What does this gospel call us to do? Is it just a little bit of sob stuff? Should I be standing in this pulpit and not doing what I am doing now, but telling you stories, telling you about myself, giving anecdotes, illustrations, telling you about how I have been reading novels during the week, or what happened to me on holiday? Is that it? God forbid that anybody should have such an idea! Or is the gospel here just to soothe people and make them feel a little bit happier for an hour or so, by getting them to forget their troubles? This old world in which we live is such a cruel world – let us pull down the blinds and forget it. Let us sing hymns and choruses and work ourselves up and feel jolly and happy and imagine all is well. Is that it?

No, no, think! The world is as it is today because it does not think. What utterly ridiculous ideas people have of Christianity. They think that people are Christians because they do *not* think and are still behaving like children. 'If Christians would only think,' people say, 'and apply their minds to what is happening in the world, they would give up their Christianity.' But it is the exact opposite. The people who watch television by the million, are they great thinkers? I wonder whether their minds are being tested as yours are as you consider these things. I am reasoning with you. I am appealing to you to think.

Yes, the gospel does that. Peter had compassion upon these people. He said: You are the people who but a few weeks ago were saying about the Holy One and the Just, 'Away with him! Crucify him!' Why did you do it? You did it because you did not think. You acted as a mob, as a mass – 'through ignorance ye did it.'

And this generation that boasts so much about its intellect does not think. If it did, it would not believe all the advertisements on the television. That is just psychology, subliminal thinking, and does not bring about active, conscious thinking. People are given information by constant repetition, and absorb it without knowing it. Thinking! This is probably the most drugged, deluded, controlled generation that the world has ever known.

This is the age of propaganda and of advertising – the negation of thinking. Obviously, not everything that is recommended is bad. No, but whether good or bad, people will buy something if they are told sufficiently frequently to do so. We had a second world war in this century very largely because people would not think; they did not want to think. They said, 'Two world wars in one century are impossible, it cannot happen.' They would not face the facts, and when one man warned them, they said, 'This man is a warmonger.' They dismissed him out of prejudice – they would not think. He was trying to get them to think, but they would not. Here is the great message of the gospel – you are called upon to think.

Furthermore, you must think again. In other words, repentance means thinking in a new way. This is what Peter was really saying. We only have a synopsis of his sermon here, his main points, but here is the way he undoubtedly put it: You are looking at this man and you are looking at us. Now you must not do that because that is just excitement. It is just rushing in, in amazement. Stop! Think, now! Take this miracle and make it the starting point in a process of thinking. You think you have thought, but you have not, so I want you to start thinking in an entirely new manner.

And that is the great appeal of the Christian gospel. Our natural thinking is prejudiced, and that is why it goes wrong. We start with certain presuppositions which we take for granted and have never examined, and then we argue round and round in a circle. Most people today who are not Christians start by deciding that there is nothing in Christianity. They have no reason for that decision except that they think it is the twentieth-century, grown-up thing to do. Then all their thinking is designed to prove that there cannot be anything in it.

I have often used this illustration. Matthew Arnold put it like this: 'Miracles cannot happen, therefore miracles have not happened.' Of course, if they cannot happen, they have not happened, but the question is: Are they impossible? Matthew Arnold was thinking badly when he laid down his postulate and then reasoned from it. The gospel tells us to come further back, and to examine this first postulate. Is a miracle inherently impossible? Think again! Now that is exactly what Peter was getting these people to do. He said: Can you not see that this man here, whom you know so well, who was born lame and has never walked in his life, is now walking, leaping and praising God? Can you not see that your thinking must have been wrong somewhere? Look at the facts staring you in the face. Here is a concrete event. Here is a revelation of the power of this risen Jesus and of God his Father. Think again. Start afresh.

And this is still the great appeal made by the gospel. In exactly the same way, it turns to modern men and women and tells them: As you see life collapsing round and about you, the call of the gospel to you is to think again and to think in the light of the teaching of the Bible. You do not just start with your own thoughts or the cleverness of the popular newspaper articles. They start with prejudices and then cleverly work them out. But that is not thinking. Start with the revelation of this book. Start with this great message. Think your whole position again in terms of this. That is what is meant by the call to repentance. So are you ready to re-examine all your thinking? Are you ready to test your presuppositions in the light of this contention? Are you ready to admit that there is at any rate the possibility that you might be wrong?

You now come to the point of saying, 'Very well, I'm prepared to listen.' That is the beginning of repentance. And is that not what is needed in this country and in every other country at this present moment? Men and women have never considered this message. They think they have, but all they have done is dismiss it. They have never faced it. They have never brought all their thinking to the bar of this word. They have never really come with an open mind and given it an opportunity. The call to repentance is a call to men and women to say, 'Perhaps, after all, we've been wrong. Is there something in this, after all?' That is the first step.

But what are we to think about? First, you must think again about God. Maybe you do not believe in God at all. You say, 'It was all right to believe in God until the middle of the nineteenth century, but science has put God out. There's no need of him. I believe in a universe apart from God. In a sense, if I have a god at all, my god is the universe.'

Now are you prepared to think again about that? That is what these apostles pleaded with their contemporaries to do. Paul says to the Christians in Rome: Can you not see that God has left his mark on the whole of creation? 'The invisible things of him from the creation of the world are clearly seen, being understood by the things that are made' (*Rom.* 1:20). They declare his Godhead and his creatorship. Can you really explain our universe without God? Does an original bang explain everything satisfactorily? Is it all accident? Where did that matter come from that was exploded and dispersed in the big bang that scientists talk about? That leaves so much unexplained, and as you look at all the order and the design and the arrangement and the perfection in nature, and at providence and history and all these things, I ask you: Are you comfortable with your neat little theories? Can you really explain the whole cosmos without God? I am simply asking you to be big enough to think again.

But I want to say a word to those who claim that they do believe in God. These people to whom Peter was preaching were Jews and they believed in God. But he told them to think again. The Pharisees were even teachers about God, but they were called to think again about him, because the fact that a man says, 'I believe in God,' does not prove that he does. Who is your God? What is your God? Where have you got the sanction for what you believe about God? People say, 'Of course, I've always believed in God.' These Pharisees had a stern legalistic God who had no compassion for publicans and sinners. He was only interested in the good and the moral and the righteous and the religious. Publicans and sinners he abominated and cast out of his sight.

Think again, said Peter. Think again, said Paul.

The Lord Jesus Christ said the same thing. We read: 'Then drew near unto him all the publicans and sinners' (*Luke* 15:1), and he began to eat with them. Then he saw the Pharisees drawing their skirts together. They were amazed that he should have anything to do with such a company. That is why he told the parable of the prodigal son. Our Lord was telling the Pharisees this: Your ideas about God are all wrong. You are the teachers about God and you are wrong. It is a vile travesty. It is an insult to him. This is God – he is like the father of the prodigal son.

And there are many others today who have yet another idea of God. They say that God is solely and exclusively a God of love. They do not believe in the God of the law. They do not believe in the God of righteousness and of justice and of holiness. They do not believe, they say, in a God who punishes sin. They do not believe in a hell or in any kind of discipline. Their God is someone who says, 'Do what you like, I love you all.' And Christ dying on the cross, they maintain, was saying, 'God still loves you, though you kill me.' There is no punishment and no retribution. To these people, also, this gospel says: Think again about God.

What right have you to say that God is only this, or God is only that? What do you know about God? Whence do your ideas arise? What is your authority? And if you ask that question, you will find that you have none. I have already reminded you that in nature and creation, we can see the traces of Godhead: 'The heavens declare the glory of God; and the firmament sheweth his handywork' (*Psa.* 19:1). Everything proclaims God – the sun, the moon, the stars, the flowers in their perfection, the rivers and the brooks – ah, they are declaring God.

But men and women have become blind as the result of sin. They have no real knowledge of God apart from what they have in the Bible. I can take you through the philosophical arguments for the being and existence of God. They are sound. They are cogent and right. But I am not going to go into them because they are not enough and have never made anyone a Christian. Beyond that, here it is, this revelation. Because he is God, men and women can never understand him. They can never ascend to the heights. But he has come down. He has revealed. He has spoken. Think again in the light of this. That is repentance. Think again about God.

And then this gospel that was preached by Peter and which I am privileged to pass on to you says: Wait for a moment, think again about yourself. Let me remind you that you have dismissed, you have denied, the Holy One and the Just. You thought you were right. You thought you could assess human nature, but do you not think you had better start thinking again? The one you rejected healed the beggar. Is there not something wrong with your mental apparatus? Look at this supreme example of re-thinking in order that you might see it once and for ever. Saul of Tarsus was a truly great man. For intellect and understanding, acuity of vision and brilliance in logic and rhetoric, none could beat him. There he was, and how pleased and how self-satisfied! When addressing Agrippa and Festus, he said, 'I verily thought with myself, that I ought to do many things contrary to the name of Jesus of Nazareth' (*Acts* 26:9).

Exactly. He and himself! They were unanimous! Such a man could not make a mistake, of course not! He and the Pharisees, they could not all be wrong, and this man, this fellow, this carpenter, this untrained individual, could not be right. Jesus of Nazareth was an impostor. They were right to get rid of him, and Paul was going to exterminate all who were mad enough to follow him still. Yes, but on the road to Damascus Paul found that he was as ignorant as these people in Jerusalem who cried in the mob, 'Away with him! Crucify him!' Paul had to think again. When he saw him, oh, Paul's wonderful scheme and system collapsed to nothing. He had to start thinking from the very ground upwards. He had to go off to Arabia for three years to think again and he continued in this way for the rest of his life.

So do you not think it is time you thought again about yourselves? Are you perfectly satisfied? Is all well with you? Do you not think you had better draw up a balance sheet? What are your assets? What is the value of your morality? What is the value of your knowledge? What is the value of your goodness in the sight of God? Think again, my dear friend. What have you made of life? What have you reached? What about your past? What about your present? What about your future? There is something coming that you cannot avoid and it is called death. Are you ready for it? Are you ready to go out of this world, to make your *quietus*? What about what lies beyond death and the grave? Have you got it taped? Is it all worked out so that you can face it with equanimity and never need give it another care? Is all well? I ask you in the name of God, and if you value your own soul, think again about yourself. What do you really know? What do you really have? How will you spend eternity? What about the judgment that is facing us all? Beloved people, think again.

Think about yourself as well as about God, and then think again about this blessed person Jesus Christ of Nazareth. Can he really be dismissed? Can he really be got rid of as merely a man, a great teacher, politician, call him what you like – can you really explain him in those terms? Do you not think you had better look at him again and consider him and listen to what he has to say? Thank God, he is ready to do with you what he did with Saul of Tarsus. You may have rejected him, and in your cleverness dismissed him thousands of times, but if you are ready just to look up to him he will look back at you and he will smile upon you. Paul says: I am a great example. Christ set me forth as a great illustration of his longsuffering and compassion.

I, too, am here to tell you that whatever you may have done with him until now, if you turn round, turn back, consider him afresh, you will not be refused. He said, 'Him that cometh to me I will in no wise cast out' (*John* 6:37). Think again about that death on the cross. Was it only the death of a pacifist? Was it just anti-war or anti-bomb? Can you not see that there was a transaction between God the Father and God the Son? Can you not see that the only explanation of it is that God 'hath made him to be sin for us' (2 *Cor.* 5:21)? 'The Lord hath laid on him the iniquity of us all' (*Isa.* 53:6). Think it through again and see through it to the glorious resurrection and ascension.

Then think again about the course of history. Can you really explain away the whole of this gospel? What is left, if you do? You know you would not even have a United States of America, but for this gospel. It was this that came to men and women and changed them, as it changed the man at the Beautiful Gate of the temple. It was this that sent the Pilgrim Fathers across the ocean, that they might worship him in freedom and enjoy him together

Thinking Again

in peace. Think again, I humbly pray you, about God and about yourselves and about the Lord Jesus Christ.

But thinking again is not enough. As I told you, the Greek word here translated 'repentance' means 'change of mind', and Peter pressed that, too, upon them. 'Repent ye therefore . . .' He said: Look at the facts. Consider them. Listen to all I have said to you and, having faced it, change your minds. That just means this: Admit that you are wrong. Admit that you have been utterly and totally mistaken, that you blundered hopelessly with all your views of life and God and self and Christ and eternity. Admit that you have been a victim of the god of this world, blinded by modern ignorance, and that your whole philosophy of life has gone astray. Confess it. Tell God about it. That is repentance.

And, of course, you cannot do that without feeling godly sorrow. The moment that men and women realize that they have been so wrong in their thoughts of God, in their arrogance and defiance, the moment they realize the enormity of it all, they do not know what to do with themselves. You cannot repent without feeling it; it is not purely a matter of the intellect. It starts with the intellect, it must, everything starts there, it is God's greatest gift to humanity, and the truth comes to the mind. But once the mind sees it, the heart responds. 'Oh,' you say, 'how could I ever have done that? How could I ever have been capable of that?' And that is a vital part of repentance.

That is why, in a sense, the apostle Paul could not forgive himself. He said, 'This is a faithful saying, and worthy of all acceptation, that Christ Jesus came into the world to save sinners; of whom I am chief' (*1 Tim.* 1:15). Oh, the proud, blind, arrogant, self-satisfied Pharisee that I was, he said, how is God able to forgive me? How can he? I cannot forgive myself. But he did. I am what I am by his grace.

Oh, once people see it, they not only change their minds, their hearts are broken. They feel contempt for themselves and for their pride and all their foolish ideas of knowledge. And as they look at their good acts, they say with the apostle Paul, 'I do count them but dung [refuse], that I may win Christ, and be found in him, not having mine own righteousness, which is of the law, but that which is through the faith of Christ, the righteousness which is of God by faith' (*Phil.* 3:8–9). So have you ever repented? Have you ever seen your wrongness intellectually? Have you ever broken your heart, as it were, when you have seen the enormity of your sins? Do you know to any extent what it is to hate yourself?

> *I hate the sins that made Thee mourn,*
> *And drove Thee from my breast.*
>
> William Cowper

Listen, said Peter, think again until you see it and feel it. Do you know, in any sense, what the apostle means when he says, 'In me (that is, in my flesh,) dwelleth no good thing . . . O wretched man that I am! who shall deliver me from the body of this death' (*Rom.* 7:18, 24)? There is repentance at its acme, as it were. I am simply asking: Do you know anything about it? If you do not, you have never thought again, you have never repented, and if you have never repented, you are not in the kingdom of God. This is essential. There is only one door that leads to this kingdom. It is repentance. The only people who ever go into the kingdom of God are those who realize they are desperate, hopeless sinners who can do nothing for themselves, who are saved entirely and solely by the death of the Son of God for them and for their sins and by his rising again for their justification.

But let me come to the last point. You must give proof that you have repented. 'Repent ye therefore, and be converted.' Turn yourselves, turn around, return to God. You have acted as you have, said Peter, because you turned your backs on God and became blind. You did not know what you were doing. Repent, turn back to God. God 'sent him [his Son] to bless you, in turning away every one of you from his iniquities' (verse 26). You see, we have to give proof that our repentance is real and that it is true. You may repent now, but you cannot be sure of the genuineness of your repentance until you have given proof in your life. Many people have taken a decision, but the next day has proved that it was a passing emotional ripple on the surface of their lives. That is why I do not 'test' people in evangelistic meetings by telling them to come forward. I believe in a repentance that comes from the heart as well as the head and that shows itself in life, in living. Turn yourselves, turn back, return to God. Not results that may please a preacher, but results that will please God and cause the angels to sing. Repentance is proved in action and in practice: 'Repent ye therefore, and be converted.' Turn away from what you are to something new. This again is essential. I cannot understand people who do not even see the logic of this gospel. If you repent, you must turn from the world. Why? Because if you have thought again truly, you ask: Why was I as I was?

And there is only one answer: I was a victim of the world, the flesh, the devil – all that is opposed to God. So I have seen that. Now what do I do? I turn my back on it. The New Testament is full of that. Read Titus 2:11–12, which puts all I am trying to say to you perfectly: 'The grace of God that bringeth salvation hath appeared to all men, teaching us' – teaching what? – 'that, denying ungodliness and worldly lusts . . .' While you go on with ungodliness and worldly lusts you have not repented.

Whatever they may have said in their minds, whatever they may have said from their hearts, those who repent deny, turn their backs upon, the world, the flesh and the devil. Oh no, they do not become perfect, but they turn their backs on it, they do not want it. They may, in their folly, be enticed to half look back over their shoulders, they may fall into sin, but they do not belong there. Like the prodigal, they have got up and have gone home.

So, 'denying ungodliness and worldly lusts', what do we do? 'We should live soberly, righteously and godly, in this present world.' In other words, if you truly believe that the world is as it is because it is in rebellion against God and is ignorant of him and his holiness, and is breaking his laws and spitting upon his sanctity, if you believe that, you will say, 'I want no more to do with it. I'm turning and getting away.' John Bunyan saw it. The pilgrim leaves the City of Destruction. His wife and children are calling, but that does not matter, he must flee. That is conversion – turning away from the City of Destruction and all that will happen to it, and turning to God, to live soberly, righteously and godly in this present world; living to the glory of God; living to keep his commandments; living to tell forth his praises, 'who hath called you out of darkness into his marvellous light' (*1 Pet.* 2:9).

'God, having raised up his Son Jesus,' said Peter, 'sent him to bless you in turning away every one of you from his iniquities.' And you have not truly repented until your will is actively engaged, and you are giving positive proof of that change. The mind moves the heart, which in turn moves the will. The whole person is involved and turned right round. A complete revolution affected Paul's entire personality. He said: I was a persecutor, a blasphemer and an injurious person, but now I am an apostle of Jesus Christ and a preacher of the gospel.

So you accept the gospel, you believe in the Lord Jesus Christ, and you take up your cross and follow him. You will be laughed at in the office, jeered at in the college, regarded as a fool in your profession, but you cannot worry. You say:

> Jesus, I my cross have taken,
> All to leave and follow Thee,
> Destitute, despised, forsaken,
> Thou from hence my All shalt be:
> Perish every fond ambition,
> All I've sought, and hoped, and known;
> Yet how rich is my condition!
> God and heaven are still my own.

Henry Francis Lyte

Repent, my beloved friends, repent, therefore, in the light of all this and turn yourselves. Why was Peter so urgent? Why am I trying to be urgent, as best I can? Why should we all be urgent? Why should we be desperate? Peter supplied the answer. He told this congregation, 'Moses truly said unto the fathers, A prophet shall the Lord your God raise up unto you of your brethren, like unto me; him shall ye hear in all things whatsoever he shall say unto you.' Then – 'And it shall come to pass, that every soul, which will not hear that prophet, shall be destroyed from among the people' (verses 22–23). Why should you repent? There is the answer. If you do not repent and believe on this Lord Jesus Christ, nothing awaits you but destruction, and everlasting destruction, not merely world wars and their devastation, no – eternal devastation. That is why Peter was urgent.

Repent and believe. Turn yourselves. Oh, do so because of the appalling calamities that await those who do not, but do so, also, for this reason: that your sins may be blotted out. I proclaim this to you in the name of Jesus Christ of Nazareth who has died, been buried and has risen, to make it possible for you. Repent and believe the gospel and your sins will be forgiven, and you will be for ever with him in the glory everlasting.